MILLION DOLLAR HIRE

MILLION DOLLAR HIRE

BUILD YOUR BOTTOM LINE, ONE EMPLOYEE AT A TIME

David P. Jones

JOSSEY-BASS
A Wiley Imprint
www.josseybass.com

Published by Jossey-Bass
A Wiley Imprint
989 Market Street, San Francisco, CA 94103-1741—www.josseybass.com

Readers should be aware that Internet Web sites offered as citations and/or sources for further information may have changed or disappeared between the time this was written and when it is read.

Limit of Liability/Disclaimer of Warranty: While the publisher and author have used their best efforts in preparing this book, they make no representations or warranties with respect to the accuracy or completeness of the contents of this book and specifically disclaim any implied warranties of merchantability or fitness for a particular purpose. No warranty may be created or extended by sales representatives or written sales materials. The advice and strategies contained herein may not be suitable for your situation. You should consult with a professional where appropriate. Neither the publisher nor author shall be liable for any loss of profit or any other commercial damages, including but not limited to special, incidental, consequential, or other damages.

Jossey-Bass books and products are available through most bookstores. To contact Jossey-Bass directly call our Customer Care Department within the U.S. at 800-956-7739, outside the U.S. at 317-572-3986, or fax 317-572-4002.

Jossey-Bass also publishes its books in a variety of electronic formats. Some content that appears in print may not be available in electronic books.

Library of Congress Cataloging-in-Publication Data
Jones, David P.
    Million-dollar hire : build your bottom line, one employee at a time / David P. Jones.
        p. cm.
    Includes bibliographical references and index.
    ISBN 978-0-470-92842-4 (hardback); ISBN 978-1-118-01750-0 (ebk);
ISBN 978-1-118-01751-7 (ebk); ISBN 978-1-118-01752-4 (ebk)
    1. Employees–Recruiting–United States.   2. Employee selection–
United States.   I. Title.
    HF5549.5.R44J64 2011
    658.3'11–dc22

                                                                2010049178

Printed in the United States of America
FIRST EDITION
HB Printing   10 9 8 7 6 5 4 3 2 1

CONTENTS

PREFACE

It might seem risky to launch a book about recruiting and hiring when the U.S. job market only recently stopped shedding thousands of jobs every day and when economists forecast only modest job growth. Even today, though, recruiting and hiring continue. Over 90 percent of the workforce is employed. In many companies, 10 to 20 percent of the workforce, and more in some companies, leaves one job to find another each year. New companies start up every day. Companies continue to promote employees to higher levels, amounting to nothing less than internal hiring decisions.

What has changed in the current economic cycle is the importance of every hiring decision an employer makes. There's no longer room to get it wrong and hope that training or time on the job will fix a mistake. Today every hiring decision needs to be a good one. That's why now is the best time to launch the ideas I cover in this book.

Today, though, we're so accustomed to speaking of billions and trillions of dollars that it sounds almost trivial to talk about "million-dollar hires." What's a million dollars when you need a billion just to keep the doors open? The answer is, If you're running a business and hope to succeed, a million dollars is still a lot of money.

Many of the mistakes that brought us today's hypernumbers were made a million dollars at a time. Many stemmed from putting the wrong person in the job or making bad decisions about people. Often these decisions continue to have a financial consequence.

That's the message in this book, and it's one for every leader who answers to shareholders and every investor who seeks a return. Billions are won or lost a million dollars at a time—and often one hiring decision at a time.

Some years back, a client told me that the recovering economy meant his company would be hiring thousands of manufacturing workers over the coming few years. He had engaged my company to design a new recruiting and hiring program to drive these decisions. The client said the program better be good, because each new hire represented a commitment of more than a million dollars when he took compensation, benefits, training, overhead, and each new hire's expected tenure into account.

He said that if his company were purchasing a million-dollar piece of software, there would be vendor reviews, proposals, presentations, and hours of professional time invested in selecting the winning vendor. Yet here were decisions with equal financial magnitude, and several thousand times over, and the company's hiring was based on information not even close to what went into buying a piece of software.

The same situation holds in many companies today. The difference in rigor between how most companies purchase a six-figure piece of accounting software and how they hire a six-figure accountant is great. Is it because software packages differ so much? Is it because accountants are all pretty much the same? As any manager knows, there are differences among candidates—greater than the differences among software packages. Yet purchasing one receives a detailed assessment, while hiring the other often involves reviewing résumés, holding a few face-to-face interviews, and doing some reference checking.

Labeling hiring events "million-dollar decisions" isn't a stretch. The million-dollar view can flow from the financial commitment that comes with bringing the person onboard. With recruiting costs, salary, benefits, bonus, and training costs, along with overhead, regular pay increases, and normal tenure expectations, it's not hard to view any six-figure hire as a million-dollar investment. Where tenure expectations are longer—the public sector, jobs with union pay and benefits, jobs in companies that stress internal promotion, jobs in locations with few competitors—mid-five-figure jobs easily join the million-dollar category.

Too, the million-dollar perspective can reflect not what the person costs but what he or she is expected to do. Individual sales jobs with a low base salary are often expected to produce hundreds of thousands of dollars in sales each year, and often more. Lower-salary jobs in health care, protective services, financial institutions, or transportation have the potential to create million-dollar events if an employee makes a mistake, has an oversight, or engages in bad behavior. Here it's not the pay package that makes the hiring decision a million-dollar event. It's the risk the company takes on when making the hiring decision.

The financial view of how we make hiring decisions has been taking shape for some time. At about the same time my manufacturing client was making his point, a link was emerging between the business and the science of hiring. Research was producing financial modeling tools to forecast the results and pin an economic value on alternative approaches to recruiting and hiring. These new tools and technologies were beginning to offer, with different levels of complexity and sophistication, ways to analyze the costs, the risks, and the payoff of different hiring strategies.

Unfortunately, most of the information about these tools, their use, and their payoff remains in academic and consulting circles. Those who play a role in the hiring process inside organizations, from first-level supervisors on up, get little exposure to these tools and the thinking behind them. I'll try to change that in this book.

Today it's not only executives in companies hiring thousands of workers who can use these tools to gain a return. The concept of making million-dollar hiring decisions applies to a wide range of jobs, and they are not just ones with high-volume hiring. They can include software designers, sales professionals, accountants, marketers, engineers, and nearly every other occupational group, including CEOs.

In the chapters ahead, we'll take a broad look at how today's recruiting and hiring tools can drive better million-dollar decisions. I won't dig deeply into the math and psychometrics—just enough to give you what you need. The focus will be on explaining what's possible, demonstrating how the tools work, and showing what to expect when the ideas are put in place. In short, I'll show how to connect the pieces that go into building world-class recruiting and hiring programs—programs that work as well in a start-up, small, or midsize company as they do for employers hiring thousands each year.

The premise is simple: nothing can build a company, turn it around, or sink it as quickly as its recruiting and hiring decisions. No decisions an executive and his or her team make can pay off—or cost—as much as their hiring decisions.

How This Book Is Organized

I like things simple, and I like them clear. This book is for those with a simple and clear objective: to make better decisions about whom to hire. The thirteen chapters follow a straightforward model: they present an idea, explain it with an illustration, and offer up real-world examples to show it works. Although there's a good deal of theory under the surface, there's no need to dwell on the theory. Most of the attention will go to showing how the theory actually works.

A few chapters to dip into math and statistics. There's no way to avoid it. If you want to add up the dollars and cents that come with finding better million-dollar hires, you need to deal with numbers. When you do, you'll use the same approach of idea-illustration-example with even greater frequency.

The book opens with some foundation concepts—ideas drawn from research, practice, and just plain common sense. These concepts frame how to set up, manage, and continuously improve recruiting and hiring systems to gain a return on investment—in other words, a payoff.

Chapter One introduces the ideas that people—candidates—are different, that the differences are large, that the differences follow them into the workplace, and that these differences can, and should, be measured before we make a hiring decision. It profiles these differences and describes the ways recruiting and hiring programs can tap into them to improve payoff.

Chapter Two shows how concepts drawn from quality control, probability theory, and risk management can inform hiring program design. It helps set priorities for gaining the best return while avoiding the risks inherent in the hiring process. And it brings precision to the concept of using people differences to predict performance differences.

Chapter Three folds together the two previous chapters and introduces the concept of hiring program validity, an idea central to setting up a program that will yield a measurable financial return. It illustrates the concept, offers a basic methodology for thinking about the value of recruiting and hiring practices, and begins the examples that continue throughout the remaining chapters.

With this foundation, I'll jump a little ahead and offer examples of the payoffs employers have seen after updating their recruiting and hiring programs in the ways I describe in later chapters. I'll offer a preview on the different types of payoff you can achieve, whether through better performance, lower turnover, fewer accidents and injuries, increased sales, or other metrics.

Chapter Four offers examples of how better hiring systems produce a payoff in hard, bottom-line measures, such as higher sales, lower turnover, better production rates, and fewer on-the-job accidents or injuries. We'll look at specific tools and approaches that move the needle on both cost and revenue.

Chapter Five deals with two concepts. First, it introduces a methodology for estimating the dollar value that results from better hiring in jobs where performance is tough to measure in hard numbers—jobs where not only *what you do* but *how you do it* is important. With the method in place, I'll show how it can be used to forecast the payoff likely to result from any revision in a recruiting and hiring program. It's a model I turn to throughout the book.

Having whetted the appetite with examples of what you can achieve, I'll turn to two of the fundamentals for getting there: how technology drives cost and risk reduction while improving quality of hire and the role played by creating clear, detailed strategies and tactics to guide the way we approach hiring.

Chapter Six shows how the world of technology has entered nearly every aspect of the recruiting and hiring process and how it brings the same faster-better-cheaper outcomes to hiring it has brought to other areas of business. I'll review how specific technologies operate to either reduce costs or increase payoff while also helping manage the risk that comes with making million-dollar decisions.

Chapter Seven shows why creating a payoff-oriented approach to recruiting and hiring calls for the same level of planning, skilled implementation, and measurement focus demanded in any other part of the business. I'll illustrate how choices made at the strategic level, and followed through in assembling recruiting and hiring tactics, are what really drive payoff.

Next, I'll move to showing how businesses operationalize strategy and tactics and how to achieve payoffs like those profiled in Chapters Four and Five. You'll begin a ride down the recruiting and hiring funnel, a process that begins by generating interest in the jobs that need to be filled, proceeds by narrowing the group of candidates considered, and ends with million-dollar decisions, with a lot of work along the way.

Chapter Eight explains how using competency models to frame what you seek, drawing on today's technology and social networking tools to build a pipeline, and narrowing the funnel through a variety of techniques feeds the best candidates into the process. It also highlights some of the tools that work best in reducing an initial candidate pool to manageable numbers, while avoiding the legal potholes that fill the road.

Chapter Nine takes up with the results of prescreening and shows how to use candidate assessment tools and technologies to filter candidates further. We'll look to an array of tools that help give a view on whether candidates possess the competencies needed to perform the job. We return to the concept of validity and the Chapter Five modeling tools to help decide how to assess candidates most effectively and how to decide when enough is enough from an assessment point of view.

Chapter Ten offers strategies for reviewing, combining, and weighting all the information produced through the prescreening and assessment phases of the hiring process. It also highlights some of the latest research in the area of personality assessment and shows tools being introduced into the hiring process for supervisory and managerial positions that seek to tap candidates' dark side tendencies—those attributes that routinely lead to derailing leaders—before the final million-dollar decision is made.

Of course, there's always a "yes, but . . ." Having reviewed strategies, tactics, tools, and technologies that drive million-dollar hires, I turn to the legal side of the matter. Although I have touched on the topic in moving through the first ten chapters, I now turn to the details, and the dos and the don'ts, that you need to consider if the goal is to focus not only on payoff but on risk reduction.

Chapter Eleven covers the basics of the laws, regulations, court decisions, and government enforcement agencies that, in effect, oversee how organizations hire. It looks back on each step in the recruiting and hiring funnel and offers advice on how to gain a payoff while reducing the risk of legal challenge to these million-dollar decisions.

I close by moving beyond the million-dollar decision and speaking to how you can make sure a good investment grows and continues to pay. I discuss how to form a strong bond with new hires, steps to take to identify any errors made in hiring, and lay a foundation for continuously improving the recruiting and hiring process.

Chapter Twelve draws on field research about how new employees best enter a new workplace and bond with its leadership. I explore the concept that "employees don't leave companies, they leave bosses" to suggest some of the first things to do when a million-dollar hire arrives for work that first day. I also review ways to track the performance of new hires, introducing a continuous improvement mind-set to the overall process.

Chapter Thirteen wraps up the book. I point to some of the resources available for those with an interest in more detail. I also put in context the costs of implementing the ideas set out in the preceding chapters.

My intent in this book is simple: plant some ideas, support them with data and facts, and show what others have been able to accomplish. Most important, I show what happens when employers bring the same level of strategy, tactics, technology, and continuous improvement to million-dollar hiring decisions that they bring to other high-value decisions in the business.

You'll probably have some questions. That's why I've set up www.million-dollarhire.com as a resource for those who want to see more examples, offer up their own for others to read, or access some of the tools referenced throughout the book. I've even set up the means for readers to pose questions and exchange ideas.

With that, let's go to work. We've got million-dollar hires to make. We've also got competition.

MILLION DOLLAR HIRE

CHAPTER ONE

THREE THINGS WE KNOW ABOUT PEOPLE

Whether starting, managing, or investing in a new business, I'm driven by two things: build it well, and gain a payoff. Hitting both targets, though, is tough. The government's Small Business Administration tells us that five of every ten start-ups fail in their first year.[1] Other sources put the number closer to nine or ten.[2] Reasons range from poor financing, to poor success in growing sales, to incompetent founders and management teams. In most start-ups, nothing is built, and no one sees a payoff.

The problem isn't limited to start-ups. Research shows that at least 50 percent of executives and managers in organizations fail within two years of taking on a new job.[3] Typically the organization doesn't go out of business, but the outcome is the same: nothing built and no payoff.

When we analyze these failures, we find that too often hiring staff made mistakes in choosing those they expected to do the building and generate the payoff. They made the wrong decisions when they recruited and hired the people they now count on. And it doesn't take a new start-up, a fast-growing company, or even a high-growth stage in a business cycle to fuel these mistakes.

For example, U.S. Bureau of Labor Statistics data for December 2009 showed approximately 131 million nonfarm employees in the United States. Separation and hiring data for the same period showed about 3.3 percent of the workforce separating from a job, with close to the same number, 3.2 percent, finding a new one. That's more than four million hiring decisions, even at a time when the economy showed no growth in the size of the workforce. Even with the recession of 2008–2009, natural employee turnover and movement led the number of hiring decisions to remain within one percentage point of the December 2007 prerecession rate of 3.7 percent.[4] Awkward as it might sound, even when businesses are reducing head count, they're hiring people, and even when the workforce is shrinking, they're making million-dollar hiring decisions—and millions of them.

And two things about hiring should grab the attention of any businessperson: a relatively high-volume event (hiring) that produces a relatively high rate of errors—people who fail. These errors have a financial consequence. At one end of the occupational ladder, hiring the wrong frontline employee in a fast food restaurant might seem like a small thing. With a close-to-minimum-wage employee, how bad can a bad hiring decision be? To find the answer, ask the national chain that employs tens of thousands of frontline staff. In designing a process that puts more focus on making the right hiring decisions, we saw percentage points added to its store-level profitability.

Higher up in the hierarchy and making a bad decision in selecting a professional or manager is easier to see as a financial mistake. Here, the cost to replace a poor decision averages about twice the position's annual salary.[5] And at this level, just one bad decision can have a major consequence. An admittedly exceptional example was the twenty-eight-year-old futures trader in Singapore whose bad bets on the Japanese market sank Barings PLC.[6] We can label that a billions-of-dollars hiring mistake.

Whenever there's a high-volume event that produces a high rate of errors with financial consequences, there's a business opportunity. For a service provider that helps employers find the best talent, there's opportunity in creating solutions to reduce errors and improve the quality of results. For an employer, there's opportunity for fundamentally changing how decisions are made, reducing errors, lowering risk, and seeing an improvement in results, including financial results.

In the chapters that follow, I draw on many of the solutions that today's recruiting and hiring professionals have created to improve the quality of hiring decisions. More important, I focus on the financial payoff these organizations gain when these tools are put to work, whether in staffing a start-up or dealing with growth and replacement in an established organization. You'll see that treating the recruiting and hiring process with the same rigor demanded in other areas of business offers more financial payoff than most managers and executives would imagine. In fact, a centerpiece in what follows is showing how to estimate the payoff that stems from improving these decisions.

Since the problem rests with people, I'll start with some things we know about people—candidates for a job and those who already work for us.

People Differ in Many Ways

People are *not* equal. This fact might not be true from a philosophical, social, and political point of view, but it is dead right when it comes to building things and producing payoffs.

Think about candidates for jobs in a manufacturing company. Some can read and use technical service guides; others have trouble reading the "Caution—Hazardous Materials" sign. Some candidates for software developer jobs are so skilled they can almost sense where to look for an error in a piece of programming; others serve as great error generators. Some candidates for customer service jobs stick with a complaint, build rapport, and leave the customer happy. Some give it thirty seconds and ask whether the customer wants to speak with a supervisor.

Some argue that training can smooth out these people differences—that all a person really needs is a fair chance to learn the job. In fact, the research evidence shows that people differ a great deal in learning ability and in the inclination to succeed. From a business point of view, the questions are simple. Are you willing to take on the expense to train for things you might instead hire for? Do you believe you can train away differences in responsibility, drive, or intellectual curiosity, for example?

Most employers would rather act on differences *among candidates* while they have a choice than deal with differences *among employees* once they're on the books. Most employers don't want to go into the training business any more deeply than necessary.

A while back, a paper industry client told me his employment office operated too much like a revolving door. He said the department was moving two types of problems through the company that were hurting the business: "dumb asses," and "smart asses." He was describing two basic differences among people that human resource professionals deal with all the time. With more finesse, we can view them as qualities that take on a *can-do* and *will-do* character—or a *can't-do* and *won't-do* character.

Can Do

We know that people differ in a host of knowledge, skills, and abilities that yield an employee who *can*—or *can't*—do the job. These are qualities gained through education, training, and firsthand experience. Some take years to build; some result from something as simple as having a hobby or growing up in a particular setting. Malcolm Gladwell's insightful book on the success of outliers points to how some of these *can-do* attributes are a function of how long one works at something, or even when, where, or among whom one is born.[7]

A person's *can-do* qualities can affect outcomes as basic as being able to learn a job. They can lead to success in problem solving, creativity, or the ability to see through the complexities of a situation that befuddles everyone else. Without these qualities, all the motivation in the world provides little benefit.

In the 1990s, one of the largest semiconductor manufacturers in the United States faced a *can-do* challenge. In its manufacturing workforce, many employees could not read or do math at even an elementary school level, yet quality improvement programs and increasingly sophisticated manufacturing techniques called for basic educational capabilities. Intense competition from Asian manufacturers had framed the decision: improve the skills of the U.S. workforce, or take the manufacturing operations offshore. A new recruiting and hiring program was created to make sure new hires brought the needed skills to the job. At the same time, employee development efforts began inside the company's U.S. operations. The company's internal university drove a companywide response to the challenge. Yes, *can do* really matters.

Will Do

Will-do qualities are different. Often we say these define an employee's personality. They distinguish a candidate who puts forth effort, works well with others, takes the employer's expectations seriously, and engages in behavior that helps, or at least doesn't hinder, putting their *can-do* skills to work.

Again in the 1990s, U.S. manufacturing companies landed on the concept of teams and teamwork. Quality improvement teams, customer service teams, union-management teams, and others became the zeitgeist. Problems in implementing the concepts, though, showed that many employees just didn't want to be part of a team. Hired with no attention to *will-do* qualities such as sociability, extroversion, or openness to new ideas, these employees often stymied efforts to gain the benefits of team-based approaches. As a result, many businesses began to pay attention to recruiting and hiring employees with a strong *will-do* foundation for collaborating in a team-based setting. But today we're learning that *will-do* qualities are not always positive; some can work against success.

More Isn't Always Better

For many years, the science of personality assessment followed a more-is-better outlook. Possessing greater degrees of sociability, conscientiousness, or openness to new ideas was shown to predict success in many jobs. The more of these attributes a candidate brings to these jobs, the better his or her chances of success, it was thought.

Recently, though, a host of more-is-worse qualities—excitability, skepticism, cautiousness, mistrust, and others—have been found to predict failure in the workplace. Differences among leaders in these areas have been shown to relate to their ability to gain commitment, engagement, and retention among subordinates. In settings with the potential for job-related accidents and injuries, differences among employees in the willingness to take unacceptable risks predicts the likelihood of being involved in such events. In workplace personality, having more of some things can be worse.

Those who design today's best recruiting and hiring programs understand the range of *can-do* and *will-do* qualities on which people differ. Rather than simply talking about *can-do* qualities, hiring professionals talk about learning ability for lower-level jobs, troubleshooting and problem-solving skills for midlevel jobs, and data integration and interpretation skills for higher-level positions. For leadership positions, concepts such as business acumen, strategic thinking, and skill at allocating resources often join the list.

Rather than simply talking about *will-do* qualities, hiring professionals talk about conscientiousness for lower-level jobs, openness to new ideas for midlevel jobs, and emotional stability for higher-level jobs. A host of other *will-do* characteristics enter the discussion as well. Again, for management and leadership positions, some of these "bright side" versus "dark side" attributes can make or derail a career or an entire company.[8]

Later, I'll review more detailed examples of the *can-do* and *will-do* differences candidates bring to an employer and ways to profile the *can-do* and *will-do* requirements of a given job. This, of course, lays the foundation for comparing candidates to the things a job actually demands, a central step in making the best million-dollar hires. For now, though, one thing we *know* is that people—candidates—differ; they differ in many ways, including major ways.

People Differences Translate to Performance Differences

Once candidates are hired and join a company, the differences continue, but now they show up in job performance. Say your company employs fifty sales reps. Those fifty reps don't all build sales pipelines of the same quality, don't all book the same volume of sales, don't all hit the same percentage of their quota, and don't all close sales that carry the same gross margin. The average performance of all fifty sales reps on any of these measures says something about the sales organization's overall effectiveness, but it's the *differences* among the fifty reps that consume management's time.

People differ in their job performance, and typically a lot. Any manager who supervises more than one employee sees the differences every day. And these aren't the differences reflected on the company's performance evaluation form where most employees range between excellent and superior, and being rated "competent" actually means god-awful. In any job, measurable differences in performance are always present.

Figure 1.1 In a highly engineered job, performance variability is generally small but still consequential

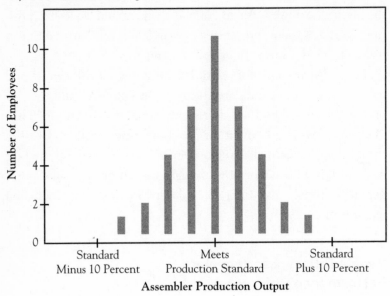

Where employees have little opportunity to influence the outcome of the work, the differences in performance can be narrowed but not eliminated. For example, a plot of individual employees' performance in a production assembly department, where work is highly automated, might look like Figure 1.1. Here, automation, engineering, and modern assembly techniques can make the job highly structured (some might say, mind-numbing). Even when jobs are simplified, though, there are measurable differences in performance among individual employees.

Figure 1.1 shows the bell-shaped distribution that measures of job performance often follow. The figure shows a few great performers at the top, a few poor performers at the bottom, and most performing in the middle of the range. In the real world, differences among employees don't always follow this perfect bell-shaped curve, but they often come close. And even small differences in performance add up. The production assemblers of Figure 1.1 who perform at 103 percent of standard over the long run make the company a great deal more money than those who perform at 100 percent of standard, particularly when hundreds are on the job. Even small performance differences matter a great deal in the long run.

In many jobs, it's just not possible to engineer out variability in performance. Jobs calling for judgment, discretion, and creativity show more performance variability. Think about the percentage of quota achieved by each of the fifty sales reps mentioned earlier. The result might look like Figure 1.2. Here, despite training, coaching, incentives, and so on, variability in individual performance is substantial.

As a rule, when jobs become more and more complex, variability in performance among individual employees increases. Nine of ten start-ups fail largely due to variability in the performance of the company founders. Some companies grow, prosper, and reward shareholders, but most don't. Any private equity investor will

Figure 1.2 In more complex jobs, performance variability is more noteworthy

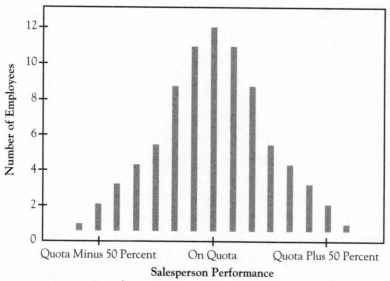

confirm that variability in the performance of newly minted CEOs has great consequences.

Variability in performance applies to high-level, single-incumbent jobs too. At these levels, though, the perspective changes a bit. It's silly to think about reducing the performance variability among your company's twenty chief financial officers (CFOs) unless it's a multinational that actually employs twenty divisional CFOs. It's not silly, though, to think about how *your* CFO performs compared to the CFOs of nineteen competitors. Here, the challenge is not about reducing performance variability *within* the organization; it's about making sure you're at the top of the performance distribution that's defined by you and all your competitors.

Performance variability leads companies to build all manner of human resource programs dedicated to *removing* it: training programs, incentive programs, disciplinary programs, and more. But think about the costs of all these "remedial" programs. All focus on removing variability among employees, particularly at the bottom of the performance distribution. All are less necessary when the quality of recruiting and hiring decisions improves.

In lower-level jobs, where performance variability is smaller, organizations typically recruit and hire the greatest numbers of employees. Here, improved hiring offers an opportunity to increase performance effectiveness by a small amount but for many employees. In higher-level jobs, where performance variability is greater, there's opportunity to improve performance for fewer employees but to a much greater degree. In short, better recruiting and hiring pay off in different ways at different levels, but both do so primarily by reducing variability in employee performance.

So another fact to build on is that whatever the job or the performance measure, people differ in the quality or quantity of performance they deliver. It's not worth arguing whether the differences always look like a bell-shaped curve. But it's important to understand the differences because they play a key role in what follows. Performance differences among employees are real, they grow in size as jobs demand more judgment and creativity, and they have major financial consequences.

People Differences Can Be Measured

The history of measuring how people differ is a long one, particularly as the differences relate to mental abilities and personality.[9] It covers research driven by two world wars, each yielding measurement tools and screening systems used to assign millions of military personnel to jobs that could benefit from their skills and abilities. The result was an array of tools for profiling differences relevant to employers too.

Beginning in the 1950s, these tools moved into the workplace as employers introduced employment testing, interviewing, work simulations, executive assessment programs, and the like. Psychologists expanded mental measurement and personality assessment to the executive level. Human resource consultants, fueled by employers who were seeking to screen candidates better, produced new ways to set up and manage hiring systems. More recent introduction of technology and outsourcing solutions has made these processes even more sophisticated.

The recruiting and hiring industry (test publishers, assessment specialists, search firms, and others) focuses on tools that deal with people differences. Annually the industry sees billions of dollars in sales. When you add in the software technology companies that support recruiting and hiring, the industry is now among the fastest-growing businesses.

Today the ways to measure differences among candidates are many. There's a test to evaluate nearly every conceivable human quality, many of them developed, tested, and proven in the workplace. The Buros Institute's *The Seventeenth Mental Measurements Yearbook*, a bible in the testing discipline, and *Tests in Print*, a similar listing, reference nearly four thousand tools that measure people differences in research and employment settings.[10]

Employers have used many of them, including those that bridge both the *can-do* and *will-do* demands of the workplace to guide recruiting and hiring decisions for decades.

But the methods available to measure differences among people that are relevant to the job extend far beyond testing. A host of methods focuses on improving the consistency of face-to-face interviews.[11] Some use realistic simulations and hands-on tools that take on the character of the job—that is, job simulations.[12] Others use software-based approaches to do things as complex as matching and scoring résumés against a job's requirements. There are measures of interests, motivation, proficiency, mental abilities, personality factors, physical capabilities, knowledge acquired through training, and almost any technical skill you can mention.

What happens when these tools are used to measure differences among candidates? Figure 1.3 shows what happened when several thousand candidates for maintenance jobs at a consumer products

Figure 1.3 People show differences in the job qualifications they possess

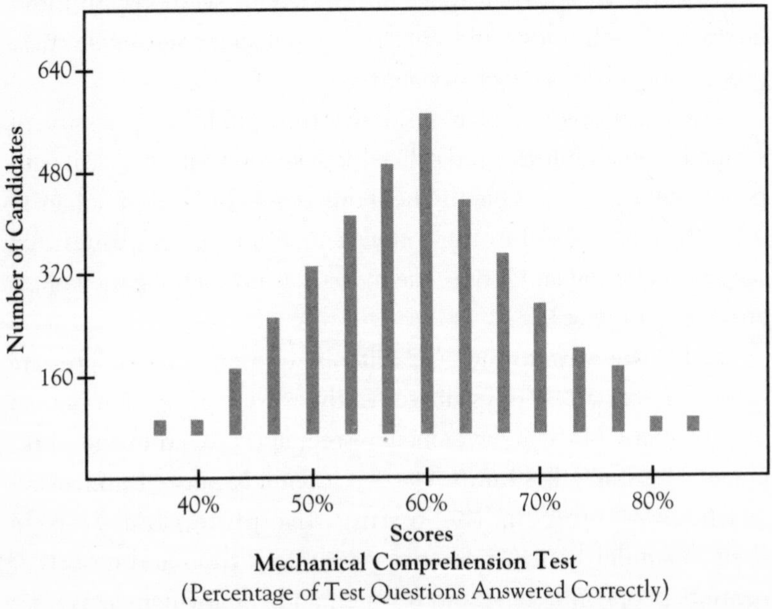
640
480
320
160
Number of Candidates
40%
50%
60%
70%
80%
Scores
Mechanical Comprehension Test
(Percentage of Test Questions Answered Correctly)

company completed a test of mechanical comprehension skills—a *can-do* measure. Scores ranged from the absolute maximum possible score to ones that would result by simply guessing. Excluding the extremes, in this case most candidates answered between 40 and 80 percent of the test questions correctly—a wide range of mastery for the knowledge being measured. And, yes, the illustration looks like a bell-shaped curve.

Candidates differ on measures of almost any knowledge, skill, ability, or personality characteristic we evaluate. For some measures, the distribution of scores is not so symmetrical, but it's often close. If an employer were to use a well-designed measure of deductive logic in screening software programmer candidates, a measure of extroversion in screening sales associates, a test of quantitative reasoning for data analysts, or a test of risk-taking inclination for the job of controller, the result would look much the same as Figure 1.3.

And it's not only tests that produce such results. Figure 1.4 shows the results when over three hundred sales candidates participated in a structured interview I designed for a recent client. In the process, teams of interviewers evaluated candidates' skills in a number of areas. The results are shown for one area: sales skills. Here, candidates received interviewer evaluations that ranged from unacceptable to superior. The total set of evaluations is close to a bell-shaped curve. Since the data are real, though, a question occurs: How did the candidates who ended up at the bottom of the distribution ever make it to a time-consuming, face-to-face interview in the first place? Was there no less costly prescreening step? Were the interviewers too critical of the candidates' skills? These are questions that carry financial implications and ones we'll tackle in detail a bit later. In this case, they're the reason I inserted a prescreening test battery to precede the interview process.

Figure 1.5 shows that differences among candidates can be measured when all the employer has to draw on is a stack of résumés. The figure illustrates that when technology-based résumé search

Figure 1.4 People differ in qualifications when measured by tools other than tests

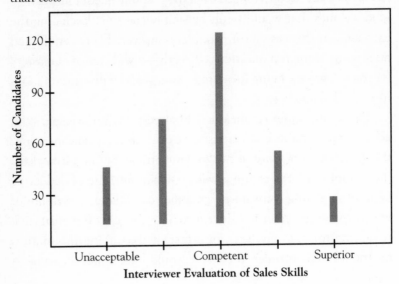

Interviewer Evaluation of Sales Skills

Figure 1.5 People differ in how well their résumés fit the job

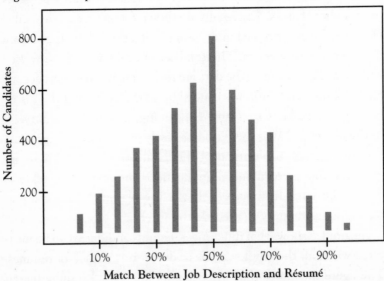

Match Between Job Description and Résumé

software reads résumés and reads the company's job description, it can produce a measure of the degree to which the information in each résumé matches the requirements reflected in the job description. Here, a few seconds of computer time devoted to reading and matching over two thousand résumés to the company's job description for an account manager job shows a familiar picture. Actually, using such a tool early in the screening process might have helped avoid inviting some of the Figure 1.4 candidates to a costly face-to-face interview process.

And so we confirm a third key fact in making better million-dollar decisions: the noteworthy differences candidates bring to the workplace can be measured accurately, reliably, fairly, and in a way that acknowledges the financial importance of every hiring decision.

Three Facts to Build On

This is where we begin, then: with three basic facts.

1. People differ. They differ in many ways, some of them major. The differences related to *can-do* and *will-do* qualities determine success on the job.

2. Once applicants are hired, the differences among people continue and show in their performance on the job. These performance differences follow from differences that existed *before* they were hired.

3. Recruiting and hiring professionals can measure the differences among candidates accurately, reliably, fairly, and in a way that produces a payoff for the business.

Space travel aside, nearly all organizations devote more financial resources to people than to any other area. Each time an employee is added to the workforce, the business makes a major financial commitment and takes a noteworthy financial risk. Each new hire, in concept, represents an entry on the organization's balance sheet, but it doesn't know whether the addition is an asset or a liability until after making the decision. If it's a liability, those who are hiring don't know whether it's a short-term or long-term liability until much later.

Next, we turn to some information about process improvement that can help limit the liabilities and the risk when employee commitments are made in making million-dollar hires.

CHAPTER TWO

FOUR THINGS WE KNOW ABOUT PROCESS

Understanding that people differ, the differences can be measured, and the differences follow people into the workplace once they're hired is a start, but we need a way to build on these facts and extract value. To do this, I assemble another set of facts—ones about process improvement.

The facts about process improvement, and the techniques they foster, are not new. Many were created as part of the manufacturing sector's quality improvement movement in the late 1980s and 1990s. They went by names such as statistical process control, total quality management (TQM), Six Sigma, DMAIC (Define-Measure-Analyze-Improve-Control), and other trademarked logos familiar to people in business today.[1] Most brought data-gathering and statistical analysis tools to bear in improving the quality of products or services. Most worked to eliminate variability in product quality, service delivery, or other measures of performance. All focused on isolating the sources of quality problems, fixing them, and putting systems in place to drive continuous improvement. For the purposes of this chapter, though, the process is hiring, and the product is new employees. Quality means quality of hire.

We Can Predict Performance

Every time a recruiter reviews a résumé and decides to follow up with the candidate, he makes a prediction. The human resource (HR) department makes a prediction when it scores a candidate's test and decides to take the next step, scheduling an interview. A department manager makes a prediction when she interviews a candidate and decides to make an offer. All are predicting the same thing: the candidate's future performance.

If the predictions work, then we've capitalized on the previous chapter's people facts. If we can *predict* the performance of candidates *before* they're hired, we reduce variability in their performance *after* they're hired. If we make accurate predictions, we reduce the risk of hiring candidates who otherwise would have populated the bottom of the performance distribution.

Predictions about candidates take many forms. Will this sales candidate hit quota or simply live off his salary draw? Will this telemarketing rep last beyond six months or leave as soon as she finds a better offer? Will this police recruit make it through academy training and succeed on the street, or decide he doesn't like taking orders? Will this consulting candidate create a client following or top out at the analyst level? Will this start-up CEO manage capital effectively or blow it, come back for more, and dilute the hell out of his investors?

Sometimes we need to make a decision: yes or no. Sometimes we need to make a choice, as when two or more candidates appear qualified. Then we need to predict which are *better* qualified and which to hire. Sometimes the predictions are not so one-dimensional. For example, we might try to determine whether a candidate for a manufacturing job will learn the job quickly *and* meet production standards consistently, show up for work regularly, and be capable of moving to a supervisory level in the longer term.

After all, we expect the software we buy to install as planned, run with minimum bugs, offer a responsive help desk, and come with regular updates. Why settle for less in recruiting and hiring systems? In fact, if only implicitly, we make a multidimensional prediction in every hiring decision. But predicting multiple dimensions of people's behavior in the future is a challenge.

Fortunately, research shows that many facets of job performance *can* be predicted, often with different kinds of recruiting and hiring tools. Different tools work with differing degrees of accuracy. And some tools might work, but are likely to bring risks such as candidate push-back, high cost, or legal challenge. In short, decades of research lead us to know a good deal about predicting people's performance on the job.

I've been asked to make some fairly detailed predictions: Which full-time financial advisor candidate will be skilled at working well with the several very different members of a wealthy family? Which Turkish production worker candidates will perform best in a cigarette manufacturing plant? Which automobile assembly candidates will not exceed an acceptable number of unexcused absences? Which future sausage-making candidates will suffer fewest on-the-job injuries? Which sales executive candidates will manage their teams to the targeted levels of sales and customer renewals? Which CEO candidate will meet the venture capital firm's growth and profitability expectations? Different jobs, different performance targets, different kinds of predictions. The solution rests in different kinds of tools.

The payoff rests in making sure the predictions we make are as accurate as possible. In talking about accuracy, I introduce a concept that hiring specialists call *validity*. The term carries a variety of definitions—ones that sometimes seem a bit convoluted, even to those in the business. But at its simplest, validity can be visualized as in Figure 2.1.

Figure 2.1 A valid candidate screening process predicts job performance levels after hiring

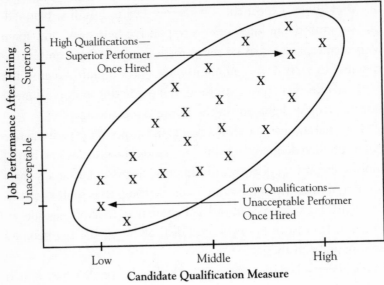

Note how the two concepts introduced in Chapter One—*people differences* and *performance differences*—are connected in the figure. Validity *is* this connection. Validity connects the dots—in this case, the X's.

Any measure of a candidate's qualifications—amount of experience, answers on a prescreening checklist, results from an interview, the score on a test—can be used to spread out candidates from low to high (the horizontal axis in the figure). If the way candidates spread themselves out on the qualification measure parallels the way they spread themselves out on job performance once they become employees, the measure is said to be *valid* for making predictions about future performance. Simply stated, a valid recruiting or hiring tool can be used to predict that those who score higher as candidates will perform higher as employees.[2]

In Figure 2.1, the X's inside the ellipse show what happens with a valid recruiting or hiring practice when candidates' qualifications are measured and the person then joins the company. The place-ment of each X shows the connection between a given candidate's qualification before hire (on the horizontal axis) and the same person's on-the-job performance after being hired (on the vertical axis). This way of depicting the validity, or value, that rests in candidate information has been used in the science of hiring system design for decades.

The figure shows a *valid* hiring process—one where information learned about the candidate forecasts his or her future on-the-job performance. As shown, though, some candidates who perform relatively better on the qualifying measure perform less well on the job than those with lower qualifications, and vice versa. No surprise there. Validity isn't about perfection; it's about making *better* hiring decisions in the long run by improving the odds of hiring, or reject-ing, the right candidates.

Use Figure 2.1 as a mental image to guide the way you think about a recruiting or hiring tool. The illustration should come to mind when you think about whether, and to what degree, a par-ticular piece of information about a candidate helps in predicting their future job performance. If the pattern doesn't hold, then why use the information? It's revealing nothing of value.

Figure 2.2 shows such a situation: a case where the candidate information bears no relationship to how well people will perform if they join the workforce. The illustration shows that whatever the qualification might be, it measures the wrong kind of experi-ence, the wrong knowledge or skill, the wrong personality dimen-sions, or the wrong interviewer impressions. The tool is *not valid*; it's irrelevant.

Unfortunately, the information that many recruiting and hiring professionals use produces results that look just like Figure 2.2. I've often found it an unpleasant conversation, after reviewing a pro-gram that a company has used for years, to show management a data plot that looks like Figure 2.2. It's particularly unpleasant when hundreds of thousands of dollars have been spent to run the

Figure 2.2 A screening process with no validity does not predict performance after hiring

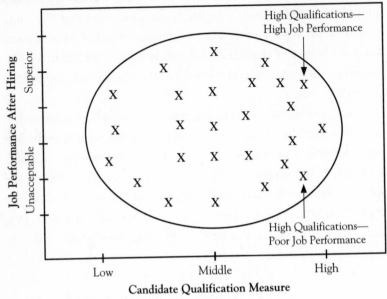

program or when a legal challenge has been filed and the purpose of the review was to estimate the company's exposure.

For example, traditional, unstructured candidate interviewing programs produce results that look a lot like Figure 2.2. Gladwell reports that IQ-oriented tests that some professional football teams use also show patterns that look like Figure 2.2 despite their hoped-for contribution.[3] In a more complex example, one of my recent expert witness assignments showed that when firefighter candidates were assessed with general mental ability tests, the tests' relationship with on-the-job performance looked like Figure 2.2, not Figure 2.1. But evidence showed that if a mechanical comprehension element were added to the firefighter test, the picture would begin to look more like Figure 2.1.[4]

That's the rub. Certain kinds of recruiting and hiring tools produce patterns that look like Figure 2.1; others produce ones that look like Figure 2.2. It often depends on the type of job, the kind of performance targeted, the kind of candidate qualification considered, or even the group of candidates. In other words, the situation gets complicated.

It's a fact, though, that we can predict employee performance. Performance on a wide range of outcomes can be predicted with reasonably good accuracy. Although there are always unique cases, recent decades have laid the foundation for improving recruiting and hiring predictions in the same way that Six Sigma and TQM process improvement techniques have had an impact on improving other parts of a business. The objective is to improve results—in many cases, financial results. I'll review a variety of examples in Chapters Four and Five and show the financial consequences associated with the predictions.

Predicting Performance Yields a Financial Payoff

In the science of process improvement, the goal typically is to take *all*, or as much as possible, of the performance variability out of a process—in our case, a hiring process. Typically the goal is to narrow the range of performance that results from a particular process so that both the right and left sides of the bell-shaped performance distribution are pulled toward a more uniform, predictable outcome. Process improvement involves removing variability so that outcomes are more predictable.

The goal in removing variability in the performance of employees is a little more complicated. Variance on the high side of the bell-shaped curve actually works to the organization's benefit. Here, sales exceed quota, production beats standards, and customer opinions are very favorable. No one would suggest that performance variability on the top side of the curve should be eliminated. In fact, it identifies the winners in the workforce.

But variance on the bottom side of the distribution always works against the business. Eliminate it, and the average performance of the overall workforce improves. Chop off a small percentage at the bottom of the distribution, and many of the company's problems are solved. For example, a trucking firm recently discovered that more than 80 percent of its accidents were caused by the poorest-performing 20 percent of its drivers. The other 80 percent had almost no accidents. The same holds for other performance measures. A small part of the workforce is generally responsible for a noteworthy portion of the problems: absenteeism, injuries, theft, waste, sabotage, and so on. That's why it's the bottom of the performance distribution that's often the process improvement target.

In recruiting and hiring, though, we can never eliminate all the variability in employee performance. The information collected about candidates and the tools for finding and screening candidates are just not that accurate. Things that happen in the workplace and at home *after* a candidate is hired affect performance too. Nevertheless, we can improve the degree to which we chop off the bottom of the performance distribution and, as a result, improve the average performance for those we hire.

Later chapters offer examples of programs that focus on lowering turnover, increasing sales, reducing accidents, increasing productivity, and increasing customer satisfaction. Many of the examples are linked to straightforward computations of the financial payoff produced when a recruiting or hiring tool targeting a given payoff metric was implemented. The examples come not only from large companies with sophisticated systems but small and midsized companies, and start-up ventures too. They illustrate that straightforward tracking of both hiring and performance data can be used to set up a continuous improvement loop where the human resource and operating departments of a company track the results gained by adjusting the types of candidate information they use.

Ask a manager, though, to describe the difference between her top and bottom performers *in financial terms*, and the answer is likely to be, "It's hard to express in dollars." Most managers have difficulty coming up with a financial outcome that describes the performance differences noted in Chapter One. In a few cases, financial metrics are straightforward—for example, with sales jobs. In most jobs, though, it's tough to translate performance differences directly to dollars. It's difficult to show, for example, that Joe is *worth* $37,000 more than Mary.

In health care, education, customer service, and even government jobs and departments such as marketing, accounting, or human resources, it's always difficult to compute the financial return gained by removing variability at the low end of the performance range. For some jobs (salesperson or production worker), it's easy. For other jobs (accountant, marketing manager, or employee benefits specialist), placing a financial value on different levels of performance is difficult.

But research has begun providing some basic rules of thumb that express performance differences in financial terms for these types of jobs too. These rules offer a simple way to place a dollar value on different levels of employee performance. And the best news is that they provide a way to estimate the return gained when better hiring programs reduce performance variability for jobs where hard measures of performance are tough to find.[5]

The statistics and economic modeling tools driving these rules of thumb can be complicated, but they can be simplified for the sake of illustration. That's what I'll do in Chapter Three. We'll review a rule of thumb that can be used to estimate the economic value gained in hiring more of the bell curve's top performers, and avoiding its bottom performers, even when hard measures of performance are difficult to produce. These tools underscore the second process fact: a measurable payoff rests in better hiring decisions, it can be reduced to numbers, and it's far larger than most would think.

But You Can Get into Trouble

There's always risk when you discriminate among people, and that's what a hiring program is designed to do: discriminate. The risk is in challenges of *illegal* discrimination and challenges to decisions about who is invited to join the organization and who is not. The challenges can come from individual plaintiffs, groups or classes of plaintiffs, and government agencies.

Let's start with a little background. Parts of the 1964 Civil Rights Act turned government attention to hiring practices. Legislators feared that some employers might use hiring programs to mask illegal discrimination in the workplace. Federal and state agencies were created and regulations were crafted to help prevent such discrimination. Of course, litigation followed.

The Equal Employment Opportunity Commission (EEOC), Office of Federal Contract Compliance Programs (OFCCP), and U.S. Department of Justice (DOJ) became the major federal agencies charged with enforcing provisions of the act related to recruiting and hiring. The EEOC took oversight of companies in the private sector, OFCCP took over employers that were holding contracts with the federal government, and DOJ took oversight of units of government.

State-level agencies were also created to enforce equal employment statutes at the local level. State to state, differences in practices resulted, with different states taking more and less aggressive regulation postures. Meanwhile, the courts began the process of interpreting equal employment opportunity legislation with a number of landmark decisions.[6] Litigation proceeded to deal with increasingly technical matters. Even the U.S. Supreme Court became involved. It remains so, as illustrated in the 2009 *Ricci* case involving not hiring but the use of candidate assessment tools to guide promotion decisions for firefighters in the City of New Haven, Connecticut.[7]

More than a decade after the act, three federal agencies, along with the U.S. Department of Treasury, published rules for recruiting hiring practices: the 1978 Uniform Guidelines on Employee Selection Procedures.[8] The guidelines advise employers about the ways to satisfy federal statutes should their hiring practices be challenged. Since the publication of the guidelines, the courts too have relied on them as something of a benchmark for evaluating employer programs.

Over the next three decades, new laws emerged. The Civil Rights Act was amended in 1991. The Americans with Disabilities Act was enacted in 1990 and revised in 2008, also addressing employers' hiring standards. Employment litigation expanded to include broadly defined plaintiff groups, based on ethnicity, gender, age, disability status, and other characteristics.

Today compliance with a host of equal employment opportunity laws and affirmative action practices is central to recruiting and hiring. Concern with the potential of legal challenge is ever present. It's not a stretch to say, in fact, that human resource professionals often pay as much attention to legal compliance as to how well their recruiting and hiring programs function, and with good reason. For federal contractors who work with the government or other government contractors, compliance can determine the companies' ongoing cash flow. The OFCCP can literally disbar a company from eligibility to do business with the government if it's not satisfied with the company's recruiting and hiring practices. The costs associated with government reviews, adverse publicity, and private party challenges are worrisome. Many executives give a clear message to their HR leadership: keep us out of trouble and out of the newspaper.

In effect, though, the rules of the road for recruiting and hiring systems set down by the Guidelines, along with additional standards produced by a number of professional organizations, now serve as fairly routine checklists for employers. For now, we'll look at these rules and guidelines as another process fact, because legal compliance calls for process monitoring and quality control steps in the work of improving hiring results. The good news is that if an employer's recruiting and hiring program produces results that look like Figure 2.1, it's likely to succeed in any compliance review or legal challenge. When all the evidence has been reviewed, it's the program's validity, in content and administration, that wins or loses the case.

Continuous Improvement Principles Apply in Hiring

One of the primary ways to avoid legal risk is to look at recruiting and hiring practices as subject to the same continuous improvement thinking that guides production or delivery of services in other areas of a business. Here, the *product* is people—new hires. The *process* is whatever practice makes up the company's recruiting and hiring program. Like any other continuous improvement effort, a company's hiring program needs to incorporate data collection, analysis, and improvement planning steps similar to those used to control variability in the quality of its products or services.

In hiring, continuous improvement is measured in terms of the performance produced by those recruited and hired. Here, the low end of the performance distribution is the target. Here, continuous improvement goes by the name *validity* or *validation* of the employer's recruiting and hiring practices. Improvement in the quality of new hires and reduction in costs or legal risk are the process improvement targets.

Today technology platforms available to even small and midsized organizations offer the data tracking and analysis power needed to drive continuous improvement that once was available only to large enterprises. The cost of access to these solutions falls in a range where using them to avoid just one hiring mistake covers the cost of an annual license. Some of the solutions provide a means for continually testing the system and identifying areas where recruiting and hiring can be done more effectively.

So the final process fact notes that continuous process improvement, and all the techniques that have grown up around it in other areas of business, applies to recruiting and hiring. In fact, that's what the rest of this book is about: putting these tools to work and measuring the results.

So Far

At this point, we've gained four more facts, all reflecting process improvement concepts that capitalize on the people facts reviewed in the first chapter. These facts involve technical tools and risk-reduction steps that predict the differences in how candidates will perform on the job. These process facts tell us that

1. With valid recruiting and hiring programs, we can predict which candidates are most likely to perform at or below the level we expect. Over time, making these predictions will help "average-up" the performance of the overall workforce.

2. Improvements in how well we predict people's performance have financial consequences. The consequences can be measured and used to estimate the financial return, whether through better performance or lower costs, that accompanies a change in the way an organization runs its recruiting and hiring programs.

3. There is a legal side to recruiting and hiring. But there also are steps that reduce the risk of challenge and cost of compliance. Although we sometimes dress up these steps with terms such as *validity*, they boil down to following the same logic that companies apply in other quality control and quality improvement initiatives.

4. Risks are reduced and payoff is increased if recruiting and hiring programs are treated with the same continuous improvement outlook applied to manufacturing, logistics, operations, financial, or other aspects of the business.

With three people facts and four process facts, it's time to bring this knowledge to life. I'll start with a few thinking models: tool kits to guide how to put the facts to work.

CHAPTER THREE

SOME BASIC THINKING MODELS

It's now time to begin building on the seven facts reviewed in the two preceding chapters. Be forewarned, though, that this chapter involves a bit of math. Since I've always found it easier to understand math and statistics when they're presented in pictures, I'll follow that model here. Most of the ideas are in the form of charts and graphs. Readers who wish more will find plenty of references to more detailed sources throughout the rest of the book.

Here's my promise: get through this, and the rest of the book will be a breeze. Grasp it, and you'll have thinking models to use in considering your own organization's recruiting and hiring practices. The real payoff will be in gaining a better framework for thinking about your recruiting and hiring programs from both a risk-reduction and financial payoff point of view.

The Materiality of Recruiting and Hiring Decisions

My first job after graduate school was with one of the large public accounting firms. Like its competitors, the firm was organized into audit, tax, and management services divisions. The last included a human resource consulting practice where people like me plied our trade.

There was frequent opportunity to attend cross-discipline meetings, where staff from one division—say, the audit practice—would explain to other divisions what they did and why it was important. Attending one such session, I learned from the audit group about materiality. In conducting a financial audit, they explained, they needed criteria for identifying transactions that were important enough to merit scrutiny—ones they considered "material transactions." For a midsize company, they reported, a transaction carrying a value of $25,000 might be considered "material."

A light went on: my work involved helping clients undertake "material transactions" too. Developing tools to hire a manager with a $100,000 annual salary was a material transaction, after all. So were collecting $100,000 to recruit, screen, and select a divisional operating officer and making sure a client's hiring program met equal employment opportunity statutes, lowering the likelihood of litigation.

At our next discussion session, I described how the human resource consulting practice guided clients through material transactions. I suggested there might be opportunity to introduce our services to some of the office's major audit clients and to bring the concept of materiality to clients' recruiting and hiring transactions. Soon after, I left the firm to start my own business.

The idea stuck, though. If recruiting and hiring a manager is not a material transaction, what is? If hiring those at the C-suite level is not a material transaction, what is? Yet there's no outside agent to review these actions and report to shareholders on whether the company followed generally accepted practices, used proper tools, or created remedies to avoid repeating any errors. Although we in HR lack the financial regulatory imprimatur, we make and evaluate material transactions all the time.

For example, Hogan, Hogan, and Kaiser describe the concept of derailed managers.[1] They point out that the costs associated with a derailed manager in "time and resources to recruit, select, and train new ones . . . and hidden costs associated with golden parachutes, lost intellectual and social capital, missed business objectives, and destroyed employee morale," range from about $750,000 to over $2 million, depending on the level of the job. Do the programs that recruit and hire failed managers have a material effect on a company? What about the executives whose actions have brought down entire companies? Was their hiring a material transaction?

Of course, these examples involve small-population, even singular, positions. But what about the group of fifty salespersons that hits only 70 percent of its annual sales target? What about the maintenance staff of twenty-five whose manufacturing lines have 20 percent more downtime than the rest of the company's plants? Do such groups have a material effect on their company? Could you say that the recruiting and hiring tools that brought them inside the company had a material effect on the business? What about the two-hundred-person call center whose customer retention numbers run 25 percent ahead of the company's other centers? All of these examples involve large groups of people—groups whose performance has a material effect on the overall business.

Viewed in the context of most financial audits, the decision made in hiring just one employee involves sufficient dollars to qualify as a material transaction if such actions were covered by rules such as generally accepted accounting principles. It's just that there are no rules or regulations that look to whether the hiring decisions companies make are good ones. No one audits them, and few shareholders question them. Except for equal employment opportunity laws, the government doesn't care about them either.

The materiality concept might seem like a cute way to make a point. The fact is, though, that there *are* generally accepted principles for recruiting and hiring employees correctly. There *are* practices that research, not regulation, shows to produce results more beneficial to the company, its shareholders, and the people involved—both candidates and employees. There *are* ways to express the materiality of recruiting and hiring decisions in a financial framework. It's just that not many companies have gotten there yet. But some have.

Improving the Odds of Being Right

What's the long-run payoff in a game of blackjack? The folks at the Cornell University Math Department tell us that under the most favorable rules, the house advantage is never less than 0.16 percent.[2] In more usual circumstances, the disadvantage to the player is about 6 percent. So if you play blackjack for the next thirty days, eight hours a day, you could expect to take home ninety-four cents for every dollar you wager. You will win some hands; you might even win big from time to time. But in the long run, you are going to lose big.

What if you could do something to improve the odds of winning by just 10 percent? It would mean that in the long run, you could expect to collect about $1.03 for every dollar you wager. Do this for thirty days, eight hours a day, and you've made some real money. That's only a small improvement in the odds but a big payoff. The longer you do it, the more you gain.

When we set out to produce a financial payoff through better hiring, we take this improving-the-odds perspective as another thinking model. Improving the odds fits the world of hiring because hiring too is a game of incremental improvement—a game where recruiting and hiring specialists can do better but will always make mistakes. No matter what strategies or tools we add to the process and no matter what due diligence we follow, we will make errors.

We can improve the odds of being correct and improve our batting average in finding the best talent. But we will continue to make mistakes—just not as many.

Validity as Another Thinking Model

A way to visualize improving the odds involves the idea of validity introduced in Chapter Two. There, I illustrated how a valid hiring program makes sure that the way candidates are selected actually forecasts their performance on the job. Figure 3.1 illustrates the concept.

In the illustration, the pattern that relates information about the candidate—his interview evaluations—to his performance on the job is not very tight, but there *is* an overall pattern. In the

Figure 3.1 Even relatively low validity improves the odds of making accurate hiring decisions
Note: An example of a qualification measure is interviewers' ratings of sales skills.

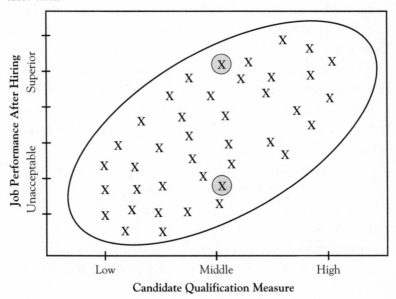

example, candidates receiving the most favorable interview evaluations tend to perform more effectively once on the job; in fact, the most highly qualified candidates turn out to be acceptable performers. Candidates receiving the lowest interview evaluations tend to perform less effectively once on the job; the very lowest-evaluated candidates produce consistently poor performers.

Still, candidates rated at a given level on the interview vary a good deal in how well they perform once on the job. This is shown by the two circled X's, representing candidates who receive generally equivalent interview evaluations but whose subsequent performance differs substantially. To put the illustration in context, it's actually better than most employers would find if they linked their interviewers' ratings of candidates to the subsequent on-the-job performance for those they hire.

In Figure 3.2, the relationship between the candidate qualification—a skills test—and performance after hire is tighter. The validity of the hiring program is greater. Most important, the odds of accurately predicting performance on the job for those who possess the same level of qualification on the test are much better. Here, the two circled X's show that those with close to the same test scores perform within a narrower (more predictable) range than illustrated in Figure 3.1.

In this case, the skills test can be said to show greater validity than the interview process. As a point of reference, Figure 3.2 is similar to the pattern one might see in using a well-designed battery of preemployment tests to predict the performance of technical employees.

The purpose in showing the two figures is to set a mental image for what we seek: better odds of hiring people who perform to expectations and better odds of being right when making a prediction about how a *candidate* will perform as an *employee*. Improving the validity of the hiring program increases the odds of identifying candidates whose performance actually falls at the level we expect.

Figure 3.2 Better validity means more accurate forecasting of performance after hiring
Note: An example is a skills test battery for apprentices.

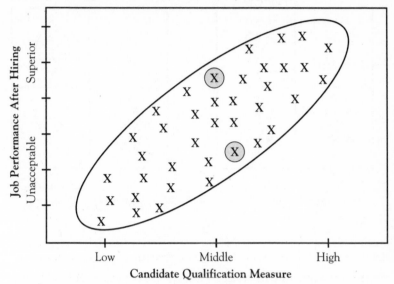

Later I link these two simple figures to a bit more sophisticated math that will help produce estimates of the financial payoff a given recruiting and hiring program is likely to offer. For now, though, *what* is important is the mental image of tightening the link between what a recruiting and hiring program considers and *how* new hires will perform on the job.

There's one more view on this thinking model that's important. Figures 3.1 and 3.2 illustrate the model for cases where the measure of candidate qualifications ranges along a scale from low to high—scores on a test, ratings from interviewers, or years of education, for example. The measure of performance after hiring also runs along a range from low to high: percentage of sales achieved, production rates, supervisor's performance ratings, and so on.

The concept holds too when the measures are not so finely tuned. For example, say you want to predict the likelihood that

Figure 3.3 The concept of validity applies to even simple yes-no hiring standards

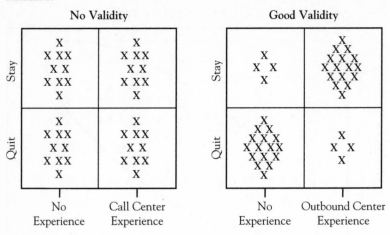

new hires will turn over during the first ninety days of employment—the bane of call center managers. Say you set out to do this using a candidate qualification measure that looks at a candidate's prior job experience with a simple level of measurement of experience versus no experience. Figure 3.3 illustrates this simple, two-dimensional proposition.

The left side of the figure shows a hiring program where prior experience is measured as possessing call center experience versus not having this experience. In the figure, results show this type of experience tells nothing about whether new hires will leave within the first ninety days. Regardless of whether they possess the experience, the number of "quits" and "stays," illustrated by the X's, is identical. The simple two-by-two exhibit actually looks somewhat like a circle, just like the illustration of a process with no validity in Chapter Two.

The right side of Figure 3.3 shows results for a different measure of experience: possessing *outbound* call center experience versus not. Here, knowing the candidate possesses such experience increases the odds he or she *will not* leave in ninety days. This simple two-by-two exhibit looks somewhat like an ellipse—the definition of a process with validity.

In the figure, one measure of candidate qualification has validity; one does not. Using one measure *increases the odds* of controlling turnover of new hires; using the other does not. Given the cost of each turnover event—recruiting costs, training costs, payroll, benefits, and so on—one hiring program reduces the turnover rate with a measurable financial payoff; the other does not.

The concept of increasing the validity in a hiring tool relates to any measure of performance after hiring, whether the tool is finely tuned, or produces simple yes-versus-no metrics. Figure 3.4 brings more detail to the illustration. The new concept is simple. Information that valid hiring tools produce can be used to make a best-fit prediction about the future performance of candidates

Figure 3.4 A valid screening process helps set a qualifying standard for hiring candidates who perform at targeted levels

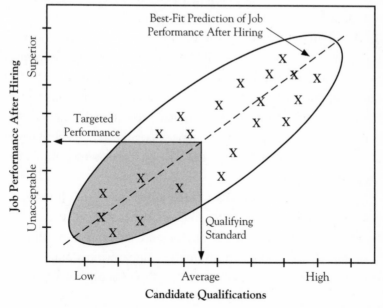

who possess various levels of a given qualification. This best-fit prediction is the straight line that passes through the X's in the figure according to a simple statistical technique called regression analysis.[3]

An employer who wants to hire candidates who perform at or above a targeted performance level can use this best-fit prediction to identify a qualifying standard that predicts performance at (or above) the targeted level.

As shown in Figure 3.4, the statistics boil down to identifying where the targeted performance level on the vertical axis connects with a qualifying standard on the horizontal axis, using the best-fit prediction to connect the two measures. Candidates falling below this qualifying standard are rejected, because the data predict they will perform below the targeted performance level. Although this process can be dressed up with other statistical terms, it's fundamentally simple.

Figure 3.5 shows that the procedure just outlined will make mistakes. Remember that the intent is to *increase the odds* of hiring employees who perform at a targeted level or higher. A valid process increases the odds, but it isn't perfect.

As Figure 3.5 shows, some candidates who fall short on the qualification measure would have been acceptable performers. Some who pass the qualification measure will turn out to be unacceptable performers. There's no way to avoid such errors, because qualification measures never predict performance with perfection. Too many factors influence human behavior, both before and after they're hired, to expect a hiring process to yield perfect predictions.

Some time ago, we hired a computer wunderkind. Just twenty years old, he helped develop some of the advanced technology solutions that impressed our clients and set us apart from competitors. He was celebrated inside the company as a young genius. A year later, we found the "wunderkind" had applied his genius in

Figure 3.5 Even valid recruiting and hiring programs make errors

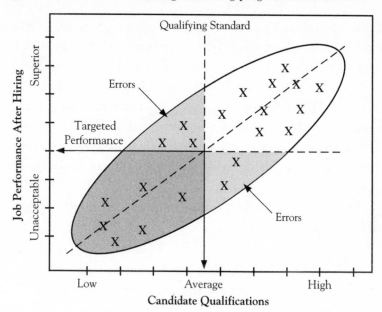

some unique ways. He'd been collecting our client payments from the mailperson and depositing them in a company he set up with a name nearly the same as that of our company. He used the money to fly to Europe on the weekends and visit casinos on the Riviera and to find an eastern European girlfriend! Now, that was a spectacular hiring error!

So, yes, there will be errors. The concept illustrated in Figure 3.5, though, shows that the hits in predicting which candidates will be acceptable versus unacceptable performers will outnumber the errors. Use a valid practice over a period of time, and a major shift in payoff results by improving the odds in your favor. When hiring volume is high, even a small improvement will produce a major improvement in the financial return that results.

What the Models Have in Common

Every HR professional and hiring manager applies the thinking models reviewed—materiality, improving the odds, and validity—every day, if only in a commonsense way. What is new are the methods for estimating the economic impact that using them produces. Field research and technology bring together statistical modeling tools that forecast the financial payoff of alternative recruiting and hiring approaches and help guide return-on-investment decisions. We enter that conversation in the following chapters.

To recap, though, the thinking models I've introduced blend together several common features:

- They rely on decades of research showing that information collected during the recruiting and hiring process can be used to make predictions about candidates' performance on the job.

- They acknowledge that predictions of performance after hiring will never be perfect; that errors always will occur, and it's lowering the odds of errors and improving the odds of being right that drive payoff.

- They offer methodologies for analyzing the quality of any hiring process and for expressing the extent to which it will increase the odds of making correct predictions. These methodologies provide a means for translating improvements in the odds of being right to estimates of actual financial return.

The upcoming chapters focus on how to make improvements in recruiting and hiring programs: using tools, technology, and support systems, for example. First, though, we'll skip ahead a bit in the next two chapters and discuss some of the financial payoff employers have seen by using such programs. I'll tie together the thinking models just reviewed and demonstrate how organizations have carried them to the level of documenting financial payoff. Chapter Four reviews payoff examples for jobs where performance is easily measured with hard, quantitative metrics—jobs where the results of changing the odds through better hiring can be tracked and documented most clearly.

CHAPTER FOUR

MEASURING PAYOFF IN HARD NUMBERS

Chapters One and Two laid down three people facts and four process facts on which to build recruiting and hiring programs. Chapter Three then supplied thinking models to use in viewing a program's financial payoff. You might expect this chapter to deal with how you actually do it, that is, how you create a program that drives million-dollar decisions.

Instead, I'll whet your appetite. Covering the how-to-do-it is going to take a number of chapters—chapters on everything from screening résumés to evaluating references, from testing to technology. It will take a chapter to review the legal pitfalls too (the how-not-to-do-it) and more to discuss the continuous improvement mind-set that really drives payoff. Here, though, I'll jump straight ahead to showing the payoff that employers have seen when the how-to-do-it ideas reviewed later are put to use.

My motivation is simple. I want to grab your attention to convince you of the returns to be gained and to show what you can count on. If I'm successful here, the how-to-do-it chapters will prove particularly interesting.

Choosing Where to Move the Needle

There are two ways to measure the payoff in better hiring. In the first, results can be tracked with objective metrics. I've already previewed some of these—measures such as sales volume, number of units produced, number of errors made, and costs incurred. Some objective measures are more administrative than performance oriented—ones like turnover, absenteeism, tardiness, and accident rate. These, like the positive ones, though, can be tracked with hard numbers.

When results can be measured in such terms, tracking the payoff from better recruiting and hiring is more straightforward. For many jobs, though, it's difficult to come up with objective performance measures: accountant, software engineer, flight attendant, even politician. In fact, in many jobs, hard measures of performance aren't as relevant to evaluating how well the person performs the central purpose of the job. Teachers, for example, can be measured through hard numbers with the standardized test scores of their students, but does this really address the central purpose of the job? In many jobs, evaluating *what you do* and *how you do* it doesn't fit a numerical yardstick.

For such jobs, it's more difficult to measure the payoff in better recruiting and hiring practices, and that requires a different thinking model. Since so many jobs fall in this category, I'll devote Chapter Five to measuring payoff when hard, quantitative metrics of performance aren't realistic.

Here, I'll deal with situations where you *can* track results with hard measures and where hard data can be used to document the impact of more effective recruiting and hiring. Among the most frequently used of these metrics are these:

- *Sales results*—the Holy Grail, typically tracked according to volume, percentage of target, retention rates, and other measures

- *Turnover rates*—the bane of call centers, retail jobs, food service, and other positions with a seemingly fluid workforce

- *Production rates*—key to more than just manufacturing jobs where the results of employee efforts can be counted not only according to quantity, but quality, cost, speed, and other metrics

- *Accident and injury rates*—low-frequency but high-cost events that are often tracked for jobs such as over-the-road drivers, construction workers, skilled trade employees, and employees in physically demanding jobs

Other quantitative measures of performance fit these broad categories, but most typically fall into one of two broad categories: those that measure the quantity or quality of *work outcomes* and those that measure *administrative outcomes* like turnover, theft, or termination. The key question in both cases is how much better recruiting and hiring programs can move the needle on such measures. What's the payoff an employer can expect to see? Let's deal with the four categories individually, with examples of real results.

Improving Sales Results

In a private sector business, working to finding talented sales staff typically receives more attention than any other occupational group. And it makes sense, since salespeople link the organization's products or services to the customers who make or break the business. Even the best products don't speak for themselves; it's the salesperson who does the talking. Create a great sales force, and even an average product can lead to success. Build a weak sales force, and even the best product won't keep the business afloat. Hire salespeople who are 10 percent more effective than the competition, and you're a hero.

As of late 2009, U.S. Bureau of Labor Statistics data showed nearly 16 million U.S. workers, or about 11 percent of the overall workforce, engaged in sales occupations. Projections called for the number to increase to about 17 million by 2018. About 2.2 million hold sales management or supervision roles, and about 8.7 million work in retail sales, 2.0 million in wholesale positions, and 1.6 million in the sale of services. This exceeds the economy's number of production employees (about 10 million) by more than 50 percent, and it more than matches the number of employees engaged in all the nation's management, business, and financial occupations combined (15.7 million).[1]

Decisions about choosing salespeople carry greater risk than most other professional positions, too. Salespeople are not only the face to leads, prospects, and customers; they make commitments, offer promises, and sometimes engage in exaggerations that few others in the company have the opportunity to do. Bad salespeople can make a great deal of trouble before they're found out.

If there's an opportunity where better recruiting and hiring can lead to higher financial gains, it's sales. It's no surprise, then, that so many vendors offer services around sales recruiting, screening, testing, and interviewing. It's also no surprise that organizations try to increase the odds and limit the risks associated with hiring sales employees. So let's review some of the results for programs that *do* work.

Table 4.1 shows five business situations where better recruiting and hiring tools produced a payoff as measured by sales results. The five cover a range of jobs and industries. They also provide examples of sales at differing levels, ranging from financial services to a pest control company. If my purpose were an exhaustive review, I

Table 4.1 Hiring Solutions and Their Payoff for Improving Sales Results

The Job	The New Hiring Solution	The Payoff
Financial services firm manager	An assessment tool introduced to match candidates to an ideal position profile created for the job.	Managers meeting the profile averaged $175,000 higher annual sales than those who did not.
Computer systems company sales professional	A Web-based tool introduced to assess candidates' sales orientation, reliability and follow-through, adaptability, and practical problem-solving skills.	High-scoring candidates performed 14 percent better in meeting quarterly revenue quotas—an average increase of $1.5 million per sales representative per quarter.
Financial advisor	Two personality and job preference surveys introduced to profile candidates against the job's total set of entry requirements.	Advisors fitting the profile added approximately a $1 million more in assets under management than others.
Cosmetics company sales representative	Tools to assess bright side and dark side personality factors introduced to identify candidates with a strong sales profile.	Those matching the profile produced an average of approximately $4 million in annual sales; those not meeting the profile sold an average of $875,000 annually.
Pest control technician	A Web-based assessment tool added to match candidates to the position's sales profile.	Technicians matching the sales profile created twice as many new account sales as those not matching the profile.

could add hundreds more examples. Here, though, the objective is to illustrate the *magnitude* of what's possible and to illustrate the variety of recruiting and hiring tools that produce results.

Whether improving the recruiting and hiring process involved adding *can-do* or *will-do* measures, results show new hires hitting their sales quota and selling more. And the new procedures produced more than minor results. Some of the examples showed a doubling of sales outcomes; others showed improvements in the millions of dollars per salesperson.

Most of the examples reflect improvements staged early in the candidate screening process—most of them immediately after initial screening steps and before a visit to the company, a hiring manager interview, and other more costly steps. Therein rests some of the added payoff not seen in the hard number results shown in the exhibit: avoiding the time and expenses wasted in meeting poorly qualified candidates.

Of note too is the fact that either basic ability or personality testing tools appear in all the examples. This isn't to suggest that other techniques fail to add value. It's just that much of the research on sales improvement focuses on these kinds of tools. In each case, the cost of implementing the new tools was less than $100 per candidate, which is trivial in light of the payoff that resulted.

There's another important point that doesn't show itself directly in Table 4.1. A good deal of research on improving the validity of a recruiting and hiring process shows that the payoff is *additive*. In other words, payoff can be increased when, for example, a structured prescreening interview is added to *can-do* and *will-do* testing. Payoff increases even further when a behavior-based interview process is added to the prescreening and testing programs. Later I'll review the kinds of tools that can be linked together in this way to get the best payoff for a given job and even show the incremental value that each can bring. For now, though, hold on to the concept that payoff can be increased by additional recruiting and hiring components to the overall process.

There is a point of diminishing returns, but as long as each tool added to the process taps another relevant competency that goes into performing the job, research shows the financial payoff of the process increases. This concept is particularly important in sales hiring.

Reducing Turnover

Every year, close to 20 percent of U.S. workers quit their jobs. That's about thirty million cases of turnover each year. In some businesses—leisure and hospitality, retail, construction—turnover averages about 50 percent. Few occupations see rates lower than 15 percent. Imagine the challenge at Walmart, which needs to replace more than 40 percent of its nearly two million employees worldwide each year.[2]

When the labor market is hot, employers pour efforts into turnover reduction. When unemployment rates go up, voluntary turnover, not so mysteriously, goes down. Do you want to predict the rate of turnover your organization is likely to face? Data assembled over more than thirty years show the nation's overall unemployment rate correlates at .86 (that is, predicts nearly perfectly) the nation's average rate of employee turnover.[3] Another way to put it is that the unemployment rate and average turnover rate across all job sectors vary together. When the first goes up, the second goes down.

But even during periods of high unemployment, turnover costs companies a tremendous amount of money. Much is spent on recruitment advertising, screening, onboarding, training, and making up for the lost opportunities that result when an employee leaves the company.[4]

When a fairly long-tenured poor performer leaves and is replaced by a better performer at an entry-level rate of pay, the event is actually beneficial. But when an effective performer leaves and is replaced by a poorer performer, turnover is dysfunctional.

Dysfunctional turnover is the most troublesome, but turnover of any type carries a cost.

When an employer adds up the tab for replacement, training, and lost productivity, studies show that the total cost of each "turn" runs between one and two times the employee's annual salary, particularly for professional and managerial positions.[5] Although some of the costs are not as directly measurable as an invoice from the outside recruiter or the relocation expense awarded to the new executive, all hit the employer. Reducing turnover is clearly an opportunity for cost reduction.

Current thinking often views turnover as resulting from events *after* an individual is hired. The popular mantra that "employees don't quit jobs, they quit bosses" drives HR efforts to make sure employees' supervisors have a clear understanding of workers' needs and aspirations, provide constructive reinforcement, and not chase the employee away through lack of engagement.[6]

If this idea rules, can better recruiting and hiring programs reduce turnover? The answer is yes: evidence shows that employee-supervisor relationships have an impact on turnover. But much evidence also shows that straightforward recruiting and hiring techniques can produce a significant reduction in turnover rates too. The two views look to fundamentally different factors. Accepting evidence of one doesn't rule out the other.

Tactically we can use recruiting and hiring tools to identify candidates who are less prone to turnover whatever the supervisory environment. The techniques focus on screening out candidates who lack either the *can-do* or *will-do* attributes that affect their likelihood of success, regardless of how their supervisor behaves. Let's look at some results. Table 4.2 summarizes real turnover reduction results, assembled from a variety of sources, involving a variety of different occupations and associated with different kinds of improvements in the employer's recruiting and hiring process.

In some of the Table 4.2 examples, a single tool produced the payoff. For example, a new assessment test was added, a personality

Table 4.2 Hiring Solutions and Their Payoff for Reducing Employee Turnover

The Job	The New Hiring Solution	The Payoff
International temporary services company office managers	Historical data reviewed score information provided on candidate application forms found to predict the likelihood of short-term turnover.	First-year turnover fell by more than 25 percent when the candidate application form was used as a prescreening knockout factor.
Financial services sales representative	A Web-based assessment tool added to the process, matching candidate values to the job's requirements.	Employee turnover fell from 48 to 18 percent. Three hundred fewer "turns" during the first year produced $4.5 million savings in hiring costs.
Telecommunications company sales positions	A test measuring workplace personality factors added to a structured interview and role-play assessment exercise and evaluated in a special use-versus-no-use tryout study.	Turnover was 27 percent in the comparison group not using the new tool but only 14 percent for those selected with the new tool. The cost of replacement was approximately $675,000 lower during the first fourteen weeks of use.
Frontline employees in a retailer of home accessories	Added a test to assess candidates' work orientation, ability to follow instructions, judgment, and the match between candidates' interests and the job environment.	A 10 to 30 percent reduction in annual turnover, with results varying by geographical region.
Auto service technician	Walk-in recruiting process was replaced with targeted Web posting, an automated prescreening inventory, and a behavior-based interview tied to a job competency model.	During the first year, turnover during the initial thirty days fell from more than 50 percent to approximately 5 percent. Hiring managers moved from hiring only one of every eight candidates interviewed to one of every two.

profiling tool was implemented, or a more formalized means for screening candidates' résumés was introduced. In others, a change in the overall approach to *finding* talent produced the result.

For the table's temporary services managers, structuring a simple review of information drawn from the candidate's résumé resulted in a more than 25 percent reduction in first-year turnover. In the financial services example, a Web-administered assessment tool seeking to match the candidate's values and preferences with the job's demands was the single change to the process. The result was a reduction of more than 60 percent in annual turnover, as well as a substantial increase in productivity. The cost was less than $100 per candidate.

Both the telecommunication company and home improvement store examples add measures of *can-do* and *will-do* attributes to the candidate screening process. Again, turnover fell substantially. Although a lower-level job, the auto technician example illustrates a broader change to the employer's recruiting and hiring process. Here, the employer was losing more than 50 percent of all new hires during the first thirty days with the company. Historically the recruitment and screening process was to accept applications from walk-in candidates, verify that the candidate possessed auto technician experience, conduct an interview, and reach a hiring decision. As noted, more than half of those who accepted the offer were gone within thirty days, often to a competing service center.

Eager to stop the revolving door, a review of the job's duties— changing oil; lubricating the vehicle; checking the battery, tires, shock absorbers, and muffler—showed the position didn't really demand auto technician training. In fact, individuals with a love of cars or a hobby related to automobiles typically could be trained to perform the job very quickly.

The company instituted a Web-based approach to posting position openings and targeting those with an interest in automotive hobbies. Service center managers then used behavior-based interviewing tools that targeted *not* technical skills but competencies, such as interest in learning about the field, motivation to grow into the job, and drive to succeed.

The overall process changed to include prescreening and more targeted interviewing, but it was the new recruiting and hiring tools that produced the result. It also was the "aha" about what the job really required that reduced thirty-day turnover by 90 percent.

Today there's clear evidence about the types of tools and process redesign steps that reduce employee turnover. As Table 4.2 illustrates, the payoff can be substantial, and the cost of implementation can be small in comparison. Many times, too, technology can take up the administrative load that comes with the improvements.

As in the discussion on improved sales results, research shows that integrating a complementary set of tools, rather than pulling just one lever, produces a better payoff. Research shows something of a bonus too. In many cases, those with a higher propensity to turn over are those who perform less well while they're with the organization. In effect, recruiting and hiring tools that reduce turnover also result in hiring better performers.

Increasing Production

Many organizations track a variety of production-oriented measures to evaluate success. Often they use these measures to track at the individual employee level: calls serviced per hour, complaints resolved per day, number of hours billed per week, number of units built per shift, time needed to set up a production run, and so on. In some jobs, piece rate systems tie compensation to these production rates.

In jobs where production matters, recruiting and hiring solutions typically focus on identifying candidates who will perform better at whichever of these measures pertain to the job. Sometimes this means recruiting candidates with prior experience in the job. Sometimes it means screening candidates for the skills they need to learn the job and come to production standards quickly. In cases where production demands bring stress and pressure to the job, it means evaluating candidates for soft skills such as persistence, drive, or adaptability.

To see that better recruiting and hiring move the needle in production-oriented jobs, look at Table 4.3.

In the examples, the concept of production takes different forms: producing additional revenue and profits, learning a job and meeting production standards more quickly, protecting current customer accounts. In each case, a range of both *can-do* and *will-do* tools shows a payoff.

Particularly in manufacturing settings, it's clear that basic learning ability, along with strong work habits and team skills, are the areas essential to reaching high levels of production. Tools have been developed that place evaluation of these *can-do* and *will-do* attributes early in the hiring process. Given the large numbers of entry-level employees who typically work in production-oriented companies, even small improvements in the hiring process at this stage produce financial results with major consequences.

Lowering Accident and Injury Rates

Accidents and injuries are a concern in fewer and fewer of the jobs in our growing professional and service-related economy. For some jobs, though, accidents or injuries to employees are a concern: excavation and construction workers, oil and gas production employees, utility workers, forest and wood products production jobs, and mining occupations, for example. For other jobs, the concern applies to those with whom the employee comes in contact, such as over-the-road drivers, heavy equipment operators, and fire service employees.

While the numbers are relatively low in aggregate, U.S. Bureau of Labor Statistics data showed 5,657 workplace fatalities in 2007. About four of every one hundred full-time workers were injured,

Table 4.3 Hiring Solutions and Their Payoff for Improving Production Rates

The Job	The Hiring Solution	The Payoff
Shipping terminal managers	A job-fit tool introduced to identify terminal managers by matching a profile based on job analysis results.	Managers hired under the new process showed an approximately 25 percent increase in revenue and approximately 50 percent lower damaged-goods complaints.
Food services retail employees	A realistic job preview for candidates, a job fit assessment, and structured interview were added to the previous process.	After one year's use of the program, the organization saw a $21 million increase in profits.
Electronics company production assemblers	A basic abilities testing battery, developed to match candidates to job requirements, was added to interview and drug-testing procedures.	Those selected with the new procedure contributed more than three times as many implementable performance improvement recommendations.
Production employees in a consumer products company	A basic abilities test battery was added to an employment interview process.	First-line supervisors reported that 70 percent of new hires learned the job and came to production standards more quickly than under the previous hiring program.
Account managers	A battery of two workplace personality tests was introduced to identify account managers better able to retain customer accounts.	Those meeting the profile lost an average of approximately $6,000 in business each year; those not meeting the profile lost approximately $10,000.

while more than two of every one hundred suffered an injury leading to time off the job. For the same year, data showed more than fifty-three thousand transportation-related job injuries.[7] Even today, the costs associated with insurance, treatment, lost time, and litigation, for example, mean that workplace accidents and injuries remain an area of concern.

Most accident and injury reduction efforts are focused on training, workplace reengineering, use of safety and protective equipment, and others. Here too, recruitment and hiring programs can offer a payoff—in two areas. First, in some cases, the candidate's tendency to take undue risks, ignore policies and procedures, and make wrong choices follows him or her into the workplace and increases the likelihood of bad outcomes. In others, the candidate's physical capabilities determine not only the likelihood of being able to perform the job but the chances of being injured in the process.

Different kinds of recruiting and hiring tools address these two situations. All consider the fact that accidents and injuries have a key defining feature: they are *low* in frequency and *high* in cost. Hence, hiring tools that target a payoff through accident or injury reduction need to work in situations where most candidates will perform without incident once hired, but a relatively few will create great cost. Therein rests the challenge.

Table 4.4 provides illustrations where recruiting and hiring initiatives produced a payoff through accident or injury reduction. The jobs cover a range from locomotive engineer to state government employee. They all show a substantial impact on unwanted outcomes after introducing tools that consumed little time to administer.

One case shows a hands-on assessment of the candidate's actual *ability* to perform the job without injury. In the latter, data showed a noteworthy reduction in injury rates. But as most police and fire agencies have noted for nearly thirty years, using physical ability testing procedures is costly and often open to legal challenge as a result of producing higher failure rates for female candidates.

Table 4.4 Hiring Solutions and Their Payoff for Reducing Accidents and Injuries

The Job	The New Solution	The Payoff
Transport drivers	A workplace personality test to assess candidates' likelihood of engaging in rules violation was added to the process.	The accident rate for drivers passing the new standard was 12 percent, compared to an earlier 28 percent.
Production employees in a food manufacturing plant	A hands-on simulation of the job's lifting and carrying tasks was added to a battery of ability tests, group interviews, and a medical exam after hiring already in use.	Data from a three-year follow-up study showed employees who passed the new tool could be expected to be involved in an accident every 1,624 days on average. Prior to the tool, the rate was one accident every 307 days. There was a fivefold reduction in injury rate.
Locomotive engineers	A workplace personality test was added to identify candidates fitting a job analysis-based profile for the job.	A pilot evaluation of the test showed that it identified correctly 69 percent of those who had been involved in accidents; the group showed a 38 percent lower incidence of accidents.
State government employees	A workplace personality test was added to predict both the incidence and cost per claim due to workplace injuries.	A follow-up study showed a cost savings among new hires of approximately $1,000 annually associated with reduced sick leave, lost time, and worker's compensation costs.
Warehouse freight handling employees	A workplace personality test was added to predict both the incidence and cost per claim due to workplace injuries.	A follow-up study showed a reduction of approximately 20 percent in the incidence of injuries and a 57 percent decrease in cost per claim.

For the other examples, measures of personality factors predicted both the incidence of accidents and injuries and the level of cost associated with each event. Apparently employees' inclinations to behave in particular ways open them to more or less frequent accidents and injuries. In short, it appears also to be more a *will-do* attribute that leads to such events. This possibility can be instructive in shaping the focus of other recruiting and selection tools to address the problem—tools such as behavior-based interviews or structured reference checks.

The potential for gaining a payoff through better recruiting and hiring practices is clear. The results illustrate a point made in the Chapter Three thinking model review: cutting off the very bottom of the performance distribution can produce a major payoff. Here, research shows that a small percentage of employees produce a large majority of accidents and injuries. The examples show that a combination of *can-do* and *will-do* tools can help identify these cases most effectively and eliminate the costs they bring to the workplace.

Big Numbers

The twenty actual examples in this chapter show that introducing new tools and better overall processes can produce better hiring decisions where objective measures of performance are the target.[8] Depending on the type of job and the type of performance metric, different phases of the recruiting and hiring process offer different levers for increasing financial payoff. Most important, different types of tools show gains in different ways and produce a payoff that far exceeds the cost of the new program.

In the cases reviewed, the payoff also involved reducing the need for programs that focus on training, motivating, or incentivizing employees to behave in certain ways after they're hired. In a sense, these programs *after* hiring reflect remedial efforts: work organizations undertake to compensate for having made suboptimal decisions from before the *candidate* became an *employee*. The point is that payoff results also from cutting the cost of remediation by hiring those who will need it least.

Recall, though, that where there are no sales, production, turnover, or other measures that fit a clear yardstick, in some cases, it's difficult to measure employee performance. That's where we go next: exploring the payoff of better recruiting and hiring when it's hard to boil performance down to quantitative metrics and need to live with soft numbers.

CHAPTER FIVE

MEASURING PAYOFF IN SOFT NUMBERS

We can come up with hard measures of performance for most jobs. Sometimes, though, relying on hard measures leads to missing what's most important about employee performance. In many jobs, it's not *how much workers produce* but *how they do it* that matters. Consider just a few of the examples: health care, education, accounting, public relations, scientific or other research jobs, or work in government. This creates a problem, though: How can you estimate the payoff in better hiring when there's no hard measure to track success?

As an illustration, take the job of account manager in a membership services company. Renewal rates and up-sells might be useful hard measures, but a big part of an account manager's performance relates to softer concepts, such as anticipating problems, finding answers to complaints, negotiating resolutions, and ensuring customer satisfaction. With performance targets like these, how can you determine whether investing in a better account manager hiring program will produce a payoff? The answer rests in research that draws on a few statistics.

Working through the numbers is worth the effort. The result provides tools for estimating the payoff from better hiring for *any* job, whether it comes with hard *or* soft measures of performance. The technique produces a simple method that helps in framing what can be expected through a small refinement or the wholesale redesign of a hiring process. Let's walk through the numbers one step at a time, with some illustrations.

Another Way of Thinking

Return to one of Chapter One's people facts: in any job, employees differ in the performance they deliver, and the results they produce spread them out over a range of effectiveness. I illustrated the discussion with jobs such as production assembler and salesperson, where performance is measured in hard numbers. But the same fact holds when performance isn't easily put to numbers. For illustration, let's stay with the account manager example.

Let's assume the data that drive Figure 5.1 are performance evaluations prepared by account managers' supervisors, a typical soft measure of performance. In the figure, supervisors describe some account managers as performing very well and some as performing very poorly. They rate most in the middle of the range. The resulting distribution shows how the department's account managers spread themselves out on supervisors' ratings.

A basic premise is key to the rest of the discussion: the range of performance reflected in Figure 5.1 has financial consequences. The premise holds that those performing at a high level *do things* and *create results* with more financial value than those performing at less effective levels. It holds that the bell-shaped distribution represents a range of *financial value*, even if the data that drive it are supervisors' evaluations.

Figure 5.1 Account managers differ in overall performance effectiveness

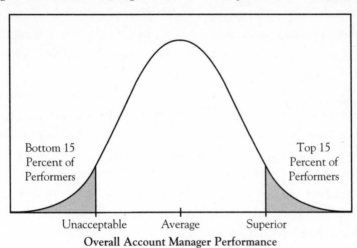

Bottom 15
Percent of
Performers

Top 15
Percent of
Performers

Unacceptable   Average   Superior
Overall Account Manager Performance

The premise applies not only when the performance measure
is a supervisory rating. It holds if the performance measure is feedback on individual account managers collected through a customer
survey. The measure might be evaluations completed by an outside
mystery shopper or results of an exercise to evaluate account managers' job knowledge and interpersonal skills. All of these are soft
measures of job performance. The premise holds that these
soft measures of performance reflect financial value and that this
value can be used to estimate the payoff in hiring people who
populate the top of the performance distribution.

Now, I'll shift from the concept of *job performance* to *employee
compensation*. Assume your company's compensation system results
in an average salary of $80,000 for account managers. Typically
setting this average salary is based on reviewing outside labor market data. The company surveys other employers with similar account
managers and uses the resulting labor market average to set a competitive rate of pay.

This typical compensation practice is based on the idea that a
competent account manager *is worth* a salary of $80,000 because

that's what similar organizations pay employees working in the same job—organizations with which yours competes for talent or will lose account managers if you try to pay less. For illustration, let's say you've selected the market average as the level of pay targeted for average performers.

Next, we draw on the results of research in the discipline of organizational psychology. The research, done with different kinds of organizations and occupations, has produced ways to attach an actual dollar value to levels of performance when we're limited to soft measures like supervisors' evaluations. These techniques draw on information about employees' average rate of pay to estimate the dollar value that rests in performance at the top, middle, and bottom of the bell-shaped curve.

Different approaches can be used to produce estimates.[1] Some of them require a great deal of analytical work but see little use in real-world settings. Some, though, are straightforward and suited to everyday settings. Here, we'll rely on one of the simple techniques, referred to as "the 40 percent rule of thumb."[2] Figure 5.2 illustrates the concept.

The rule of thumb assumes that the compensation system is set up in a logical, systematic way, and that the *average rate of pay* is intended to attract and motivate *competent employees*. What comes next is more interesting, though, and more useful in estimating the payoff that comes with better hiring.

Research that produced the rule of thumb shows that employees whose performance falls among the top 15 percent of those in a given job produce results with economic value approximately 40 percent greater than that of average-performing employees. Statistically, the top 15 percent of employees deliver performance that falls about one standard deviation above average performance. The same holds, in reverse, for the bottom-performing 15 percent of employees. These employees produce results with an economic value approximately 40 percent less than that of average-performing employees.

Figure 5.2 Rule of thumb: The economic value of top versus bottom performers differs by at least plus and minus 40 percent of average employee pay

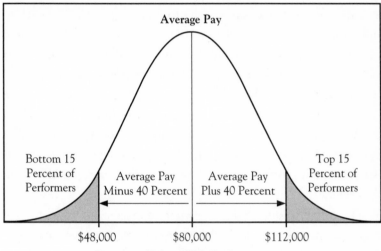

Economic Value of Job Performance
(Account Manager Example)

I'll illustrate with the data shown in Figure 5.2. The rule of thumb says that top-15-percent-performing account managers can be expected to deliver performance *worth* 40 percent more than their average-performing colleagues. As the compensation system has already established, average performers are *worth* $80,000, the going rate in the labor market for competent performers. So top-15-percent-performers are *worth* at least $112,000, or 40 percent more than the typical $80,000. Top performers are *worth* this amount regardless of what the organization actually pays them. This is an important concept because it's where the payoff in hiring better account managers originates.

Research that produced the rule of thumb shows employees who perform in the bottom 15 percent produce results *worth* 40 percent less than those of average performers. If average performers are *worth* $80,000, these poorer performers are *worth* no more than $48,000, and less if they are truly bottom performers.

The 40 percent rule of thumb isn't just an idea that statisticians have made up.[3] The concept flows from research where hard measures of performance (on sales, production rates, error rates, and so forth) and soft measures of performance (supervisory ratings and customer reviews, and so forth) are collected and compared for the same job. For example, in a review summarizing fifty-eight individual studies, the top 15 percent of salespersons produced 39 percent more sales.[4] Although results vary from one study to the next, when hard measures of performance are available to test the concept, research shows that estimates based on the rule of thumb hold up well; in addition, they sometimes actually underestimate the magnitude of the difference between top and bottom performance.

The rule of thumb holds too when managers are asked to give it a commonsense check. Ask the manager of an account management department with one hundred people whether her top fifteen employees are worth 40 percent more than her average performers or whether the bottom fifteen are worth 40 percent less. The answer will be something like this: "Yes, but you've underestimated the difference. The top is worth more, and the bottom is really worth less, or worthless!"

Think about jobs in your own organization where you track hard measures of performance and compare the results to the rule of thumb. Think about the sales force. Do your top-15-percent salespersons return 40 percent more value than the average salesperson? Do the bottom-performing 15 percent produce 40 percent less value than the average salesperson? Most sales managers say, "Yes, but the real difference is way more extreme."

The rule of thumb lets us translate soft measures of performance like customer reviews or supervisory evaluations onto a scale that captures the financial value that might otherwise appear hidden. This is a big step. With it, we can estimate the return that comes with hiring more top performers and avoiding the bottom of the curve.

Top Performers Are Worth a Lot

To carry the illustration further, for every $48,000-*value* account manager avoided through a better recruiting and hiring program to land a $112,000-*value* employee, the organization gains a $64,000 increase in economic value—almost the equivalent of one extra employee. The process also averages up the value of the overall account manager workforce.

Of course, hiring *only* candidates who become top-15-percent performers is a tough assignment. The business needs a recruiting and hiring program with high accuracy (validity). In addition, finding and then retaining only top performers is expensive. Unless the organization has a competitive advantage, the labor market will work against this degree of selectivity.

While recruiting and hiring *only* top-15-percent performers is a challenge, any employer can begin seeding the workforce with a higher percentage of this group. With each hire, the average level of performance increases, as does the value of the job's talent pool. Any manager knows that averaging up produces a payoff. Like compound interest, the payoff in top performers accrues each year.

Bottom Performers Cost a Lot

If it isn't practical to hire *only* top-15-percent performers, it's certainly possible to aim at eliminating those who fall in the low-performing group. With this group, the organization really doesn't get what it pays for. From a compensation point of view, employing the group makes no sense. If employees' average salary is indexed to labor market rates for competent performers, then this group is overpaid. Also, the group leads employers to host all manner of HR systems: performance improvement programs, disciplinary programs, severance programs, and others.

Let's take a view on this group that blends hiring and compensation concepts. Typically employers set a range of pay for each of their jobs. The lower part of the range is where new people are hired; the top is where they move with seniority, solid performance, and growth in value to the company. The middle part of the range is typically indexed to the average rate other organizations that compete for the same kind of talent pay. As noted, the middle of a pay range, the midpoint, often is set at the average rate the surveys of other employers' pay practices identify.

For a job at the account manager level, an employer typically sets a range of pay with the minimum falling about 20 percent lower than the midpoint and the maximum falling about 20 percent above the midpoint. Overlaying these compensation concepts on Figure 5.2 produces Figure 5.3.

The only difference between Figure 5.3 and Figure 5.2 is the pair of dashed vertical lines, reflecting a typical pay range for an account manager job. The pay range shows a minimum (new hire, learning the job) pay level of $64,000 and a maximum (senior, very solid performer) pay level of $96,000, both framing the $80,000

Figure 5.3 Employers get both less than they pay for and more than they pay for

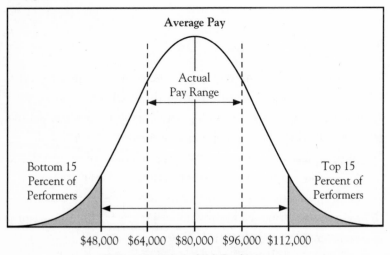

$48,000 $64,000 $80,000 $96,000 $112,000

Economic Value of Job Performance
(Account Manager Example)

midpoint that the labor market information suggests. In compensation language, this is a 50 percent pay range; the $96,000 top of the range adds 50 percent to the $64,000 bottom of the range. In practice, all of the company's account managers' base pay will fall within this range.

Remember that the bell-shaped part of the illustration shows the *range of performance* over which all the account managers spread themselves. Now focus on the bottom portion of the distribution. According to our rule of thumb, the bottom 15 percent of employees perform at a rate that is *worth less* than the very minimum the company pays any account manager. With these employees, the company doesn't get what it pays for. If they perform at low levels because they're new and just learning, they need to improve to justify even the minimum salary at which they entered the company. But not all of the employees in this portion of the performance curve are necessarily new hires. Some are likely to be *long-term* poor performers.

At the same time, the company gets *more* than it pays for from the top 15 percent of employees. While those performing in the top-15-percent group contribute $112,000 or more in economic value, the pay range tops out at $96,000. This group is paid less than its value. In a sense, it carries the load for the poor performers. Only this group's performance justifies the fact that the total group of account managers is drawing an average rate of pay that matches the labor market's $80,000.

It would be nice to continue getting more than we pay for at the top of the performance distribution, and eliminate cases where we don't get what we pay for. Some HR programs focus on doing just that. General Electric's Jack Welch used a program that focused on eliminating the bottom 10 percent of performers each year.[5] The intent was to continually replace the bottom of the curve and thereby continually increase the average level of performance.

As an alternative, or at least an addition, why not *avoid hiring* those likely to populate the bottom of the performance distribution and skip the disruption of eliminating them later? Using better recruiting and hiring programs eliminates risk by stopping the flow of unacceptable new hires, and it still builds the upside by averaging up performance with each new hire.

Blending the Concepts of Validity and Payoff

I'll put an actual value on the upside to expect from better hiring by using the rule of thumb to estimate the expected payoff from almost any recruiting and hiring program improvement. This will be our deepest dive into statistics, but in the end, it will produce a very simple, straightforward tool.

Recall from Chapter Two that some recruiting and hiring programs have a greater level of validity than others. Figures 5.4 and 5.5 illustrate the comparison.

The relationship between information the company uses to guide hiring decisions and measures of a person's performance after hiring is expressed as a statistic: the validity coefficient.[6] The validity coefficient has a value of zero when there is absolutely no relationship between the information collected on candidates and their performance after hiring (see Figure 5.4).

Using such information makes no sense; it's worthless. For example, using the candidate's day of birth during the year (measured from 1 to 365) as a "qualification" to predict his or her future performance would produce a validity coefficient near zero.

As the relationship between candidate information and performance after hiring becomes more aligned (see Figure 5.5), the illustration becomes more and more elliptical in shape, and the value of the validity coefficient approaches 1.00. If the coefficient had a value of exactly 1.00, all the X's would fall on a single straight line. Of course, this never happens, but the goal is to use information that produces the largest validity coefficient and tightest relationship possible.

Figure 5.4 A screening process with no validity does not predict performance after hiring

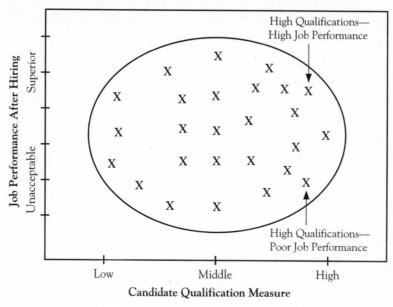

Figure 5.5 A valid hiring process predicts job performance levels after hiring

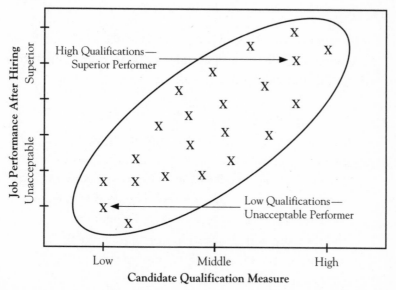

Different kinds of recruiting and hiring tools produce different levels of validity. I'll cover more on this topic in later chapters that review the levels of validity typical of different recruiting and hiring tools. In fact, I'll provide summaries of thousands of validity studies and use them to forecast the validity likely for various hiring tools when the tools are used individually, and in combination.[7]

With the concept of the validity coefficient in mind, I'll introduce a model for computing the payoff to expect by improving a hiring program's validity and, at the same time, adjusting other levers that go beyond the concept of validity: hiring volume, selectivity, tenure expectations, program cost, and so on. I start by laying out a mathematical formula, defining a few terms, and making some assumptions about the recruiting and hiring environment in our account management department. First, the formula:

$$
\begin{array}{l}
\text{Net dollar} \\
\text{value gain} \\
\text{for year's} \\
\text{hires}
\end{array}
=
\begin{array}{l}
\text{Increase} \\
\text{in} \\
\text{program} \\
\text{validity}
\end{array}
\times
\begin{array}{l}
\text{Year's} \\
\text{no. of} \\
\text{new} \\
\text{hires}
\end{array}
\times
\begin{array}{l}
\text{Avg.} \\
\text{new} \\
\text{hire} \\
\text{tenure}
\end{array}
\times
\begin{array}{l}
\text{\$ Difference} \\
\text{in top vs.} \\
\text{bottom} \\
\text{performance}
\end{array}
\times
\begin{array}{l}
\text{Candidate} \\
\text{screening} \\
\text{selectivity}
\end{array}
-
\begin{array}{l}
\text{Year's} \\
\text{increased cost} \\
\text{of program} \\
\text{administration}
\end{array}
$$

The formula combines all the principles discussed so far, yielding an estimated dollar-value payoff for a new recruiting and hiring program. I'll start by defining the terms.

- *Net dollar value gain for year's hires.* This is the financial payoff to expect from implementing the new recruiting and hiring program. It expresses the dollar value of performance improvements that result from avoiding hires who would have populated the bottom part of the performance distribution. The term shows the net return from just one year's use of the program, after taking into account administrative costs.

- *Increase in program's validity.* This term takes into account the new program's validity coefficient compared to the validity coefficient for the prior program, that is, the increase in program validity. Remember from Figures 5.4 and 5.5 that the higher the validity coefficient, the more accurately it predicts performance after hiring.

- *Year's number of new hires.* Obviously the payoff of the new program depends on how many new higher-performing employees will be hired during the year. This is the volume driver in the equation.

- *Average new hire tenure.* The longer the year's higher-performing employees are on board, the longer their performance will produce a payoff.

- *Dollar difference in top versus bottom performance.* This is where the 40 percent rule of thumb comes into play. This term takes on a dollar value and amounts to 40 percent of the average salary paid to those in the position that the company is hiring to fill.

- *Candidate screening selectivity.* This term takes into account two concepts: how selective hiring professionals will be in screening candidates, and the score level of new hires on the qualification measure used in screening them. Selectivity is the proportion of candidates the company expects to hire. The candidates' level on the qualification measure is expressed in z-score terms, where an average score on the qualification measure is zero and departures above and below the average are expressed in standard deviation units. The actual term entered in the equation combines these concepts in a value that is easy to find in published statistical tables or through software routines easily accessible on the Internet.[8]

- *Year's increased cost of program administration.* This term makes the assumption that the new program comes with an increase in the cost of administration. In fact, more effective programs sometimes decrease the cost of program administration. For example, they screen out noteworthy numbers of candidates who previously took up resources in the face-to-face interview. If this is the case, a reduction in cost is captured here as well.

Now I'll build on the account manager example to show the value gained through one possible improvement to the job's recruiting and hiring program. I'll compute the economic payoff expected from using a new program for one year.

First, assume that the change in the hiring program is to introduce a combination of basic ability testing and behavior-based interviewing. Research shows that the combination of these tools can be expected to show a validity coefficient of about .60.[9] For simplicity, assume that the prior hiring process used no testing tools and followed an unstructured interview program that produced a validity coefficient of .15—again, a research-based assumption.[10]

Second, assume that turnover (say, 20 percent) and company growth (say, 10 percent) leads to a need for thirty new account managers during the first year the new program is in use. Also assume that those hired will remain with the company before turning over or being promoted for an average of four years. Third, the 40 percent rule of thumb for the account manager example indicates that the distance between average and top-15-percent-performance is $32,000.

Fourth, assume we will screen five candidates for every one we actually hire. The value entered to capture this level of selectivity and the associated qualifying score for those hired come from the tabular look-up noted above. Finally, assume the new behavior-based interview costs no more to administer than the previous unstructured interview, and that the basic ability test is administered at a cost of $50 per candidate (a high estimate).

Once we assemble these assumptions, the formula for computing the financial payoff for one year's new hires is as follows:

Year's total net $ gain = $(.60-.15) \times (30) \times (4) \times (\$32,000) \times (.2789+.20) - 30(\$50)/.20$
$= \$2,402,196$

The projection for using a relatively straightforward recruiting and hiring program improvement for one year to add thirty new account managers is a payoff close to $2.5 million in improved job performance over the new hires' expected four-year tenure. The payoff results from reducing the rate at which poor performers are hired and increasing the rate of hiring for better performers. The mechanism in this case, the screening tools, carries a known level of validity compared to the prior selection process.

The result takes into account the rule-of-thumb value attached to performance at various points in the distribution of employee performance. Importantly, the payoff pertains to those hired during *the first year of use*. During the second year, if thirty new account managers are added again, hiring results will add equivalent value.

Achieving this result didn't require a costly capital investment, a major operating system change, or a program that affected the current workforce. It didn't require terminating or retraining any of the current poor performers. It didn't expose the company to significant employment litigation risk. It required only applying behavior-based interviewing techniques to replace an unstructured approach and introducing a valid testing program. In fact, it could be argued that administering the new process will cost less than the prior program since in day-to-day use, candidates failing to pass the basic ability test won't take up interviewer time as they did in the past.

True, it will take the group of thirty new hires all of their four-year tenure to produce these results, but during their first year, the company can expect to see one-fourth of the payoff—a more than $600,000 increase in economic value. Let's even assume that it will cost $100,000 in internal and external expenses to design and validate the behavior-based interviewing and testing program, train those responsible for administering the new program, and put data tracking procedures in place. This is a high estimate, but it helps produce a conservative estimate of payoff. Also, let's say that the thirty new hires are brought on board throughout the year, so that on average, each puts in only one-half year on the job.

Even adding these constraints, the payoff resulting from just one year's hiring of thirty new account managers produces the following cumulative economic payoff and rate of return on the initial design and implementation investment of $100,000 (this is net of the initial $100,000 design and implementation cost and assumes that new hires are spread evenly throughout the year):

Year End	Cumulative Dollar Value of Improved Performance	Return on Initial Investment
1	$200,274	2 to 1
2	$800,823	8 to 1
3	$1,401,372	14 to 1
4	$2,001,921	20 to 1

Although the initial group of new hires is producing an approximately $600,000 economic payoff through improved performance during years 2 through 4, additional new hires are joining the company as well to cover turnover and continued growth. Factor in these additional new hires, and the payoff and rate of return for the new program become truly inspiring. Note too that the examples of payoff cited in the preceding chapter, where hard numbers were available, parallel those presented here very closely.

Say the company wants to do a little better and is willing to add a behavioral integrity test to the process that will cost $50 per candidate (a high estimate). With all else the same, research shows we might expect a validity coefficient of approximately .65 for the process.[11] The new four-year payoff for year 1 hires is $2,662,440, a 10 percent addition to the payoff of the initial program improvement. Now we have a decision to make. Is an additional test worth the effort given the payoff?

The point is that recruiting and hiring professionals can alter any of the terms in the equation. They can consider the costs and benefits, and choose an update to the hiring program that's affordable, consistent with the company's ability to administer it, and targeted on areas with the most potential to make an impact. In this way, the HR department has raised its analysis of recruiting and hiring practices to the level followed by other areas of the business as they look for productivity improvements or cost reductions.

But, But, But . . .

It's easy to be skeptical, though, when a formula says you can gain over $2 million more value by simply using a test and changing your approach to interviewing. Some might say that it's just statistical mumbo jumbo, that the forecast payoff never really arrives. But look to the evidence of the previous chapter.

There, hard measures of payoff made no assumptions about the dollar value of performance. The examples required no mathematical formulas to estimate payoff. Yet the magnitude of the payoff summarized in these more easily measured cases paralleled the results for the account manager example very closely. True, the account manager illustration might seem less tangible than the examples of the previous chapter. But there, adding a basic personality test to the hiring process for sales representatives produced hard numbers showing that turnover fell from 48 percent to 18 percent, with a $4.5 million reduction in costs.

Employers who have implemented the rule of thumb often report that the returns they forecast actually underestimate the increases in productivity they see. The higher we move into professional, managerial, and executive levels, too, the more the rule-of-thumb approach tends to *underestimate* the true value of improved hiring.[12]

You might argue that in a tight labor market, there's no way to hire only top performers. But it's not about hiring only the best; it's about changing the risk and reward rules. It's about avoiding bottom performers and averaging up the total workforce, one hire at a time. If you're concerned about being able to screen five candidates for each one hired, as in the account manager example, plug your own hiring ratio into the payoff formula.

Some might challenge that these approaches will lead to hiring overqualified people who will grow frustrated with the job and be more likely to leave the company. It may be a nice theory, but there's no evidence that this is the case. More talented people produce more effective results. Period. Unless you plan to recruit Ph.D.s to work as call center staff, there's little danger of this problem. Research often shows that candidate qualifications and performance after hiring correlate linearly. In other words, the higher the level of candidate qualification, the higher the level of subsequent on-the-job performance will be.

Finally, some might argue that hiring like this can lead to legal challenges that offset all the gains with litigation costs. But as I review later, there are clear standards tested in the courts, for implementing valid screening tools. Today less litigation takes place in the hiring arena than in the past because employers know these standards. Most litigation today focuses in the areas of promotion, termination, and, increasingly, compensation.

A Simple Approach to Estimating Payoff

The advantage to the approach reviewed here is that it offers a general model for estimating payoff when it's neither feasible nor practical to gather hard performance measures. With the rule of thumb, it's possible to ask "what if" questions. It's possible to consider the features of a new hiring approach that might offer a payoff and take into account the costs that might cancel out part of the gain. If it takes hard measures of results to convince you, then by all means add them to the process. But don't wait on the hard results to start thinking about payoff. Rely on the rule-of-thumb approach to complete new program design, and then begin tracking results with hard performance measures that also make sense.

The forecasts produced by this simple approach beg a question: Why would an employer rely on practices such as a quick review of a candidate's résumé, an unstructured interview, and a background or reference check of unknown validity to make a hiring decision—a million-dollar decision? Why is so much invested to remediate hiring mistakes through training, incentives, performance improvement, and motivation-building programs? These HR efforts are not supported by payoff information. Most exist to compensate for poor hiring decisions.

Many employers *are* implementing these more effective solutions. Some are following through on internal quality-of-hire initiatives to recast both the tools and hiring processes they follow. Some are turning to recruitment process outsourcing providers who blend these tools with high-volume expertise. Some turn to best practices consulting companies to help frame programs that build on the concepts of increasing validity, limiting downside performance variability, and introducing efficiencies through technology solutions.

Adding Even More Value

Three questions can help judge the financial payoff of better recruiting and hiring:

1. What's the difference, in dollar terms, between superior, average, and unacceptable performance for the job?

2. What's the validity of the new approach to recruiting and hiring compared to that of current practices?

3. How selectively will we use the new program?

With these fundamentals, you can begin framing recruiting and hiring programs with the objective of gaining a clear financial payoff and with clarity regarding each of the levers to pull to accomplish the outcome. When you put the tools to work, you will realize that the way you recruit and hire can hold a greater payoff for your business than nearly anything else you do.

As substantial as the financial payoff is in improved performance, there's additional upside. Decades of research in human performance show that better-qualified new hires

- Learn the job faster and achieve performance standards more quickly. Hence, the group that enters through the new program will consume less training time and resources.

- Hold potential for more demanding positions and serve as a talent pool so the company can rely on internal promotion rather than seeking outside talent to populate higher-level positions.

- Are less likely to be terminated or to quit. Hence, estimates of payoff are typically conservative, given that new hires can be expected to remain with the company longer than those hired without using the measures set out in this book.

- Will consume less time in disciplinary actions, retraining efforts, or performance counseling. Hence, the demand for overhead HR programs to deal with poor performers will drop.

An additional possibility is buried in economic projections. If the new recruiting and hiring program produces a workforce whose performance outshines that of previous employees, the company has the opportunity to run its operation with *fewer* employees.

For example, extend the account manager illustration into years 2 through 4. For simplicity, assume the number remains at thirty new hires each year. By the end of year 4, essentially the entire account management department will have been replaced. Among those hired during years 1 through 4, each contributes approximately $22,000 in improved job performance *value*. This means that the one hundred account managers who now populate the department contribute approximately $2.2 million more value annually than their predecessors. By the end of year 4, this amount represents approximately one-fourth of the department's total base salary budget, assuming that annual salary increases parallel typical inflation rates.

So if the job performance of the one hundred account managers now resident is this much better than that of their predecessors, does the company really need one hundred account managers to do the work of the department? Enter the next phase of continuous improvement: restructuring and head count reduction.

In conclusion, we're left with these essential points:

- Tools are available to estimate the payoff of improved recruiting and hiring for jobs where hard measures of performance aren't available or relevant.

- Even for jobs where quantitative measures are available these tools can be used to produce a quick estimate that shows how results will be affected through improved hiring.

- The introduction of valid hiring tools results in substantial financial gain, even in a relatively small work group.

- The financial impact of improved hiring is so substantial that it can be a platform for other restructuring or reorganizing initiatives that also produce economic benefits driven by having better talent.

There's yet another way to gain a financial payoff from better recruiting and hiring solutions—a way that brings technology to the fore. We take a look in the following chapter.

CHAPTER SIX

TECHNOLOGIES COME TO RECRUITING AND HIRING

Chapters Four and Five showed the payoff that comes with better recruiting and hiring: stronger sales, higher production, lower turnover, fewer accidents—in fact, better performance on nearly any measure you can name. Now it's time to begin the how-we-do-it discussion and dig into the tools that produced the payoffs we reviewed.

Our first stop colors nearly every how-to-do-it concept we'll deal with: technology. As in every other area in today's workplace, technology has had an astounding effect on recruiting and hiring practices, making things happen faster, better, and cheaper.

If the goal is making better million-dollar hires, though, the concepts of faster-better-cheaper need to work in sync. Go for speed alone, and you risk making the wrong hires—and at blinding speed. Go for quality alone, and you risk that the competition will snap up the best candidates. Go for the lowest cost alone and—well, you know. The good news is that today's recruiting and hiring technology delivers all three outcomes.

It's All Changed

Not long ago, hiring was a paper-intense role of the HR department. Magazines, newspapers, radio, and TV built the employer brand needed to attract candidates. Job openings were posted at the company and in ads in newspaper and professional publications. Paper applications were mailed or handed out at the employment office. Résumés arrived in the mail, by fax, or through the early versions of e-mail.

If education, experience, or salary history were prerequisites, they were verified through telephone interviews or written sendouts. If tests or other assessment tools were part of the process, they were administered in paper-and-pencil and then scored, interpreted, and logged by HR staff. Interviews by HR staff and hiring managers were documented on paper forms. Background checks, drug tests, and reference checks were tracked on paper by the HR department too.

Candidates were followed through the process with paper files, spreadsheets, or stacks of manila folders. Contact with them was through letters or telephone follow-up. None of the information collected for a candidate was linked in a systematic way. Large-scale hiring events such as start-ups or staff expansions created a paper blizzard.

In the late 1980s, I was an expert witness in an employment case for a company of about twenty-five hundred employees. On my first visit, I was taken to a double-wide trailer parked outside the HR department. Inside, the walls were stacked from floor to ceiling with candidate files copied and organized for the litigation. The space was filled with paper but for a small room set aside for the paralegal. Even the simplest question about hiring practices required someone to pore through boxes of paper, tally results, and determine how decisions had been made, all at incredible cost.

Then three things happened: computers, HR software, and the Internet. The world of recruiting and hiring, and litigation, changed forever. Already several generations of recruiting and hiring technology have unfolded. Installed software has expanded to on-demand solutions. The Internet, along with an expanding array of social networking tools, continues to change recruiting and hiring practices seemingly every month. What once required hours of labor can be accomplished in seconds.

Today all the different information that goes into hiring decisions can be integrated, linked, and made viewable through any prism you wish. Technology came to finance, accounting, and customer management first, but it's arrived in recruiting with a bang. And the cost of hiring technology has followed the same downward curve that's come with technology solutions everywhere else.

Here, I'll offer an overview of technology's role in driving better million-dollar decisions. I'll stay at a summary level, though. A complete review would take a book, not a chapter, and there are many detailed sources for IT-oriented readers who want to dig deeper.[1]

Here my purpose is to describe what's possible. In fact, a good part of the payoff in the examples in the two preceding chapters resulted from hiring programs delivered through technology platforms. Take away the technology, and you lose much of the payoff. The intent, though, isn't to remove human judgment and face-to-face contact from the hiring process. Technology's role is to provide tools that support the best judgments and bring people into the process when and where they make the most effective contribution.

In what follows, I'll review where technology supports better million-dollar decisions by staging the discussion into the basic steps that make up the recruiting and hiring process: the hiring funnel shown in Figure 6.1.

Figure 6.1 Technology plays a role at every stage in the hiring funnel

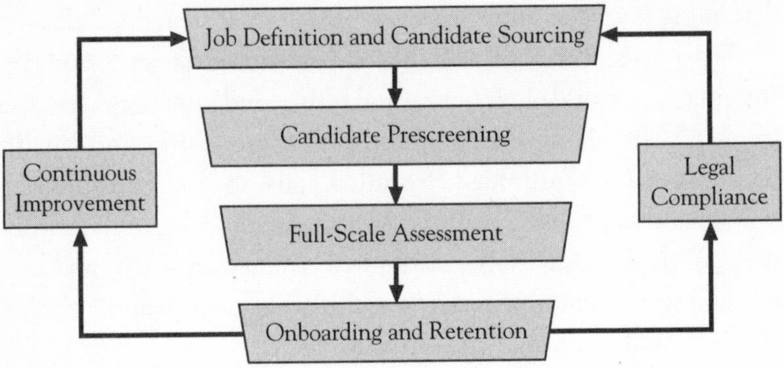

I'll survey what technology offers at every stage, from launching a candidate sourcing strategy, to prescreening, assessing, and selecting those deemed to be the best investments. I'll also profile solutions for onboarding new hires, laying a foundation for employee retention, monitoring legal compliance, and, importantly, setting up a continuous improvement loop in order to fine-tune the system regularly. Each of these topics will unfold in later chapters, but for now, we'll stick to the basics.

Candidate Sourcing

I begin with a caution: ten minutes after I finished writing this section, it was out of date, or so it seemed. Today everyone remembers the dawn of monster.com, careerbuilder.com, and similar businesses trailblazers in the job board world. Early to capitalize on the Internet, these businesses set out to help employers move from the age of paper to the era of digital candidates. When launched, the companies offered completely new ways to get the word out for both companies and candidates.

That was only the start. Today many view Facebook, MySpace, Twitter, and other sites as ways to keep in contact with friends, link with long-time associates, engage in a little narcissism, or make sure Grandma sees the grandkids' photos. But these social network-ing tools are changing the recruiting world dramatically too. Today there's not a recruiting firm in business that's not plumbing all the social networking tools as deeply as it can.

Today employers offer virtual tours of their company and its open positions on the company Web site. They highlight their corporate vision and values and offer video testimonials from employees and new hires. They send out "spiders" to creep around the Internet; find résumés, profiles, and bios that fit the company's open positions; and bring the results back to the recruiting depart-ment. Hundreds of companies now offer technology solutions that focus on finding better candidates, faster and cheaper, and on beat-ing the competition to making first contact with the top candidates. Linguistic sciences are even being used to create computer "brains" that read résumés at a conceptual level, match them to a company's job descriptions, and deliver a list of the best recruiting prospects scraped from the Internet. Figure 6.2 highlights examples of the technology-driven sourcing tools available today.

Figure 6.2 Technology helps define what we're looking for and build a strong candidate pool

First, technology solutions can help define exactly what the company seeks in a candidate. Tools to clarify qualifications that once required substantial time for HR staff to create can be produced quickly by tapping large dictionaries of job competencies, preloaded into software packages. The result is a detailed picture of the skills the company needs and the qualifications to use when reaching out to candidates. (I review some of the tools in Chapter Seven.)

Once you know what you're looking for, technology provides a platform to "post out" your position on the thousands of second-generation job boards created since monster.com and careerbuilder.com blazed the trail. Today there's a job board specializing in seemingly any occupation, profession, position level, geographical area, or other category you can imagine. Already, though, some say that job boards are giving way to social networking tools as the best possibility to recruit talent or find a job if you're a candidate on the hunt.[2] Some say the job boards of today will be gone within ten years, suggesting that only a little more than 10 percent of the jobs filled today come from job board postings.

Today advice to those seeking jobs focuses on personal branding, using platforms such as Facebook, LinkedIn, Twitter, and MySpace, complemented by personal Web sites, blogs, and other tools people use to put themselves out there in the world of the Internet. Employers also use these tools to market their companies and jobs in a way that's attractive to the new generation of job seekers. Professional associations are jumping into the act, sponsoring networking venues for members, where their participation leaves a trail that recruiters can pick up and follow.

Résumé search technology is opening completely new sourcing opportunities too. Here, software tools grab résumés as they arrive in an employer's inbox or search Internet sources to find candidate information that matches the employer's job opening. Created to sniff out, read, and process megavolumes of information in seconds, these solutions are becoming part of corporate HR departments' repertoire for finding candidates who fit a given job—and before the candidate even knows there's a job to be had.

All of these job-defining and candidate sourcing tools require a platform to manage the process and a place to house the information they collect. Enter the current generation of applicant tracking systems (ATSs). Designed to orchestrate the outreach and candidate tracking process, ATSs capture the results of sourcing and begin managing contacts with those who appear to be good prospects. Today ATSs are a platform for orchestrating all stages in the hiring funnel. They're the means for integrating information drawn from different sources and from different service providers who play a role in the hiring process. Today candidate sourcing is the level in the hiring funnel experiencing the greatest proliferation in technology solutions. Chapter Eight digs into what all these tools do to improve the payoff of the hiring process.

Candidate Prescreening

While sourcing focuses on spreading the word and finding candidates who fit the job's profile, there's a downside: the volume that often results. The Internet can stuff an employer's e-mail box to overflowing with résumés or social network profiles. Lots of résumés are good. Too many are not.

Prescreening offers a solution by sorting through an initial group of candidates using basic qualifying factors as objective and job related as possible to find a group of candidates for further review. These tools don't focus on finding the best; they try to find those who warrant investing further attention. They also focus on saving costs wasted if poorly qualified candidates were permitted to take up time moving down the hiring funnel.

In some cases, prescreening reduces large numbers of potential candidates to a manageable size, for example, in the start-up of a new facility where many thousands apply for hundreds of jobs. In other cases, prescreening eliminates candidates who clearly don't match the job's profile—for example, by eliminating retail sales clerks from consideration as new home sales representatives.

For the moment, let's sidestep policy and legal compliance topics: for example, whether to accept unsolicited résumés, how long to retain records, what actually constitutes "an applicant" for a given opening, and so forth. I'll come back to these later because they are important from a risk-reduction point of view. For now, let's just deal with how technology can turn thousands of résumés for a single opening into a good thing.

Figure 6.3 shows some of the options. To broaden the appeal, I'll direct the discussion not only to what a Fortune 500 company can afford but to what's feasible for an organization with five hundred employees.

Résumé extraction, and search and match, technology can replace humans in reading, interpreting, and deciding the degree to which a résumé or personal profile matches the requirements of the job. Using concepts as advanced as latent semantic analysis, computer software can actually read and compare documents, and

Figure 6.3 Technology helps manage candidate volume and identify the best follow-up choices

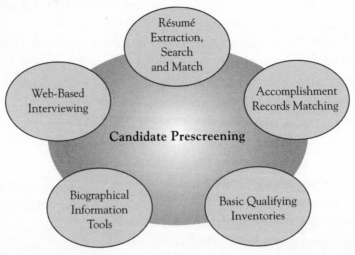

compare a candidate résumé to a job description based on similarities in the concepts reflected in the document's narrative.[3] The old days of keyword matching are gone. Technology now looks for concepts, themes, *and* key words. It can serve up a rank-ordered list of résumés, stacked in order of how well they match the position description or hiring profile. It can even match candidates to the résumés of star performers hired in the past.

The same tools automate another prescreening process born decades ago—something called an accomplishment record. The accomplishment record was designed as a tool to collect, through candidate self-report, a summary of work history and experiences that highlight candidate accomplishments most relevant to the position at hand.[4] Technology today can match the concepts and themes embedded in a candidate's answers to questions about what he has accomplished in his educational or career history to details of the job description for the open position. It can determine which candidate accomplishment records match the requirements of the job best.

Basic qualifying inventories or biographical information tools can be e-mailed to candidates whose resumes appear qualified for further review. These tools collect simple checklist answers to questions about education, experience, training, compensation requirements, and so on. They can be used to prescreen candidates based on their answers. Biographical checklists typically present multiple-choice questions, also collecting answers by e-mail send-outs. Such checklists evaluate general work orientation, job preferences, career interests, or specific experiences that can be used for filtering down the candidate group.

Finally, those who appear to fit the job can be scheduled for a Web-based interview, using teleconferencing technology to conduct an initial prescreening interview. Today's tools can place the candidate on one side of the computer display, with an interview script displayed on the other, so interviewers can be prepared and consistent, and accurately capture their observations in real time.

Together these solutions focus on gaining high-quality information, processing it accurately and consistently, and saving the cost associated with bringing underqualified candidates on-site. The technology typically provides a way to capture information, and then archive it in the employer's applicant tracking system too. If the candidate isn't a fit for the job at hand, the information is there when a position that's better suited to the candidate opens or for study when continuous improvement analysis of the company's hiring standards calls for review of prescreening decisions made in the past.

Full-Scale Assessment

Assessment focuses on finding the best. Technology-delivered testing, work simulations, and other assessment platforms examine knowledge, skills, abilities, and personality characteristics in the candidate pool. Recruiters, HR staff, and hiring managers responsible for face-to-face interviews also can use a variety of technology-driven platforms to meet, interact with, and collect information on qualifications that demand in-person assessment.

Full-scale assessment also extends to collecting information from prior supervisors or other employment references, offering a way to verify and expand on information that's been learned during earlier stages in the hiring funnel. It also extends to steps such as drug and alcohol testing, background checks, or medical examinations after the offer.

All of these activities focus on gaining an understanding of the whole candidate. There are other benefits too: consistency and fairness. The structure that technology brings to assessment dictates that every candidate receive the same opportunity to show his or her qualifications. Figure 6.4 shows examples of how technology supports the assessment process.

All manner of knowledge, skill, and ability assessment tools are available to help evaluate candidates. Today tests once administered

Figure 6.4 Technology helps create a picture of the whole candidate

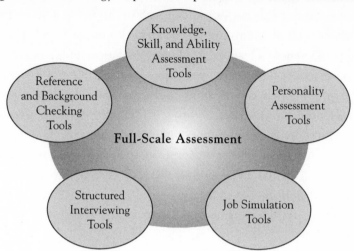

in paper-and-pencil format are delivered through Web-based platforms that administer and score them, report results to the employer, and archive the data. There's hardly a skill, ability, or higher-level technical knowledge that such platforms don't assess. Labor costs related to administration, scoring, and interpreting these tools once discouraged their use, but this is no longer the case. In 2005, research indicated that about 70 percent of companies in North America planned to move to technology-based platforms for administering their candidate assessment activities.[5]

In cases where the demands of the job call for a particular personality profile—salespersons, managers, or executives, for example—Web platforms also deliver assessment tools. The more complex scoring and interpretation requirements of these tools are handled by software solutions that create profiles, produce machine-generated narrative, and offer hiring recommendations in a strengths-and-weaknesses format. Some even offer developmental guidance should the company choose to put the assessment information to use in planning for initial development activities once the candidate is hired and on the job.

Technology also brings job simulation tools to the assessment process. Some evaluate a candidate's ability to use common office software such as Microsoft Word, PowerPoint, or Excel spreadsheets. At a more advanced level, job simulation tools can present managers with facts, data, and other information and ask them to assemble a plan for resolving problems embedded in the data. Sometimes simulations involve interacting with a scripted role player by telephone or computer connection. The goal is realism, involving the candidate in showing what he or she can do in a simulated version of the job. Technology makes the process efficient by eliminating the need to draw on company staff in administering, scoring, and summarizing the results of the process.

Every hiring decision uses an interview at some stage in the process, and technology has entered the system here too. Structured interviewing tools once required staff time and professional resources to create. Today technology platforms used to identify the competency requirements of a job can also generate lists of interview questions tapping the competencies, create the forms interviewers use, capture interviewers' notes and opinions, and add them to other candidate data archived in the employer's ATS. The tools even send out an interviewee's answers to employment references to verify (or not) the details.

Technology also drives reference and background checking tools. Platforms automate the collection of information from a candidate's references, comparing references' input against the position's competency requirements or using them as a cross-check against answers the candidate provided in an accomplishment record or interview. Automation makes it easy for an employer to draw information from its ATS and reach out to a candidate's references to ask: "The candidate says he accomplished this, with these results. Is this true, and if so, what did you think of the result?" Of course, the process of background checking has been nearly completely automated too.

All of the stages in full-scale assessment were once labor intense, paper intense, and open to legal challenge because of inconsistent administration. As a result, only the largest employers worked to build and rely on such systems. Small and midsize employers shied away, fearing high costs and legal challenge. Today technology diminishes both challenges. It's now possible for small employers to bring the same rigor to million-dollar decisions that a Fortune 500 company followed in the 1990s. Today a small employer can evaluate talent just as effectively as the big guys can.

Onboarding and Retention

Assessment ends when the employer reviews the information, evaluates it, and makes a decision. With technology, steps as disparate as reviewing the candidate's résumé, evaluating her performance on various assessment tools, considering interview results, and folding in employer references and background information can create a total candidate portfolio. Since the information comes from different sources, the process starts with integrating information into a single platform and generating reports and displays to help guide the final decision. Here technology implements any systematic rules the employer chooses to follow: specific hurdles, cutoffs, or patterns sought in the candidate's profile, for example.

Technology offers tools that support making hiring decisions, onboarding, and retention-related activities. Figure 6.5 shows some examples.

Today's ATS platforms provide data integration tools that sweep together all the information collected as candidates proceed down the hiring funnel. The tools organize this information in formats that help guide final selection decisions. They also archive the information for later use in both the continuous improvement and legal compliance steps discussed later. The more effective of these assemble qualifying information as the candidate proceeds down the hiring funnel and serve it up in reports and displays that

Figure 6.5 Technology helps guide candidate onboarding and drives retention

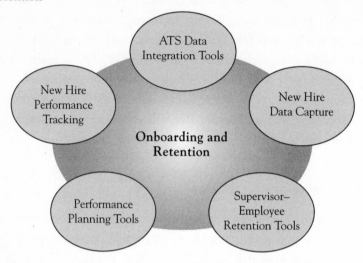

people participating in the hiring process can use to make the best decisions. Here, technology hands off decision-making data so that HR department and hiring managers can make better job-related decisions.

Technology tools also support data capturing for new hires, so that information needed to populate the company's compensation, benefits, tax, and other programs can be collected directly from new hires without the need for extensive paperwork and data entry time. Once a hiring decision is made, the employer and employee enter a transition period when both are taking a risk that there will be a fit and neither knows the other very well.

Research shows that this is the time when a foundation is laid for a productive, long-term relationship—or for a shorter, less positive one. Using technology-driven tools to help manage a new employee's transition into the new employment setting is proving important in building employee retention.

Research in turnover reduction shows that facilitating a hand-shake between the new hire and supervisor plays a major role in reducing turnover. Technology solutions help supervisors learn about a new hire's interests, preferences, career outlook, interest in feedback, and other information. They help build this information into how the employee and supervisor interact during the initial stages of employment—solutions unknown just a few years ago.

Finally, in addition to supplying all the information that goes into enrolling the new hire, the onboarding process provides an opportunity to build on information the company gathered about the new employee when he was still a candidate. A wealth of information is collected during the prescreening and assessment stages of the hiring process. Today, employers no longer toss this information away as the transition to employee status takes place. They use it to lay out initial plans for training, development, and transition management.

For example, the technology for administering candidate assessment tools is being used to summarize the new hire's strengths and weaknesses and populate performance planning tools set up during the onboarding process. In effect, these tools turn candidate assessment information into employee performance planning information, a step taken less frequently in the past when paper-based systems made it too labor intensive to add such information to the onboarding process.

In the same way, ATSs that track candidates during the hiring process have evolved to include performance tracking features too. These tools capture information about performance during training or note whether the new hire turns over in the short term. As a result, they provide data used in continuous improvement reviews of the overall hiring program.

Again, most of these activities were once paper intensive and called for significant staff involvement. Bringing them to technology platforms has encouraged broader use and opened avenues for ensuring that the best decisions are made during the risky period of a new hire's transition into a new position.

Legal Compliance

Legal compliance in recruiting and hiring involves ensuring that an employer designs, administers, and tracks its process in a way that meets federal and state statutes and the case law that has emerged over the years; it's a long list. Its focus is making sure that recruiting and hiring results serve up the same opportunities to all ethnic, gender, national origin, and other groups protected by law. (Chapter Eleven addresses the complexities of this challenge.)

Ensuring compliance rests on analyzing the outcomes of recruiting and hiring decisions made for a given job, business unit, and overall organization. It involves looking at the results produced at each stage in the hiring funnel, not just the bottom line. Since decisions might satisfy requirements in one area of the business or at one stage in the hiring process but be digging a compliance hole in others, a number of analyses are required to reduce legal risk. That's where the analytical power that comes with technology helps support what needs to be done. Figure 6.6 provides some examples.

Figure 6.6 Technology helps ensure recruiting and hiring practices meet legal requirements

For example, ATSs today offer tools that examine an employer's affirmative action plan and determine whether a given opening is one where there's a need for special attention to affirmative action. If so, candidate sourcing, prescreening, assessment, and hiring can be linked to the need.

Today's ATSs also provide a platform for undertaking applicant flow analyses. These reviews look to whether, for example, male and female candidates have fared the same at each stage in the hiring funnel and at the bottom line. The basic question is: Does the process present higher hurdles for one group than another? In programs that pose multiple screening hurdles, these analyses can be complex. Today's technology automates such reviews, so both real-time and periodic reviews of potential problems can be made.

In fact, today's ATSs assess an employer's degree of risk by automating adverse impact analyses too. These are the statistical reviews that compliance agencies use to determine whether step-by-step and bottom-line hiring decisions are sufficiently different from the initial flow of candidates to warrant a preliminary conclusion of discriminatory hiring. Reporting features embedded in these systems help make decisions about taking another look at certain candidates, replenishing the candidate pool, or proceeding with a hiring decision in a way that's informed from a risk management point of view.

The same systems help employers take a step that federal enforcement agencies strongly recommend: looking at alternatives that are equally valid but less adverse to members of protected groups. This process can involve a great deal of "if-then" review that we'll cover later. The analytical power of technology, though, permits employers to pose and answer questions about the operation of a hiring process. It can help avoid challenges that the practices might be valid, but that others would work just as well, and produce less negative impact on the opportunities of protected groups.

Finally, analytical tools that come with technology make it possible to investigate the validity of every step in the recruiting and hiring process in both real-time and periodically. In effect, these platforms help write the story that's used to defend an employer's practices in the event of a challenge. There is no longer a need to search through boxes of paper files built up over the years; today's tools produce answers in a matter of minutes and keep the answers fresh. In a sense, technology has become the legal department's best friend in helping to find, calibrate, and remove legal risk from a recruiting and hiring program.

Continuous Improvement Hiring

A decade ago, because of legal compliance issues, employers spent a great deal of time and money studying and proving the effectiveness (validity) of a hiring program before they implemented it. In the 1990s, for example, I completed many large-company and industry-wide projects to design new recruiting and hiring systems in the United States and internationally. The projects sometimes required several years to analyze the employer's jobs, try out various recruiting and screening tools, validate the processes, and analyze the way the process would affect the opportunities of legally protected groups. The studies went forward while the employer continued to use a prior system or simply waited until the R&D was finished. Payoff was delayed, hiring mistakes were made, and R&D brought costs with no offsetting improvement in the quality of results.

Today technology helps ensure that new recruiting and hiring concepts are implemented quickly. It means hiring results can be monitored the same way as quality control programs used in manufacturing, logistics, or other areas of the business, just like Six Sigma and other continuous improvement strategies. Technology makes it possible to track the legal compliance of a new program as it's launched, examine its validity as it's used, and modify it to

Figure 6.7 Technology brings a continuous improvement perspective to recruiting and hiring

produce better payoff and better compliance, all in real time. Figure 6.7 illustrates some of the underlying tools.

Here, the data capturing capability that comes with ATSs provides a way to keep a running scorecard on metrics such as time-to-hire and cost-per-hire for a job, a department, an outside recruiter, or the overall organization. These tools provide HR leaders with a quick view on where there might be problems and where there's progress. Some put a recruiting dashboard on the HR department's computer screen to provide a depiction of how well the system is operating.

Performance tracking capabilities provide a way to track successes and failures very soon after a hiring decision is made. For example, some platforms reach out by e-mail to a new hire's supervisor at the end of a predetermined period of time and ask questions about this person's day-to-day performance, strengths, and weaknesses. The information is then reflected back on data gathered when the employee was a candidate. If the employee is a star, the system can search for clues that could have forecast this outcome.

If the new hire seems a poor choice, the information can be used to find where changes to the overall process can leverage better payoff—for example, where the data might point to opportunities to fine-tune the system and make better predictions of performance in the future.

That's where return-on-investment analysis tools help the HR department show what it has contributed from a financial payoff point of view. Using analyses like those reviewed in Chapters Four and Five, as well as other quality control-based approaches, technology can help the HR department serve up detailed summaries of the costs saved and the better performance results achieved.

Tomorrow—More for Less

This chapter has covered a lot but only scratched the surface. Hiring stage by hiring stage, though, it has hit the major areas where technology is supporting the recruiting and hiring process and where it's guiding companies to better million-dollar decisions.

Technology vendors have made strides in bundling together the capabilities reviewed here, integrating them onto single platforms so that employers need not deal with a dozen software providers to execute all the stages in the hiring funnel. Like all other technology solutions, the costs of these capabilities continue to fall. What once cost millions of dollars to implement now costs thousands. Capabilities a few years ago affordable to only the largest employers are now at the fingertips of small companies. What recently came through installed software and hardware now comes through the Internet.

The path forward is likely to involve more attention to removing administrative costs and increasing hiring speed. More attention to better candidate fit and quality of hire is in the offing as well. There will be more focus on integrating all the stages in the hiring process through components that talk to one another, with more emphasis on building in tools and metrics that document the payoff gained and underscore where the next continuous improvement tweak should be made. That's why, even in small HR departments, it's important to encourage staff to gain a basic understanding of recruiting and hiring technology and to encourage them to bring a mind-set about bringing faster, better, and cheaper to their assignments.

So with the thinking models in place, ideas about where technology can help in mind, and a preview of the payoff that comes from better hiring behind us, it's time to focus on the how-to-do-it. Chapter Seven begins a review of the steps that drive the best million-dollar decisions. I'll start by reviewing how to lay out an overall hiring strategy, choose tactics, and set up the tracking tools that will reveal what contributes to the bottom line.

CHAPTER SEVEN

SETTING STRATEGY AND CHOOSING TACTICS

Organizations, particularly businesses, are built on a web of strategies: product and service strategies, financing strategies, marketing strategies, sales strategies, organic growth versus acquisition strategies, and, most important to the topic here, talent strategies. Strategies lay out the big picture and present the overall objectives. They're the forest, not the trees. Tactics step in to make the big picture clear and focus on the trees that might get in the way.

For a new enterprise, the strategies are captured in a well-crafted business plan. For an established business, they're refreshed with each new planning cycle. Nonbusiness, government, and other public entities are not as economically driven, but they nevertheless frame strategies to help them become what they hope to be and accomplish what they hope to do. The business literature is full of guidance on developing strategies and tactics.[1] Here I'll cover the topic with a specific application in mind: how to set the best strategic and tactical foundation for a recruiting and hiring process. And I'll keep the discussion both practical and applied.

Within HR, leadership typically sets a strategy for each of the areas in which it's held accountable. For example, HR leadership commonly works with senior management to define a compensation strategy for the enterprise.[2] There's always a compensation strategy. After all, compensation captures everyone's attention. An example might look like this:

> We will target average base compensation at the seventy-fifth percentile of our labor market competitors and offer a blend of base and incentive compensation that puts us among the top 10 percent of companies with which we compete for talent. This, along with other HR initiatives, will yield workforce retention among the top 10 percent of competitors, and our external workforce surveys will place us in the top 10 percent of benchmark companies on metrics of employee commitment, engagement, and level of effort.

The strategy is the game plan. Details of the strategy can differ for individual business units, groups of jobs, geographical locations, and others. Once the plan is set, though, HR leadership can move ahead to assemble the tactics and tool kits needed to accomplish the strategy's targets. Strategy then shapes the communications that flow from senior management and provides guidelines for day-to-day decisions about individual employees.

Every company has compensation tactics too. Companies implement their compensation strategies by creating role descriptions that define what employees are expected to do. They undertake job evaluation reviews to attach a value to the work performed in different jobs, complete surveys of labor market competitors to determine what others pay for similar work, create compensation policies and procedures to guide day-to-day decisions, set up performance evaluation tools to guide individual rewards, and set up audit tools to make sure they stay consistent with the overall strategy, and with legal compliance standards. After all, everyone from the CEO to the groundskeeper wants to know "how compensation works around here."

An organization's recruiting and hiring strategies often get far less attention than its strategies about pay. Fewer than half the organizations I've worked with have an adequate response to the opening question: "Let's start by looking at your overall recruiting and hiring strategy, and then talk about how it's shaped to your operating units, okay?" The responses often cite "hiring people who fit our culture," "working closely with our hiring managers," or "choosing people who can grow with our business." Although there's nothing wrong with any of these concepts, the question is how you know when you get there, how you catch on when the plan isn't working, and how you make sure you're gaining the best payoff with the hiring decisions you make. Imagine the sales function describing its strategy as "selling as much as we can."

Why a Recruiting and Hiring Strategy?

- *Question to C-level executives:* Do you work with HR leadership to create a clear strategy for finding the single most costly asset in your business: people? Do the plans carry the same level of detail as ones that guide your product development, new business acquisition, geographical expansion, marketing, sales, customer retention, or even compensation strategies? If not, doesn't the strategy that supports all your other strategies—how you find people—need attention?

- *Question to managers and supervisors:* Have you met with the HR department to learn how the company's recruiting and hiring strategy, and tactics, are shaped around the needs of your part of the organization? When you look at the candidate qualifications targeted, the tools used to screen people, and the flow of candidates you see day to day, does the output of the strategy measure up?

- *Question to investors:* Does the business plan you're reviewing cite a strategy for recruiting and hiring the management team and workforce in which you're being asked to invest? Does it tie the plan to the company's financing needs? Does it give you confidence the management team asking for your money knows how to get where it needs to go? After all, it's not the glib guys you meet on the road show who make your investment yield a return. It's the people they hire.

These questions aren't intended to harp at producing written plans, spreadsheet projections, rules, or bureaucracy. They're intended to underscore three facts. First, like financing or acquisition strategies, there are best practices for creating and driving an organization's recruiting and hiring strategy. Second, there are tools and technology to make the plan work. Third, if a business is going to spend time designing a strategic plan anywhere, it should probably start by creating one to define how it hires the people who create and implement all its other strategic plans.

I've founded, run, and invested in businesses. I've made mistakes, and almost every mistake rested in what I've done, well or poorly, to evaluate talent. Hiring decisions made too quickly, or investment decisions that stopped short of looking closely at the competence of the company's CEO and management team have cost me. Targeting the right skills, measuring talent in the right ways, or seeing through the thin veneer of a new CEO looking for money have paid off. I don't know how else to say it: if you're interested in success or a financial return, you need a strategy that finds the right talent.

What follows isn't an exercise in the science of strategic personnel planning. That topic already has many excellent guides.[3] There the focus is on anticipating how many people will be needed, when they will be needed, and in what part of the organization they will be needed. Expansion, retirements, promotions, management reorganizations, staff reductions, and other areas are addressed in strategic personnel plans and typically emphasize the number and timing of staffing decisions. Sometimes such plans set out to add talent and sometimes to subtract. They also address the need for internal programs to develop talent and help balance the use of outsourced or temporary resources versus making permanent staff additions.

Here the focus isn't on developing a strategy about *how many* and *when* or about how to *develop talent* internally. Rather, the focus is deciding on the target, going hunting, and choosing the tools to get the job done.

Choosing a Strategy—Critical Needs and Low-Hanging Fruit

The compensation strategy outlined in the opening of the chapter has three features. It indicates the organization's overall objectives—*where it wants to focus*—citing workforce retention and engagement. It indicates the metrics to be used in tracking progress against the objectives—*how it plans to measure success*—citing a variety of survey tools. Finally, it indicates the targets the organization plans to hit—*where it wants to be*—citing specific comparisons to competitors.

The recruiting and hiring projects I worked on that gained the greatest payoff were those where we framed a strategy around these three elements, and then followed with tactics that experience had shown to work in similar circumstances. We've avoided generic strategies like this one:

> We will recruit and select talent with the ability to accomplish our organization's strategic objectives and with the skills to adapt and change as our business changes. We will build a workforce that is diverse, committed, and aligned with the vision and values of our organization. The result will be talent that stands out among the competition.

Nice, but what's the next step? How do you implement such a strategy? More important, how do you know when you're there? This might reflect a useful *vision*, but it does little to help run the business, track success, or gain a return on hiring investments.

Instead, gaining a payoff calls for a strategy that's much more targeted. Figure 7.1 captures the concept.

Setting a recruiting and hiring strategy starts with identifying hiring-related objectives particularly critical to the business, fitting metrics and targets around the objectives, and then assembling tactics that experience shows are most likely to accomplish the strategy. It's important to recognize, though, that different tactics drive different outcomes, so you need to know the objectives before you assemble the tactics and tool kits to achieve them. We'll dig deeper into tactics shortly.

Here's a simple example. Millions of employees work at entry-level positions in the fast food and casual dining sector. Front-of-

Figure 7.1 Three elements of a recruiting and hiring strategy

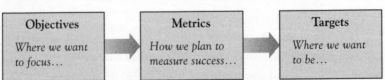

the-house positions take orders, interact directly with customers, and engage in a bit of up-selling. Back-of-the-house positions deal with food preparation, support front-of-the-house staff, and see to the cleanup and general appearance of the restaurant. Wages are typically low, experience and training requirements are minimal, and career progression isn't a key expectation. Employees aren't asked to create new systems and procedures, bring new ideas to the business, or launch a career. Some do, but they're the exception.

To determine what senior management should target in framing a hiring strategy for jobs at this level, think about what's most important to the business and what's achievable. In this business, employee turnover is rampant—sometimes more than 200 percent for entry-level staff. The cost of replacement isn't high, but costs are driven by volume and the time that's required of store managers to make it happen. They add up fast. In a highly competitive space, customers' satisfaction with service and the increased revenue that comes with up-selling—"Would you like a dessert with that?"—also are important to driving store-level success.

It's all pretty simple: reducing turnover brings down costs, and adding sales and customer retention raises revenue. Subtract one from the other, and you've got profit growth, a nice objective. A business that is planning to upgrade recruiting and hiring with these objectives and metrics in mind, even at this relatively low level in the labor market, might develop a strategy that looks something like this:

> We will recruit and hire entry-level store talent in a way that lowers 180-day turnover by 20 percent per year from our current level and achieve a 24-hour replacement time for all entry-level positions, at an average recruiting and hiring cost of $500 per replacement. As we roll out the new program, we will achieve a 1 percent first-year increase in store-level net profitability for units coming online with the new system.

Figure 7.2 A recruiting and hiring strategy brought to life

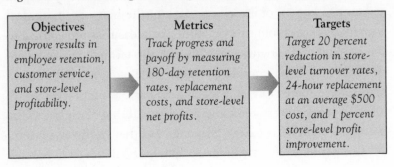

Objectives	Metrics	Targets
Improve results in employee retention, customer service, and store-level profitability.	*Track progress and payoff by measuring 180-day retention rates, replacement costs, and store-level net profits.*	*Target 20 percent reduction in store-level turnover rates, 24-hour replacement at an average $500 cost, and 1 percent store-level profit improvement.*

All three elements of strategy are there: where to focus, how to plan to measure success, and where the business wants to be. Figure 7.2 adds detail to the strategy introduced in Figure 7.1. There are no glittering generalities or visionary positioning. Simple, straightforward business metrics compose the strategy. Of course, things the company does *after* people are hired will affect the metrics and payoff targets cited too. After all, it's a system, and everything affects everything else. Training supervisors to build teamwork and engagement, providing compensation that holds employees, and bringing technology to administering the process all affect the outcome measures. The recruiting and hiring strategy, though, focuses on improving the raw material that enters the system so that other initiatives have an additive effect.

Working with one of the largest employers in the sector, we built a hiring strategy much like that summarized in Figure 7.2. It incorporated four objectives: reducing turnover, improving customer service, increasing store-level profitability, and remaining legally compliant. In the end, we hit the targets, even store-level profitability. The system was simple, and the payoff came very quickly. Legal compliance was built into the monitoring process from the outset. I'll review the tactics that accomplished the strategy shortly. The point here is that success rests in deciding what payoff you want to accomplish in a recruiting and hiring strategy and translating that objective to a specific focus and metrics.

As in the fast food example, the strategy can be framed around objectives central to the business. But a strategy also can take a somewhat shorter-term focus, aiming at areas that represent low-hanging fruit—outcomes where experience shows that following an easy-to-implement strategy will yield a substantial gain by fixing simple problems quickly.

A client in the home-building sector was hit with unacceptably high turnover in its sales professionals. Its previous recruiting and hiring strategy had focused on attracting experienced sales professionals, identifying those with a record of success, and using turnover and sales performance targets to measure the program's success. At a tactical level, those hired had to make it through a résumé screen, a battery of skill and ability tests, a series of management interviews, and the traditional background and reference checking process. So, what more could be added to the strategy to fix the turnover problem?

Analysis of the company's turnover data showed that its recruiting and hiring strategy needed one final revision. Review showed lower turnover among new hires who brought a five-year background to the job in four areas: working against individually set sales targets, accepting completely commission-based pay, regularly working weekends, and showing an inclination to understate rather than exaggerate their past accomplishments. Salespersons with these attributes showed less than one in three chances of turning over during the first two years of employment. New hires lacking the characteristics were twice as likely to turn over. Hiring them made little sense: two of every three would be gone soon after they began hitting their sales targets.

Not surprisingly, all four of the candidate characteristics that forecast longer tenure linked directly with the company's work environment. Sales employees were expected to take on individual sales targets. Compensation was totally commission based. As you might expect, weekends were a peak time for making sales contacts. And in the company culture, the emphasis was on producing, not talking about producing.

The analysis altered the overall recruiting and hiring strategy in a simple way. The focus of recruiting and initial screening changed to targeting those with all four of the characteristics where possible and avoiding those who met only one or two of the four unless circumstances made it simply not possible.

Sometimes a simple review of metrics and targets—in this case, ones focusing on turnover rates—suggests simple solutions. In these cases, changing the overall recruiting and hiring strategy can yield dividends in the short term. Tracking outcomes once a strategy is implemented can be the key to finding these minor changes that pay off well. Here, the strategy was tightened to focus on candidates whose experience fit the company's work environment more closely.

What becomes clear is that an organization of any size and complexity is likely to need multiple recruiting and hiring strategies. Different parts of an organization often focus their strategies on very different objectives, metrics, and targets as they execute recruiting and hiring programs. The customer call center and help desk segment of a software producer will have a very different strategy in recruiting and hiring talent—building customer satisfaction and controlling employee turnover—from the development side of the house, where innovation, teamwork, productivity, and hitting time commitments are key objectives. At senior levels, strategy is likely to focus on finding talent that will meet individual objectives, build workforce engagement, and avoid the dark side tendencies that derail about 50 percent of today's leaders.

In summary, major segments of a business's operating management can communicate to HR leadership where they need to focus, how they want to measure success, and where they want to be. Then HR can translate the discussion into a recruiting and hiring strategy that fits each segment's needs and also inform operating management about the effort, cost, and risks likely to come with the strategy.

Using the tactics and tools profiled in later chapters, HR leadership can then set up the best conditions for success with each strategy. At the highest level, an overall organization's strategy might look like the rather generic statement cited earlier. At the operating level, though, gaining a payoff demands a strategy far more buttoned down. It also demands a clear set of tactics.

Assembling the Tactics and Building in Risk Management

The best reason to lay a clear, measurement-driven strategy is to guide the choice of tactics. Experience shows different recruiting and hiring tactics produce different types of results. So a strategy targeting a specific objective calls for assembling specific tactics proven to achieve the targeted outcome. Simply put, knowing the metrics you want to hit directs the choice of tactics most likely to drive success.

It's much like a business choosing a strategy to increase revenue by acquiring other companies versus one that focuses on organic growth. Choosing the acquisition-based strategy implies different tactics: more need for financing, less product development focus, and less emphasis on recruiting new talent. Under an organic growth strategy, the company seeks out and develops talent, who then mature as the business grows. Under an acquisition strategy, though, the tactics for finding talent can rely on what some call a merge-and-purge approach: reviewing and assessing acquired talent and deciding which to hold and which to release. A great deal of material in the coming chapters deals with the concept that different recruiting and hiring tactics produce different outcomes and different types, and even levels, of payoff.

Let's go back to the fast food example. The strategy is to reduce short-term turnover, improve customer satisfaction, and boost store-level profitability. But even this simple example becomes more complex when we set out to make it happen. Which of the three

Figure 7.3 Three tactical elements for accomplishing a strategy

Tool Kits	Technology	Tracking
What we'll use to get it done . . .	*How we'll make it deliverable, scalable, and cost-effective . . .*	*What we'll use to monitor, measure, and make course corrections . . .*

metrics targeted should be the major focus? For example, might reducing turnover actually drive the other two metrics by lowering hiring costs and giving longer-tenured staff a chance to learn the company's customer retention techniques? Even this simple strategy requires choices about which tactics will produce the best return on the metrics underlying the strategy.

Figure 7.3 shows the main features I've found most helpful in expanding a recruiting and hiring strategy into a set of tactics to guide its implementation.

As with strategy, three components shape the model. First is choosing tools that experience shows to work best in meeting the strategy's objectives. As we'll see, there are countless tools available to compose the new, what-we'll-use-to-get-it-done part of tactics. Second, as reviewed in the previous chapter, technology is an area that pervades the world of recruiting and hiring today. Choosing a technology platform to support the tools selected is essential. Today technology sets up much of *how to make the tools deliverable, scalable, and cost-effective.* Even things as basic as face-to-face interview protocols are now created and delivered by technology platforms.

Finally, the tactical plan needs a dashboard to show how to monitor, measure, and make course corrections. This part is sometimes supported by, and sometimes linked to, the technology side of tactics. It's sometimes driven by in-house HR information systems. It ensures we track progress and identify opportunities as soon as possible to fine-tune or adjust the tactics. Without a strong tracking component, we don't know whether we're hitting the targets set in the strategy, and we don't know whether we're on the road to trouble with respect to legal compliance, cost overruns, or potential pushback in the candidate pool.

Tactics can differ for different business units, locations, and groups of jobs. Each business unit needs to spend time with HR leadership thinking through what amounts essentially to a tactical plan for "where we want to be and how we're going to get there." Layering in best practices, prior experience, and limitations from budgets, current staffing, and local labor market conditions all help shape what goes into the tactics that management decides have the best chance for payoff and the best level of risk mitigation.

Let's go back once more to the fast food example. As we worked with the client to move past strategy and build a tactical plan, we found there was no trouble attracting candidates. Nor was there a problem with the range of talent that candidates brought to the screening process. Recruiting was not the challenge, so recruiting tools were not a focus in laying out the tactical plan. Instead, we based the tactical plan on three things we knew from research with similar entry-level jobs in similar settings.

First are the people facts: candidates differ in what they bring to the job. Many of these differences can be measured reliably and economically. We know that differences among candidates in *will-do* characteristics do a reasonably good job in predicting the likelihood of their quitting early. They also work reasonably well in identifying whether candidates are likely to behave badly enough to be terminated (show poor customer service, demonstrate high absenteeism, fail to follow instructions) versus falling at the other end of the scale on such metrics.

Captured by workplace personality dimensions such as conscientiousness or responsibility, these characteristics can be assessed with simple-to-administer screening tools. In the example, we decided to add such a tool in screening the restaurants' entry-level talent as the first step in building our tactical plan.

Second, given the high volume of hiring, the tactical plan needed to provide for delivering the new screening tool through a computer-based platform that could administer the assessment at the store level, score and interpret it, and provide store managers with immediate feedback. The technology also needed to provide feedback to the store managers about areas they might want to probe if the candidate proceeded to a face-to-face interview. Importantly, it also needed to administer the screening process in less than twenty minutes to avoid turning off the typically young, low-attention-span candidate pool.

Third, the tactical plan called for using the same technology platform to provide data tracking capabilities by linking with the company's human resource information systems to monitor the tenure of those hired, capture store managers' reviews of their performance, and provide a way to track store-level profitability. These data tracking tools provided a way to monitor candidate hiring and rejection rates too, so that equal employment opportunity objectives could be measured to avoid potential legal compliance problems.

Figure 7.4 captures the basics of the tactical plan.

Figure 7.4 A tactical plan brought to life

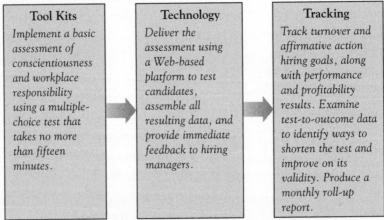

Tool Kits	Technology	Tracking
Implement a basic assessment of conscientiousness and workplace responsibility using a multiple-choice test that takes no more than fifteen minutes.	*Deliver the assessment using a Web-based platform to test candidates, assemble all resulting data, and provide immediate feedback to hiring managers.*	*Track turnover and affirmative action hiring goals, along with performance and profitability results. Examine test-to-outcome data to identify ways to shorten the test and improve on its validity. Produce a monthly roll-up report.*

Controlling Risk and Keeping It Legal

One of the process facts set out in Chapter Two introduced the ways that legal compliance surrounds the world of employment decision making. As noted, federal, state, and local laws raise the risk of legal challenge to an employer's recruiting and hiring decisions. Some laws and regulations require regular reporting to government agencies on hiring, placement, and other employment activities when an organization reaches a certain size (typically fifty employees) or does business with units of government. Other laws and court decisions require that steps be taken to demonstrate the validity of employment practices that affect one group of candidates differently from another.

Chapter Eleven reviews how recruiting and hiring tactics can control the risk of legal challenge. I'll discuss not only the most likely sources of challenge, but offer some do's and don'ts that come from major court decisions and compliance agency guidelines. I'll note some of the areas in a recruiting and hiring program most vulnerable to challenge based on how the courts have decided cases in the past.

I raise the topic of legal risk here because the best time to think defensively is while laying an overall strategy. Such thinking is particularly important when you are assembling the tactics that drive the strategy. Agency challenges, court decisions, research studies, and private party suits challenging companies' recruiting and hiring practices have laid a generally clear path. Today there's good precedent for what to do and, most important, what not to do in framing the components of a tactical plan: tools, technology, and tracking systems. Some of the precedents suggest tactics that clearly reduce the risk of legal challenge. Some put up stop signs that can't be ignored.

Because costs are high in defending, losing, or even responding to legal challenge, it's important that every idea going into a new strategy and set of tactics receives an overview for potential risk while it's being created. The review will come at a cost, but the price is lowest now, before pulling the trigger on a new plan. Having been an expert witness in the area for more than twenty years, I've learned that challenges often come from parts of a new process where they're least expected. And the challenge is much harder to deal with if it comes in an area where things have been going awry for some time and no one has noticed. That's why the HR function today operates almost as a legal department when recruiting and hiring tactics are being formed. It's just good business from a risk-reduction point of view to take a legal review at the outset.

Deciding Whether to Outsource the Process

Another decision that comes with assembling a tactical plan is one that often is intertwined with the choice of tools, technology, and tracking. It's the decision about whether part, or all, of the recruiting and hiring process to be implemented should be handed off to an outside service provider, that is, whether it will be outsourced. Today this is a decision that a noteworthy number of employers are making. In fact, the decision to outsource sometimes begins even as the company is creating its overall strategy, and development of the tactical plan is then the first activity that's outsourced. Recruitment process outsourcing (RPO) providers are one of the fastest growing segments of the market servicing businesses today.

The long-used model of handing recruiting assignments to fee-based or contingency recruiters began to morph substantially in the 1990s. New HR outsourcing concepts, new technology, and newly formed business offerings redefined the concept of using outside recruiting support to fill an organization's talent needs. As shown in Figure 7.5, some of the offerings that emerged were targeted solutions, taking on a tightly defined piece of the overall recruiting and hiring process.

In the early 1990s I tapped the technology that marketing companies were using to send out customer surveys using fax, ask those

Figure 7.5 Examples of levels in recruitment process outsourcing

Targeted Solutions	◆ Outsourced job board to post position openings ◆ Social network or résumé search technologies to find candidates ◆ On-demand applicant tracking solution ◆ Web-based testing or assessment services to screen candidates ◆ Web-based new hire onboarding tools and technology ◆ Web-based employee retention tools for new hires
Event-Based Solutions	◆ Find and screen candidates to support a new product launch (for example, sales reps) ◆ Recruit and staff a new location, additional work shift, or international opening ◆ Fill seasonal hiring (for example, retail) or beginning-of-cycle hiring needs (for example, educational institutions) ◆ Recruit, screen, staff a one-time event (for example, sporting event, entertainment venue, volunteer event)
Overall Solutions	◆ Outsource all hiring activities for a single job (for example, call center rep, account manager, programmer) ◆ Outsource all hiring activities for an occupational area (for example, manufacturing positions, college new hires, retail sales staff) ◆ Outsource all aspects of recruiting and hiring for a business unit, location, country, or overall organization

receiving them to bubble-in answers to marketing questions, and fax back the results. We shaped the same technology to send out and receive bubbled-in answer sheets for candidate screening tests. The technology let us pull the test answer sheet directly into computer software that scored the test, determined the candidate's qualifications, sent a fax-based report to the hiring manager, and archived the results into a database for later use in payoff analyses.

This narrowly targeted solution took test administration, scoring, reporting, and databasing off the shoulders of the field HR staff: no more local test administrator burden and no more leaking of test answer keys in the field. Recruiting, sourcing, interviewing, and all other aspects of the hiring process remained with the hiring company. Just this single piece of the process was outsourced to achieve faster, better, cheaper results. In months, it became the most profitable part of our outsourcing business.

As Figure 7.5 shows, other targeted RPO solutions populate the market today, from job boards, to résumé search technologies, online applicant tracking systems, testing, and onboarding or retention-building tools. All of these activities were once created or administered *inside* the organization. Today they're used to reduce staff time and address specific recruiting or hiring needs.

As rifle-shot offerings took hold, broader offerings evolved. These covered more aspects of the hiring process. As Figure 7.5 indicates, many of these solutions addressed event-based recruiting or hiring needs. In the mid-1990s, for example, my company took over most of the blue-collar and skilled-trades hiring activities for a number of the major automobile manufacturing companies and their tier 1 suppliers. Here, everything from accepting applications, to skills testing, interviewing, and administering group assessment exercises was bundled as an outsourced offering to deal with the start-up of a new shift or expansion in head count to deal with a new manufacturing line.

Versions of these offerings also were used in what were known as greenfield start-ups, where we took over the recruiting and hiring for entire new facilities in the United States and internationally. In the mid- and late 1990s, we moved from Turkey, northward through the Czech Republic, Hungary, Poland, Russia, and the Baltics, even Kazakhstan, starting up manufacturing facilities for a major U.S. manufacturer. We adapted the approach to fit the local cultures, but the outsourced model fit the needs of U.S.-based companies moving into environments where recruiting and hiring practices had not yet matured. Employers loved the flexibility to turn on recruiting and hiring resources when the need was high and turn them off when the need for employees dropped.

These were the initial steps toward building a business sector that's known today as recruitment process outsourcing (RPO), a rapidly evolving part of the HR space that's fundamentally redesigned the way many employers find talent. The scope of capabilities offered in the RPO sector means that while assembling a tactical plan, we need to ask, Should we outsource any, or all, of this?

Sometimes the decision can be to draw on a third party to provide one piece of the overall solution, as we did by providing the outsourced test administration, scoring, reporting, and payoff analyses in the fast food hiring example. Sometimes the decision is to outsource the overall recruiting and hiring process, and even the design of the strategy and tactics that drive it.

The pharmaceutical industry, for example, often launches a major hiring campaign to build its cadre of pharmaceutical sales representatives as part of launching a new product. It's not unusual for the company to engage an RPO provider to source, attract, screen, select, and provide offers to hundreds of new sales reps. Here, RPO providers marshal the recruiting staff and technology needed to find candidates quickly, process and evaluate them, forward them for any necessary internal interviewing process, and complete the onboarding process. For the pharmaceutical company to complete the work itself in a short time span, it would need to expand its staff and purchase new technology platforms. For the RPO provider, it's just part of doing business.

Finally, as Figure 7.5 shows, some companies actually off-load all their recruiting and hiring programs, along with the job of defining the tactics. In these cases, it's not a short-term hiring objective that drives the decision. It's the decision to involve service providers who hold expertise in talent acquisition. For example, among other areas of focus, my former employer, Aon Consulting, runs an RPO offering that takes over physician recruiting and hiring for health care providers. Other offerings take over recruiting and hiring for groups of jobs, a business location, or even an entire business.

At this level, the decision is to rely on outside parties who know where and how to source talent, how to assess and select it, and which tool kits and technology to assemble at the lowest cost. Like any other decision to outsource, the choice is driven by the belief that someone else can do it better, faster, and cheaper.

As we move forward to the chapters that deal with each stage in the recruiting and hiring process, I'll provide examples of RPO solutions. For now, though, we need to add "to RPO or not to RPO" to the list of decisions an employer makes in crafting a solid tactical plan. In fact, this is a decision that often comes *first*, once the business has set a strategy that senior management supports. Creating the strategy often opens the door to hearing from RPO providers about the tactics they propose for bringing the strategy to life.

Holding the Plan to Return-on-Investment Review

We now have a strategy and tactics. Both have been held to a risk management review. We might even have an outside RPO helper. The final step is to make sure we're ready to hold the process to ROI review. With the tactics in place, we have everything we need to do this. It's just a matter of reminding ourselves we won't simply implement the process and let it run.

I take the view that recruiting and hiring is essentially a major quality control initiative. Here's where we find whether we've created a valid approach and where we measure the results in dollars. It's just like a manufacturing process, but here it's the quality of hire and the cost we monitor. Just as a manufacturing process is continually tracked, measured, and revised to maintain and improve the product, a recruiting and hiring process needs to be held to the same standards of quality control.

Today HR makes increasing use of recruiting and hiring dashboards that not only the HR department but hiring managers too can monitor. Some are embedded in technology solutions, some are offered by RPO providers, and some are crafted in-house as part of running the company's applicant tracking system or overall human resource information system. Most dashboards track basic measures—metrics such as time to hire, cost per hire, average number of openings, and related metrics. Some monitor results such as average new hire turnover rates and equal employment compliance statistics, for example.

A few tracking systems even reach out to hiring departments and collect supervisors' input about the performance of new hires as they finish their initial ninety days, first six months, first year, and so on. These tools help drive data-mining activities that seek to find which components of the recruiting and hiring process have had the greatest effect on the ultimate metric: employee performance. Do particular recruiting sources produce the best performers? Do those who performed better on certain testing or interviewing tools perform better on the job? Do those with particular résumé profiles stay longer or perform better? As in other areas of the business, mining recruiting and hiring data to answer these questions is where the true payoff rests.

It's one thing to take up a set of tactics because they reflect the best practices for accomplishing a given strategy. It's another to look at the first year's results and put numbers to the outcome. If you run a customer service department, you do it. The sales department does it. If you're in manufacturing, you do it. If you've invested capital in a new venture, you do it. The recruiting and hiring department can do it too. Today it's an increasing practice and the foundation for coming up with results that show the true value gained by framing better practices.

In summary, the everyday pressure of running an HR operation can make a discussion of strategy and tactics seem a bit academic. If HR is going to generate the payoff it's capable of, though, its systems must be given the same level of rigor as the rest of the organization. The recruiting and hiring function can produce a payoff just like other departments. When strategy and tactics are created in the ways reviewed here, the size of that payoff will surprise most other segments of the business. It just takes running the recruiting and hiring function with three things in mind:

1. Laying out a recruiting and hiring strategy that sets the objectives, metrics, and targets the HR department will pursue for its client departments
2. Creating a tactical plan that assembles the tool kits, technology, and tracking procedures that current best practices show have the greatest chance of accomplishing the strategy
3. Deciding if, and where, outsourced resources can add a faster, better, and cheaper element to the process

Link it all together with ongoing quality control, and the organization's most costly asset, its talent, begins to produce a payoff. Through the following chapters, this is the model. Planning, executing, and tracking results: it's the only way I know to run a business.

CHAPTER EIGHT

CANDIDATE SOURCING AND PRESCREENING

With strategy and tactics set, we can turn to ways to source and prescreen candidates. This chapter discusses how to build a profile of basic qualifications and competencies for candidates. It illustrates how software tools can search the Internet, find potential candidates, and compare them to the job's requirements. It also shows how large groups of candidates can be filtered to a smaller, better-qualified list. It takes the first step in narrowing the field while avoiding challenge from a legal compliance point of view. Finally, it continues the return-on-investment focus, showing how sourcing and prescreening the best candidates balances cost of hire, speed of hire, and quality of hire.

Defining What You're Looking For: Basic Qualifications and Competencies

The recruiting process begins with deciding what you need. Typically it starts with a hiring manager's signature on a staffing requisition. The recruiting team then verifies that the job description accurately describes the "what you do" and "what it takes" aspects of the position. This helps ensure that the recruiters assigned to the opening screen candidate qualifications in a way consistent with the makeup of the job. Basic qualifying standards are drawn from the job description, including the education, experience, technical training, degrees or licensure, and specific skills needed to perform the job. This information serves as the guide to recruiting advertisements, job postings, recruiter outreach, and other candidate-sourcing steps.

Even in today's technology-based applicant tracking system (ATS) platforms, most of these steps remain part of the process. In fact, sign-off and approval at each of these stages is part of the work flow implemented using most ATS software. Finding payoff here requires making the process as fast, simple, and consistent as possible. It depends on reducing labor, as well as documenting the trail in a way that reduces the risk and cost of a legal challenge.

Today, though, many organizations have learned that dealing with the ever-broadening nature of jobs requires them to focus not only on the tasks and duties of the job description, but also, and to a greater degree, on the basic competencies demanded. Some have even abandoned the idea of job descriptions, and others have added information about the job's competency requirements to traditional job description formats.

The concept of competencies surfaces here because it bears on how candidates are sourced and how information about their fit to the job is used to prescreen them. It's also relevant here because using competencies, and what have come to be called competency models, helps from a payoff point of view. Thinking in terms of competencies provides additional structure to not only the sourcing and prescreening process, but also to candidate assessment, onboarding and orientation, and longer-term performance development in ways far more effective than offered by traditional job descriptions. Much has been written on the topic.[1]

As an example, Figure 8.1 shows about half of the competency model I developed recently for sales executive positions in a professional services firm. The purpose in constructing the model was to create a foundation for sourcing, screening, assessing, and hiring candidates into the role and for follow-on performance management. Of course, sourcing also was driven by basic qualifications drawn from the company's job descriptions—factors such as specific levels of training, experience, sales responsibility, and industry experience. The competency model helped frame how recruiters reviewed initial information they received from those with an interest in the job. It provided a clear definition of what the employer was seeking and served as a common frame of reference as it was shared with everyone involved in the hiring process, from external recruitment process outsourcing (RPO) recruiters, to internal recruiting staff, HR interviewers, and hiring managers who participated in the final interviewing stages of the process.

A competency model depiction of what it takes to perform the job is more constant over time than a traditional job description. It's less subject to change than a traditional job description when job duties are reshuffled or performance objectives change. Competencies focus more on defining *what we seek* in terms of attributes that candidates possess.

Today competency models are used to frame a sourcing strategy, prescreen those who express interest, and assemble assessment tools used to drive hiring decisions. Employers use them to frame the content of recruiting and hiring tools, from Internet job postings, to prescreening questionnaires, test batteries, candidate interview formats, and reference-checking protocols. They apply equally well to labor and manual jobs as to senior executive roles.

In sourcing, one of their payoffs rests in gaining clarity inside the organization about the type of individual sought. Will the salesperson be expected to behave like "hunter," a "farmer," or a "hungry shark"? Will fostering long-term customer relationships be part of the job, or will an account manager step in once the sale

Figure 8.1 Examples of competencies making up a sales executive model

Implementing Sales Strategies

Identifies creative ways to accomplish the company's overall sales strategy, along with personal objectives. Draws on practical experience and skill at assessing market forces, business climate, and potential customer attitudes. Analyzes wins versus losses to determine where changes in tactics of individual sales opportunities are necessary.

Prospecting with Insight

Follows a disciplined approach to targeting needs and opportunity openings in sales situations. Listens to prospects. Identifies the decision maker, likelihood of closing, and scope of the opportunity. Follows through to recommend products and services to match the opportunity.

Building Credibility

Works to establish immediate credibility. Follows a consistent program of contact, passing on helpful information, gathering further qualifying information, and working to achieve the status of a trusted advisor. Shows a proper balance of persistence and relaxed follow-up.

Presenting Ideas Clearly

Writes clearly and concisely. Communicates well to different size groups, at senior levels, and in different formats. Shows strong presentation skills and effectively manages group communication agendas. Listens well and responds effectively to questions. Manages the communication of ideas skillfully, whether scripted or unscripted.

Focusing on the Customer

Assesses customers' immediate interests. Listens to and shows understanding of requests or reports of problems. Follows through on commitments to find answers or solutions. Takes responsibility for responding to complaints. Seeks out feedback on the customer's satisfaction. Willingly takes on the role of customer advocate in working with internal resources.

Demonstrating Product and Service Knowledge

Grasps the features and relevance of company offerings. Maintains a current knowledge on products and services. Shows a sound grasp of product objectives, performance characteristics, and how each meets various needs. Keeps current with company offerings and those of competitors. Advises management where new offerings might represent opportunity areas.

is made? Does the job demand strong technical knowledge, or will product engineers support the sales process? All of these questions are answered as the competency model is created. The partial list of competencies shown in Figure 8.1, for example, addresses all of these questions. The answers drive the candidate sourcing, pre-screening, and assessment process.

Through the 1990s, building competency models was a revenue mainstay for many HR consulting companies. Today, though, it's hard to come up with a competency that has not already been cre-ated, at least in part. Libraries of competencies are available to produce a model specific to a given employer's jobs with little time or expense or to create a customized version. Today what takes attention is making a competency model come alive inside by work-ing with the organization to refine the various choices available in generic models to fit its culture and needs. At a minimum, a com-petency model needs to be socialized through meetings with leaders, where they're given a chance to contribute to the final tool.

To illustrate where a competency model can go once its general features are framed, Figure 8.2 expands on the level of detail illus-trated in the Figure 8.1.

Taken from a project I completed for management positions in a financial services provider, the competencies illustrate expec-tations in operational aspects of the jobs for those hired. The example shows how different jobs can be woven together and cov-ered by an overall competency model, identifying the increasing expectations that come with increasing position level. This illus-trates the usefulness of competency models at this level of detail in guiding the sourcing and hiring process.

At a more general level, it's possible to frame competency mod-els that drive sourcing and prescreening practices across an overall organization. For example, Figure 8.3 shows the architecture of a competency model I recently created to drive recruiting and hiring systems design for virtually all the jobs in an organization, regard-less of the occupational group a given job might represent.

Figure 8.2 Competency models can extend to cover multiple jobs

Supervisor	Manager	Group Manager
Developing and Implementing Strategy — Provides creative input to strategies underlying change, repositioning, or growth in the business, whether at the company or operating unit level. Contributes to implementing strategies, whether they involve overall changes in company structure and mission, or department-level changes in work practices. Builds upon existing capabilities at both the strategy development and implementation stages; effectively translates strategic ideas into action.		
• Effectively translates general operating goals into specific assignments for direct reports. • Regularly provides feedback to direct reports on how their day-to-day assignments affect company metrics such as profitability and customer service. • Brings to superiors recommendations on work practice design changes that would improve the unit's operating results.	• Works with direct reports and others across several departments to identify where shared efforts can help implement broad management goals more effectively. • Uses group-level strategic objectives to drive staff and employee development planning; links people strategy with the group's business strategy. • Provides analysis-based feedback to senior management on areas of strategy most difficult to implement at the group level; suggests specific actions for improving implementation.	• Paints a picture for others regarding the steps to be followed in improving the operation; leads others through visioning future operations. • Incorporates a risk management perspective into the development of business strategies and operating plans. • Scans the competitive horizon, identifies trends, and translates such information into actions that will improve the operation of the business.
Demonstrating Technical Expertise — Applies own specialized knowledge, training, and experience to enhance the performance of both the unit and the firm. Stays abreast of technical developments in own area of specialization, and keeps up with general trends in the marketplace, the competition, and the regulations pertaining to the operation of the business. Expands expertise at using general business tools such as information technology, financial planning, and human capital management strategies.		

◆ Provides coaching and hands-on technical training to direct reports; is skilled at translating knowledge into practice for the group; recognizes situations where exceptions or alternatives to standard practice are appropriate and adjusts as needed. ◆ Applies new techniques and practices quickly; shows flexibility in choosing the proper approach for a given situation. ◆ Uses job knowledge to create opportunities, prevent errors, and minimize problems for other groups.	◆ Knows and oversees changes to standard practices and technical approaches in the work group. ◆ Demonstrates and spreads to the work group knowledge of technical trends in the delivery of client service and execution of the overall business; serves as a group resource for communicating and applying what's new in more general areas of the business. ◆ Keeps up-to-date on required technical certification.	◆ Contributes to the business by serving as an internal technical trainer, speaker, or mentor with respect to specific technical areas, trends, or business issues. ◆ Demonstrates skills sufficient to represent the company on industry platforms and in the media. ◆ Interprets technical intelligence on the competition; applies this knowledge to further the achievement of firm objectives.
Using Creative Problem-Solving Approaches — Approaches problems in an innovative manner, building practical solutions. Brings a systematic, structured approach to problem analysis. Considers alternatives and assesses the costs and benefits of each before deciding on a course of action. Weighs technical, business, and human issues when considering alternatives. Shows intellectual curiosity and openness to new ways of solving a problem.		
◆ Applies structured, logical thinking to problems within the work group; identifies the underlying interrelationships among the set of facts that define a problem. ◆ Creates innovative solutions to day-to-day operating problems; is willing to consider new alternatives rather than adhering rigidly to current practice. ◆ Shows the intellectual curiosity needed to try new ideas, test them out, and share solutions with others.	◆ Addresses business, technical, and human considerations in the problem-solving process; effectively balances technical elegance and business practicality in arriving at solutions. ◆ Creates solutions to unique problems; goes beyond past precedent and incorporates ideas not yet part of the group's current standard operating procedures. ◆ Builds productive problem-solving teams; creates a climate of brainstorming, while maintaining a focus on the issue.	◆ Applies broad strategic and business analysis. Evaluates alternative solutions against the operating objectives, risk, and staff capabilities needed to implement them. ◆ Coordinates disparate disciplines to solve problems that cut across several parts of the operation. ◆ Monitors operating metrics for own area and assembles resources to prevent problems from developing.

Figure 8.3 An example of organization-wide competency models

Managers and Executives	• Leading organizational action • Exercising business skills • Solving problems and making decisions • Building and maintaining relationships • Managing and developing people • Showing drive and motivation • Demonstrating integrity and professionalism
Professionals	• Delivering professional expertise • Exercising business skills • Solving problems and making decisions • Building and maintaining relationships • Showing drive and motivation • Demonstrating integrity and professionalism
Sales and Customer Support	• Creating sales results • Exercising business skills • Solving problems and making decisions • Building and maintaining relationships • Showing drive and motivation • Demonstrating integrity and professionalism
Technicians and Specialists	• Demonstrating technical skills • Solving problems and making decisions • Building and maintaining relationships • Showing drive and motivation • Demonstrating integrity and professionalism
Administrative and Clerical	• Exercising job skills • Solving problems and making decisions • Building and maintaining relationships • Showing drive and motivation • Demonstrating integrity and professionalism
Operations, Trades, Services, and Support	• Demonstrating technical skills • Solving problems and making decisions • Building and maintaining relationships • Showing drive and motivation • Demonstrating integrity and professionalism

The figure shows the basic families of jobs addressed by each set of competencies composing the overall model, followed by the broad categories of competencies assembled under each family. Then full competency details, like those shown in Figures 8.1 and 8.2 are assembled for any given job. (To explore the full architecture, visit www.million-dollarhire.com for more details.[2])

So there are many payoffs in creating a competency model to expand on a job's basic qualifications as the first step in sourcing and prescreening. First, pulling HR, department managers, and hiring managers into a review of the job's competencies clarifies the kind of candidate being sought and identifies the more and less important elements of what the company is looking for in the new hire. For example, knowing that you want to recruit sales candidates from the professional services industry with at least ten years of experience and an annual sales target of at least a million dollars is helpful. But knowing the competencies the company seeks helps communicate expectations to candidates and helps frame how recruiters review those who express interest.

Second, building the sourcing, prescreening, and later stages of the hiring process on a foundation of competencies helps reduce the risk that candidates will challenge the process from a legal compliance point of view. The framework that a competency model provides supports an argument that the overall process is objective, job related, and insulated from biases that might enter a more subjective approach. The competency model provides a paper trail to explain how the recruiting and hiring process focused on truly job-related qualifications.

Finally, a competency model not only serves as a tool to drive sourcing, prescreening, and other steps in the hiring process. It also supports orientation, goal setting, and performance management actions for new hires. In describing clearly and concisely what the company expects of those it has hired, a competency model communicates how this person will be called on to set priorities, allocate time, pursue development, and perform over the longer term. In short, a competency model frames the performance management and development process.

Information provided by a competency model is added to the list of other factors (experience, credentials, industry background, and compensation level, for example) to identify when sourcing and prescreening steps begin. But its true payoff reaches much further.

Taking Advantage of the Internet in Candidate Sourcing

Building an employer brand to attract candidates, creating recruitment advertising to get the word out, engaging outside recruiting resources, and making sure there's strong relationship management once candidates show an interest have driven candidate sourcing for decades. All focus on feeding the best raw material into the top of the hiring funnel. The outside services that employers purchase in this area amount to billions of dollars annually.[3] All of these aspects of the recruiting process are evolving with new offerings and expanding technology, but it's candidate sourcing that has undergone a true revolution.

Employers continue to use traditional tools to find candidates. Some still place ads in newsprint, attend job fairs, send out college recruiting teams, receive résumés by mail, and hand off assignments to outside recruiters. At senior levels, executive recruiters still find talent and engage in matchmaking. Much of the tried and true is still in place, and works. *On Staffing*, by Burkholder, Edwards, and Sartain, provides one of the best summaries of the elements, traditional and emerging, that frame world-class recruiting programs.[4]

In some areas of candidate sourcing, change is moving fast, and practices vary substantially from one employer to another. For example, a recent survey by the search firm ExecuNet showed that more than three of four businesses surveyed use the Internet to source and screen candidates.[5] As noted in Chapter Six, Web-based job boards such as monster.com and careerbuilder.com are familiar to anyone seeking a job or a candidate. Nearly everyone knows how to access both of these. More focused job boards, dealing with specific types of occupations, professional organizations, geographical locations, and other characteristics number in the thousands.

Today most employers have agreements with one or more of the job boards, where they post job openings and résumés appear. Some rely on their ATS provider to integrate links with a variety of job boards, making the choice of the board used to fill a given job a simple point-and-click process. Some rely on their RPO provider to identify the best job boards for a given assignment and integrate them into the RPO's sourcing steps. There are many how-to guides to job boards that dig deeper than we will here, and, as noted in Chapter Six, some even see the demise of job boards as they're structured today. I don't think that's going to happen. Like any other business proposition, they'll evolve.

Then again, unless they're a free service provided by a professional organization or nonprofit entity, job boards essentially *sell* candidate information to employers for a fee. That's why the fast-growing alternative of social networking platforms is creating a tidal wave in the recruiting industry. For example, whereas monster.com makes over 150 million résumés available to its clients for a fee, Facebook has over 100 million members, and access is free. LinkedIn has more than 60 million users. That's why employers, and the recruiting software and services industry that serves them, are tapping social networking sites more and more. These sites are becoming a growing part of the candidate sourcing process. Although employers aren't abandoning traditional job boards, they're certainly adding social networking platforms to the candidate sourcing process. There already are how-to guides for both employers and job seekers that explain how to use Facebook, LinkedIn, MySpace, Twitter, and other social networking platforms to source candidates and jobs.[6]

At least three things come with this evolution. First is a change in the cost of access. Accessing social networking platforms, whether by setting up a Facebook page to announce a recruiting initiative or using Internet technology to search Facebook and other sites to find candidates, doesn't carry the per-use or licensing costs that come with job boards. A creative recruiter can use social networking sites to search out candidates quickly, particularly when the open position is one likely to attract age groups made up of dedicated followers. The work essentially carries only the labor cost of the time the recruiter devotes to it. Since reduced administrative costs feed payoff, that's a good thing.

Second, although job boards produce employment and résumé-related information, social networking sites offer the opportunity, at least in concept, to look at candidates more deeply. Some argue that these sites give a broader view about how a potential candidate behaves in real life compared to the image he tries to create on his résumé. Everyone has a story about the candidate who looked good on paper but whose Facebook photos, comments, or affiliations convinced the recruiter to move on to the next candidate.

But third, as always, risks come with relying on social networking sites. Consider the example I just mentioned. In effect, what limits a recruiter from looking at information that has no bearing on the individual's likelihood of performing the job effectively? The door is open for a candidate, who gets word that her Facebook site was viewed, to challenge a decision not to hire her as being based on subjective interpretation about information on the site. In short, how does an employer using social networking sites document the fact that *only* relevant, job-related information was viewed during the sourcing or prescreening process? Service providers who help employers access these new sources of candidates are offering advice on the topic.[7]

One piece of advice already being given is not to rely exclusively on social networking sites as a sourcing tool. Don't even rely on them substantially. Approximately 13 percent of the U.S.

population is African American, and just over 15 percent is Hispanic. But only about 5 percent of LinkedIn members are African American, and only 2 percent are Hispanic.[8] When a plaintiff attorney or federal agency asks where an employer recruited to fill a position, an answer that sourcing was undertaken largely through social networking sites might be interpreted as evidence of discrimination.

Finally, candidate sourcing solutions that involve broader technology offerings are emerging. These solutions bundle together technology that, for example, posts openings to selected job boards, searches social networking sites, extracts information gathered from all the various sites, and builds a candidate profile that's richer than just a résumé, Facebook page, or www.zoominfo.com profile. Their objective is to assemble a richer image of the potential candidate than offered by current solutions. As they evolve, of course, they're likely to face scrutiny from privacy and equal employment opportunity points of view, but the result is likely to offer employers faster access to richer data.

Sometimes, More Interest Than You Can Count

All of these solutions offer benefits: access to more résumés or applications and faster exchange of information from company to candidate and back again. All deal in a medium that's becoming the accepted way of communicating and forming work relationships. But there's also a downside: more résumés or profiles will arrive than you can imagine. Candidate volume is good, but it produces the need to deal with what has come in and find the diamonds hidden in the stack of Internet-collected résumés.

As technology began entering the world of recruiting, well before the social networking solutions did, tools to process résumés, documents, and applications were among the first offerings to arrive. Most were based on searching résumés for key words or phrases: *sales executive, C+ programming, Six Sigma experience, retail sales training*, and so on. Early tools provided ways to load résumés and other documents onto a computer platform, sort through them, and group them according to whether keyword matches suggested they should receive more attention. Some still remember Resumix and Restrac as trendsetters in the industry.

Later solutions could handle résumés, whether they were word processed documents, faxes, scans from paper copies, or in some other format. These tools were capable of extraction, which amounted to finding and pulling pieces of information from the résumé, such as name, address, telephone number, current position, colleges attended, and degrees attained. More recently, tools that use latent semantic analysis principles can differentiate whether the entry "Virginia" on a résumé refers to the candidate's name, home state, university, or favorite vacation spot.

Such tools now extract information from a résumé and use it to populate ATSs. They capture a copy of each résumé too, linking it with basic qualifying information the extraction technology pulls off the document and places in the ATS database. As a result, the ways to search a large database for particular types of candidates, and then select their résumés for review, has taken a step forward.

Today, technology merged with linguistic sciences offers even greater capabilities, producing solutions that essentially, read a résumé, extract key information, and then do processes that were once the realm of human recruiters. Tools now "read" each résumé, read a job description or competency model, and search out the résumés that best match the concepts reflected in these benchmark documents. Some tools even rank-order résumés according to their *degree of match* with the documents and offer ways that recruiters can interact with the system to refine the search parameters and then cycle back through the résumés that result.

I tested one of these résumé search and matching technologies recently while working with a client to hire account managers. We assembled a database of nearly two thousand résumés we received from an outside recruiting company. Internal recruiters used the résumés to execute the company's prescreening and assessment process. They did not use the technology solution.

After the fact, we used the narrative from the company's job description and competency model as the benchmark for searching and rank-ordering the résumé database and posed these questions: Did the résumé search technology rank the résumés similarly to the way internal recruiters had reviewed and identified résumés for further attention? Did the technology rank the résumés similarly to the way candidates performed on the company's selection test battery and internal interview process? Did it forecast who had been hired, or how they performed once on the job? In effect, if all the people-driven decisions had been based on the technology alone, would the results have been the same as those produced through the human effort spent in prescreening, assessing, interviewing, and making final hiring decisions? If so, the solution might offer a way to draw substantial payoff by reducing the labor that went into candidate processing in the future.

Did it work? It depends where you look. The way recruiters selected résumés for further attention had little in common with the way the technology ranked the résumés in terms of their match with the job description and competency model. However, résumés that the technology ranked as among the highest and the lowest, that is, the extremes, came from candidates who tended to drop out during the company's selection testing and hiring manager interviews. It makes sense that the résumés ranked low. Follow-up showed that many of the résumés at the very top of the ranking came from candidates considered overqualified for the position or from ones earning more than the company could afford to pay for the position. It's not that the technology was wrong in ranking them highly; it's just that the candidates did not fit other aspects of the job.

Finally, although the number of account managers hired was small at the start, the correlation between their technology-based résumé ranking and their performance against the job's financial objectives was statistically significant. In short, although the study produced nearly as many questions as it answered, it also showed that the technology-based approach to reviewing and evaluating résumés held promise from a payoff point of view. We're continuing the project.

For now, the technology available to find résumés and applications, extract information, populate ATS platforms, and search résumé and applicant databases is a great labor-saving device. Our small-scale review showed performance payoff as well, particularly with regard to finding those who ultimately performed well on the job.

Using these tools requires attention to what they actually do as they sort through résumés. It's important that steps be taken to track the tools' effects on equal employment opportunity compliance and that their use in defining exactly who will be considered a candidate and which individuals will be tallied in applicant flow and other statistical reports is understood. This is an area where substantial labor savings can be plugged into the payoff model. But it's also one where some legal advice and direction is a good idea, particularly as the technology continues to develop and as those who regulate the hiring process learn how it works.

As Always, There's a Caution

As these sourcing and prescreening technologies began to proliferate in the software market, federal agencies responsible for monitoring equal employment opportunity compliance—the Equal Employment Opportunity Commission (EEOC), the Department of Justice, the Department of Labor and its Office of Federal Contract Compliance Programs (OFCCP), along with the Office of Personnel Management (OPM)—became interested. They realized the technology had potential both to change employer practices and alter their record-keeping obligations under the statutes and executive orders associated with equal employment opportunity (EEO) hiring.

These agencies often require employers to track and report on the results of their recruiting and hiring programs. Their periodic reviews then examine the success rates of applicants from different race, ethnic, gender, and other groups protected by law. As this technology has proliferated, one question leaps forward: Who's an applicant? Is it the one whose résumé was submitted in response to a job board posting? Is it the one found by an Internet robot looking for particular résumé profiles? Is it the one resulting from a conceptual search of a résumé database on hand internally or accessed externally? Where's the line?

Not surprisingly, these questions have led to new rules. As of early 2006, employers under oversight of OFCCP, that is, those who are federal contractors or subcontractors, faced the Internet Applicant Recordkeeping Rule.[9] The rule defines "Internet applicants" as those who apply for work through the Internet or related technology and, in certain cases, those found through the various Internet posting, searching, scraping, and social networking technologies. The rule is important because it defines who is an applicant when these tools and technology are unleashed over the Internet and other platforms.

Defining who is an applicant is important because federal contractors and subcontractors are required to maintain and, if audited, report data on how they process applicants. When asked, they must report the results of applicant processing from an EEO point of view as they screen, assess, and make hiring decisions. The rule boils down to determining which respondents to count in these record-keeping and reporting activities.

In the past, this was relatively simple. An applicant was someone who submitted an application. The Internet Applicant Recordkeeping Rule, though, is not a simple proposition. It's new and complex, and the technology that affects it is changing every day. The result is that companies covered by OFCCP should seek advice from an employment law attorney. OFCCP's Frequently Asked Questions Web site is a good place to begin.[10]

I won't dig deeply into the rule here because details are likely to be clarified through enforcement actions in the future. In general, though, the growing number of employers that use the Internet in shaping their candidate sourcing and prescreening processes must understand its requirements. Among the more important points for federal contractors or subcontractors to keep in mind are these:

- The OFCCP considers technology platforms that might yield an Internet applicant to include e-mail submissions to the employer, résumé databases that the employer or outside sources maintain, job banks, electronic scanning technology, ATSs or ATS providers that hold information on potential applicants, or outside services that screen and deliver information to the employer.

- An individual is *an applicant* if he or she posts or submits an expression of interest through one of these vehicles, the employer considers the expression, the individual is found to possess the basic qualifications for the position, and the individual doesn't remove himself from the hiring process before it's concluded. In other words, if you find individuals, scan their basic qualifications, and see that they possess the job's basic qualifications, you are dealing with "applicants."

- If the number of individuals who express interest and possess the basic qualifications is large, it's not necessary to consider all of them as applicants. Rules for narrowing the field, though, call for using approaches that essentially *randomly* eliminate the

surplus, set upper limits to the number that hiring
professionals will consider, or follow some
other approach that does not extend to
reviewing qualifications more deeply. If it does
consider qualifications, then all those reviewed
are *applicants* and subject to record-keeping
requirements.

- If those submitting expressions of interest fail to meet
  any of the job's basic qualifications, they are *not*
  applicants. Hence, defining and communicating
  reasonable, objective, relevant basic qualifications
  becomes a key part in defining an Internet applicant.

- The basic qualifications for the job must be set *before*
  the review process begins. If a large number of
  expressions of interest arrive, it's not permissible to
  come up with additional basic qualifications to help
  filter the group and forestall a decision regarding who's
  an applicant.

- A record needs to be maintained of criteria used to do
  automated reviews of résumé databases. If a search
  tool, extraction tool, or other technology-driven
  process identifies a résumé as meeting the job's basic
  qualifications but it does not open and view the
  résumé, then the individual is not considered an
  applicant.

- If an automated review tool goes beyond looking at
  basic qualifications, then résumés that do not meet the
  expanded standard must be filed as applicants, because
  the search now takes into account qualifying
  information and enters the realm of a selection
  process. If technology is used to review and rank
  résumés against the job's basic qualifications, then the

résumés entered into the ranking process reflect
applicants.

- Once an individual meets the definition of an Internet
  applicant, the employer must collect and maintain
  race, ethnicity, and gender information on the
  individual, and analysis of screening and hiring results
  must now incorporate these individuals into the mix of
  applicants that the company finds by more traditional
  means.

- Using an outside agent to search databases and find
  candidates doesn't relieve an employer from keeping
  records or requiring the outside agent to maintain
  them and keep them available for review.

The crux of all this is that the OFCCP wants to track an
employer's recruiting, screening, and hiring practices to monitor
any evidence of noncompliance with federal EEO requirements.
The Internet, and all the tools being generated for employers by
the technology sector, makes it more difficult to see clearly what's
being done, what results are being produced, and how the outcomes
affect EEO results. The Internet Applicant Recordkeeping Rule is
a way to help the agency dig into an employer's records, analyze
the outcomes, and decide whether there's evidence of noncompliance. It amounts to making sure that new technology doesn't mask
actions the agency wants to see more clearly.

This is an emerging area. Of all the topics referenced from a
risk management perspective in these chapters, it warrants tracking
for new developments. No major litigation has taken place to date,
and no major employer actions have been taken by the agency,
but that's likely to change. Today an HR department needs to
operate with a clear understanding of all the technology it uses
to source and prescreen candidates, and it needs to have a clear
definition of who's an applicant.

Making the Initial Cut—Solutions to Prescreening Candidates

Despite the complexity, there are points in the sourcing process where it's clear that companies are not dealing with applicants: when they post a job opening and a thousand résumés arrive in the recruiter's inbox. And they also reach a point where it's clear they *are* dealing with applicants: for example, after eliminating the 60 percent of résumés that don't meet the job's basic qualifications and decide to shoot out a more detailed qualifications checklist to the 40 percent who do.

So what employers look at, and what they do with what they find, affects whether they then are dealing with an *expression of interest* versus an *applicant* and the record-keeping requirements that result. With this concept in mind, let's review some of the prescreening approaches that help complete this first narrowing of the hiring funnel. As shown in Figure 8.4, prescreening initial expressions of interest to determine who qualifies as an applicant can follow a number of classic approaches. Options include reviewing résumés or applications against basic qualifications requirements; brief telephone prescreening interviews to verify basic qualifications; or sending out follow-up questionnaires or checklists by mail or e-mail to collect qualifications information from those having expressed an interest.

Basic qualifications prescreening can also draw on technology solutions. These might read résumés or applications, extract basic qualifying information, compare it to the basic qualifications of the job, and alert HR to those who meet the job's basic requirements. All represent a preliminary screen—one that indicates whether the individual meets the minimum standards of the job. All drive the first narrowing of the funnel using basic qualifying factors such as education, experience, geographical availability, salary requirements, or licensing or certification requirement to begin screening.

Figure 8.4 There are a variety of approaches to candidate prescreening

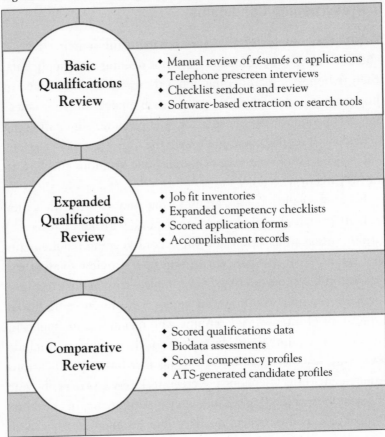

Basic
Qualifications
Review

- Manual review of résumés or applications
- Telephone prescreen interviews
- Checklist sendout and review
- Software-based extraction or search tools

Expanded
Qualifications
Review

- Job fit inventories
- Expanded competency checklists
- Scored application forms
- Accomplishment records

Comparative
Review

- Scored qualifications data
- Biodata assessments
- Scored competency profiles
- ATS-generated candidate profiles

Figure 8.5 shows a report generated through a technology-driven system that collects a basic qualifications checklist from individuals expressing an interest in a position. In the illustration, the position is that of account manager in a software company. This simple report indicates areas where the individual meets the job's basic qualifications, memorialized in the job description, as well as three areas where he does not. In this case, the individual does not enter the applicant flow since he does not meet the job's basic qualifications.

Figure 8.5 Internet interview candidate report for account executive

Basic Qualifications—Red Flag Questions

Candidate:	John Simpson
Job:	Account Executive
Net Interview Date:	6/24/2011

Shown are the results of the Net Interview Prescreen conducted for this candidate. The interview combines red flag questions the company has identified as go versus no-go conditions of employment, job fit questions that measure candidate qualifications against basic job requirements, and competency fit questions that evaluate whether the candidate describes himself or herself in a manner that aligns with the competencies found to be most critical to success for this job.

Questions	Answers	
1. Do you have U.S. work authorization?	Yes	(Green Flag)
2. Have you been convicted of a felony?	No	(Green Flag)
3. Do you have a college or university degree?	Yes	(Green Flag)
4. Are you able to begin working within 60 days?	Yes	(Green Flag)
5. Are you willing to travel at least 50 percent of the time?	No	**(Red Flag)**
6. Are you willing to relocate?	No	**(Red Flag)**
7. Do you have at least four years of sales experience?	Yes	(Green Flag)
8. Do you have software sales experience?	Yes	(Green Flag)
9. Do you have experience writing proposals?	No	**(Red Flag)**
10. Have you worked for an organization with more than 5,000 employees?	Yes	(Green Flag)

Quickly attention expands to gathering additional information, permitting the company to screen individuals against additional criteria before investing in more costly assessment techniques. Now the list of qualifications includes information hiring professionals are probably not comfortable declaring to be basic qualifications but are nevertheless relevant and useful in guiding prescreening decisions. These might include specific types or durations of experience, the average time over which past positions have been held, general interests or job preferences, and so on. Attention turns from determining who's basically qualified to learning who's *better* qualified. Here, the employer is crossing the line and beginning to deal with applicants rather than candidates. From this point onward, EEO regulations require tracking results and providing reports.

A variety of tools define best practices at this expanded stage of prescreening. All gather additional qualifying information, frequently focusing on competencies. For example, Figure 8.6 reflects the second page of the candidate report introduced in Figure 8.5. Here, though, the e-mail-based query that followed receipt of the individual's résumé asked questions that help hone in on his job fit by asking questions that look to past basic job experiences and preferences. In some cases, we might argue that these questions too reflect basic qualifications. In the assignment that produced this report, we did not. The purpose was to produce a scored profile that ultimately could be used to compare this candidate to others. As noted earlier, when comparative use is made of the information, individuals involved become applicants under the Internet Applicant Recordkeeping Rule.

Finally, initial prescreening also can extend into collecting initial competency assessment information. Figure 8.7 takes one final step for the individual profiled in Figures 8.5 and 8.6.

Here the individual has answered a series of questions designed to explore evidence as to whether he possesses competencies relevant to the job versus ones *not* relevant to it. The answers are summarized and scored to produce the initial version of a competency matching process. Collected through an Internet-based outreach, answers to these questions produce information relevant in initial prescreening. Of course, steps need to be taken to ensure the questions underlying Figures 8.5 through 8.7 are job related and defensible. All have the possibility of screening out candidates. All might affect one group protected by EEO statutes more negatively than others. In effect, all the information used in this example needs to be held to review and analysis to determine how

Figure 8.6 Internet interview candidate report for account executive (continued)

Job Fit Questions		

Number of Questions: 7 Maximum Score: 35 Minimum Score: 0 Candidate Score: 18 Candidate percentage of maximum: 51%	18 (51%) 0 5 10 15 20 25 . 30 35	
Questions	**Answers**	

1. Have you sold ERP systems?
  a. Yes (5 points)
  b. No (0 points)
	a. (5 points)	

2. Do you have experience selling professional services?
  a. Yes (5 points)
  b. No (0 points)
	b. (0 points)	

3. What is the largest sale you have closed personally?
  a. Under $100K (1 point)
  b. $100–$300K (2 points)
  c. $300–$500K (3 points)
  d. Over $500K (5 points)
	b. (2 points)	

4. Please indicate the most important factor in choosing your next job.
  a. Stability (1 point)
  b. Salary (3 points)
  c. Flexibility (4 points)
  d. Growth opportunities (5 points)
	c. (4 points)	

5. How much of your total compensation would you expect to be fixed salary?
  a. $75–95K (5 points)
  b. $95–105K (4 points)
  c. $105–115K (3 points)
  d. Greater than $115K (2 points)
	a. (5 points)	

6. In the past what percentage of your annual income resulted from sales commissions?
  a. 31–30% (0 points)
  b. 31–40% (1 point)
  c. 41–50% (3 points)
  d. Greater than 50% (5 points)
	a. (0 points)	

7. What has been the focus of your past sales experience?
  a. Farming (0 points)
  b. About equal hunting and farming (2 points)
  c. Hunting (5 points)
	b. (2 points)	

Figure 8.7 Internet interview candidate report for account executive (continued)

Competency Fit Questions	

| Number of Questions: 8
Maximum Score: 8
Minimum Score: 0
Candidate Score: 5
Candidate percentage
of maximum: 63% | 5 (63%)
0 1 2 3 4 5 6 7 8 |

Questions	Answers

1. People would describe me as someone who:
  a. Influences others by making appeals to values, sentiments, or emotions (Correct)
  b. Effectively schedules people and resources
	b. (1 point)

2. People would describe me as someone who:
  a. Conducts detailed analyses to solve problems
  b. Quickly determines customer buying criteria (Correct)
	a. (0 points)

3. People would describe me as someone who:
  a. Gathers and interprets technical intelligence on specific technical areas, trends, or business issues (Correct)
  b. Aligns product, market, sales, delivery, and people strategies
	a. (1 point)

4. People would describe me as someone who:
  a. Listens attentively to others before responding (Correct)
  b. Helps others accept and implement new processes
	b. (0 points)

5. People would describe me as someone who:
  a. Challenges others to identify inefficiencies
  b. Tailors language and examples to audience when presenting (Correct)
	b. (1 point)

6. People would describe me as someone who:
  a. Monitors daily progress of others
  b. Maintains frequent contact with customers (Correct)
	b. (1 point)

7. People would describe me as someone who:
  a. Redesigns processes to adapt to changing demands
  b. Researches answers to customer questions not immediately available (Correct)
	b. (1 point)

8. People would describe me as someone who:
  a. Ensures efficiency goals are met
  b. Asks questions to clarify customer needs (Correct)
	a. (0 points)

well it forecasts future performance and how it affects individual candidate groups.

Another prescreening technique, known as an accomplishment record, can be distributed by mail or e-mail as well. This technique asks candidates to provide information about past accomplishments in areas relevant to the job, often mapped to the competency requirements identified for the job. Figure 8.8 shows a portion of the accomplishment record protocol created for the sales executive job whose competencies are previewed in Figure 8.1.

Figure 8.8 An accomplishment record data-gathering format

Candidate Record of Past Accomplishments
Sales Executive Role

Candidate Name:	Date of Application:

As part of applying for the position noted above, tell us about your most noteworthy accomplishments in your current position and/or in ones you have held elsewhere. The questions parallel the most important qualifications for the position to which you have applied. By asking you to point out your most noteworthy accomplishments in these areas, we can gain a better understanding of your capabilities, and give you a chance to tell us what we need to know about your candidacy.

In answering each question, please be concise and speak directly to the question. Do not provide hypothetical answers, only answers that actually illustrate things that you have accomplished in past work experience. Try to provide *two different examples* to illustrate your answer to each question.

Prospecting — Describe a time when you had to determine a customer's interests and buying power. What was the situation? How did you make your estimates? How did this influence your sales or renewal activity? What happened?

The concept is straightforward, if a bit less structured than the checklist tools illustrated in Figures 8.5 through 8.7. In essence, it asks: Is there an accomplishment in your past that will help the employer understand how your background fits the competencies they're seeking? The candidate's answers can be reviewed, rated, and used to make a prescreening decision. They also can drive interviewer questions if the candidate proceeds to the interview stage of the process.

A final category of prescreening information not only compares the candidate to the job's qualifications but to other candidates. In these approaches, it's not that different information is collected; it's that different *use* is made of the data. Rather than comparing candidates to the requirements of the job, this prescreening information is used to determine how each candidate compares to others and which are more and less qualified. Prescreening now turns from comparing the candidate to the job to comparing candidates to one another.

Figure 8.9 carries the example in Figures 8.5 through 8.7 from the single candidate assessment of fit to the job to a comparison of whether the candidate fits the job better than other candidates.

The distinction might seem a fine one, but the transition is an initial step in migrating from basic prescreening to candidate assessment. Now the information collected about basic qualifications, job fit, and candidate competencies is used to array candidates according to their level of qualification and, in many cases, to determine who will receive more detailed attention, such as an interview invitation. The goal isn't necessarily to produce a literal rank-ordering of candidates. Instead, rationally or empirically based scoring algorithms can begin building a picture of whether candidates seem to cluster together in their qualification profiles, separate themselves into distinct groups, or show a profile that sends recruiters back to the job boards.

Of course, algorithms used to summarize candidates' qualification profiles need to be based on information that's relevant, job related, and, ideally, validated according to the models reviewed

Figure 8.9 Net interview reports comparison

Account Executive Group Report as of: 06/24/2011

Shown below are the results for all candidates having completed the Net Interview through the date of this report. Results show each candidate's scores on red flag, job fit, and competency fit components of the interview. Candidates are listed in order of their combined job fit and competency fit scores.

Candidate Name (SSN)	Date of Net Interview	Red Flag Questions		Job Fit Questions		Competency Fit Questions		Total Job and Competency Fit	
		Status	Problem Areas	Score	Percentage of Maximum	Score	Percentage of Maximum	Score	Percentage of Maximum
Jane Jia	06/22/2011	○		33	94%	7	88%	39	93%
Kelly Banks	06/16/2011	○		31	89%	7	88%	37	88%
James Johnson	06/20/2011	○		24	69%	8	100%	32	74%
Gloria Lopez	06/23/2011	○		18	51%	5	63%	23	53%
John Doe	06/22/2011	●	Question 1	21	60%	7	88%	28	65%
Robert Ashton	06/22/2011	●	Question 2	18	51%	4	50%	22	51%
Ricardo Sanchez	06/21/2011	●	Question 3 Question 6	10	29%	6	75%	16	37%
Kate Hamilton	06/19/2011	●	Question 3 Question 7	12	34%	3	38%	15	35%
Mary Johnson	06/21/2011	●	Question 3 Question 4 Question 5	11	31%	3	38%	14	33%

in Chapter Three. If they are, then decisions made at this prescreening phase of the process can be held to the payoff models. In this way, decisions about the proportion of candidates who will be reviewed further can even be driven by payoff computations like those outlined in Chapter Five.

When you approach the prescreening stage with this level of quality control, the payoffs are many. Candidates with a higher probability of succeeding in the hiring process receive attention first. HR and hiring department interviewers spend less time with candidates they're likely to take a pass on. Test administration, travel, reference checking, and other costs are reduced by spending time with fewer, more qualified candidates than if prescreening had provided little distinction among candidates. Just like the payoff model presented in Chapter Five, you can compute the results expected when you use the tools illustrated here and capture information about their operation over time.

Taking a Review

As recruiters prescreen and filter those expressing interest in a job, it's important to take stock of what's being produced. Although some hiring follows a defined time line, where work stops once positions are filled, the work is continuous in many cases. This often is the case in filling sales, account manager, production worker, health care support, hospitality, and other roles where large numbers of employees and natural turnover mean hiring is always under way. When hiring doesn't take on a continuous aspect, it's easy to stop, take stock, make a course correction if necessary, and then proceed. When it's continuous, taking a snapshot at regular intervals helps show where you stand and what's working.

Several areas need attention in these spot checks. First, from a legal compliance point of view, this is where trouble can begin. A simple decision about where and how to reach out for candidates, followed by decisions about who is accepted as a candidate and judgments about how candidates will be prescreened, open the process to scrutiny. From a compliance point of view, the need is to review the mix of applicants who enter more focused assessment stages of the hiring process. If you're operating with an affirmative action plan (AAP), as many employers do, it's important to compare the group of candidates assembled to the parameters of the plan. The question to ask here is, Given the ethnic, gender, national origin, and other hiring objectives of the AAP, is the candidate group likely to provide a way to accomplish the plan? If not, where do we need greater numbers of candidates, and what can we do to find them?

Second, has anything done in the prescreening process resulted in eliminating certain groups targeted in the company's AAP disproportionately? I'll define in greater detail the mistakes employers can make when dealing with legal issues in Chapter Eleven. For now, though, the key question is whether you've used an educational, work experience, or other basic qualification that hits certain groups more negatively. If so, be sure the qualification is indeed required—it's job related and you believe you can defend a challenge to using it. If not, it needs to be taken out of the process.

Of course, such a review of basic qualifications should come at the tactics-building stage of the hiring process, but the results of relying on the qualification need review now that data are in hand. Outcomes need review from a legal risk point of view where you might decide to alter the qualifying and prescreening criteria.

Third, it's also time to do some forecasting. I advise clients who need to meet tight hiring time lines to draw on the recruiting data they've collected over time to set up forecasting models that feed off the ATSs they use. It's possible to use simple modeling techniques that draw on last year's ATS database to predict whether a given group of candidates is likely to make it through upcoming steps in the hiring process and successfully fill all the positions at hand in the time line we need to meet.

For example, it's possible to draw on historical data to analyze the likelihood that a group of candidates reflecting given recruiting sources, educational, experience, prior employment, and related qualifications will be successful in the assessment, interviewing, reference checking, and other stages of the hiring process. The forecast can help determine whether sourcing and prescreening effort needs to be extended and, if so, with what focus. Forecasting can tell whether current hiring needs are likely to be fed with what's in hand but not others. ATS technology and the various recruiting dashboards vendors can make this a relatively straightforward process.

Fourth, and related, the results of this initial stage in the hiring process can help identify where changes in the tactical plan might be needed. Which of the job boards to which you subscribe produced no acceptable candidates? What feeds into social network media are producing follow-through by interested individuals? What percentage of those who visited the company Web site abandoned the process of completing an expression of interest in the position? How far into the process did they proceed on average? Are the résumés that score well against your résumé-reading tools producing candidates who follow through and enter the prescreening process? Did any particular prescreening questions in the automated Internet interview knock out a percentage of candidates that raises concern? Are you asking any questions that everyone passes?

All of these questions help determine the payoff realized at this initial stage in the recruiting and hiring process and highlight tactical components not performing as expected or as needed. These steps to take stock of results are all essentially quality control and continuous improvement in nature, but some are risk mitigation in outlook too, particularly those that look to the legal compliance aspects of sourcing and prescreening.

If the process runs continuously, then monitoring and revising this initial phase in hiring on a real-time basis can help improve quality, scrub out costs that pay no dividend, and make sure a record of legally risky decisions is not being created. If the process ceases once positions are filled, then taking stock can likely wait until the position is filled and a broader review of all the steps can be taken.

At this stage, the basic product is a pool of candidates. Using the tools and technology brought to bear by your tactics, you now have an interested pool of candidates who bring the basic qualifications required by the job, have survived prescreening against requirements you know to be job related, and is ready for further review. You also composed this pool in a way that gave strong consideration to risk reduction—both the risk of finding no new hires and the risk of being challenged as to how you went about the process. Next is a detailed assessment of the candidate pool and clearer information as to whether you have found the right raw material.

CHAPTER NINE

ASSESSING THE WHOLE CANDIDATE

Having asked candidates to jump a few low hurdles in prescreening, we now need to review them against the qualifications that drive hiring decisions. Some think it's all about candidate sourcing, but that's only the beginning. Good sourcing generates volume, builds a healthy pool, and attracts people in whom the company *might* have interest. But the most creative or high-tech recruiting and sourcing tools do little to distinguish among candidates. Done well, they're a good first step, but if the assessment stage of the process is poorly executed, candidates who truly possess what recruiters are looking for can be overlooked. Worse, awful ones, with a shiny résumé and a smooth story, might be invited to join the family.

In my experience, the payoff comes in assessing candidates against as many of the competencies the job demands as is sensible. The overall focus in this chapter is on finding techniques that yield accurate predictions—million-dollar predictions—about a candidate's future performance. Of course, you have dealt with this in building the strategy and tactics that guide the hiring process, as reviewed in Chapter Seven. This chapter, though, covers the specifics of assessment tactics that create a payoff-oriented hiring plan. Work begins where the last chapter ended: digging deeper into the competencies of candidates who made it through pre-screening.

Deciding What to Assess

The simplest way to assess qualifications is to hire people and see how things work out. What better way to measure a person's ability to learn and perform the job than to let him or her punch in and go to work? And this model actually is used in some settings. For lower-level jobs with few requirements, employers sometimes use a temporary-to-permanent approach. The concept helps keep staffing levels flexible but also offers a way to assess which of these people the employer wants as a permanent employee and which ones not. Unfortunately, this "let's give it a try" model doesn't work very well in attracting technical, professional, or management candidates. Candidates at this level seek stability and hold out until they find it.

Assessment is all about collecting information used in predicting the future. As we saw in Chapters Four and Five, what we set out to predict can cover a wide range, ruled largely by the purpose of our business and the nature of the job. We might set out to predict how quickly a new hire will learn the job and come up to productivity standards. We might predict at what level or how stable he'll perform in the longer term. We might want to predict whether, and how fast, she'll be ready to assume more complicated assignments. Finally, we might want to predict whether he'll quit, miss too much work, become a behavior problem, or something else. Predicting more and more things about a candidate's future broadens the range of information we need during the assessment process and broadens the set of tools to assemble.

Figure 9.1 Four ways to view the whole candidate

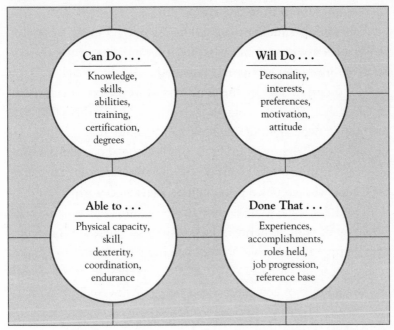

The previous chapter discussed using competencies to help frame the recruiting and sourcing process, guide how to compare an initial pool of candidates to what recruiters need, and prepare for comparing candidates. In thinking about assessment, you can view these competencies as tapping fundamental areas that together define the whole candidate. Figure 9.1 illustrates the point with a simple model for viewing candidate competencies. It also begins to suggest some of the basic types of assessment tools to assemble.

First, an assessment process can help predict whether the candidate *can do* the job, that is, whether she or he has the knowledge, skills, abilities, training, and so forth needed to learn and perform the job's day-to-day responsibilities. For trainee, apprentice, and fresh-out-of-school positions, assessing *can-do* competencies helps predict whether a candidate brings the capabilities needed to master the training and the role he's about to take on. For jobs that demand experience, they help predict when she's ready to perform up to expectations from the start.

Predicting a candidate *can do* the job doesn't mean she *will do* it. We also need to predict whether the candidate brings the personality, interests, motivation, and other qualities that convert *can-do* competencies into the performance we expect. Much recent research shows that the competencies that make up these two areas are quite independent of one another.[1] It shows that ignoring one or underweighting one produces predictions about performance that can miss the mark. Smart people aren't necessarily personable, and those with troubled personalities aren't necessarily dumb.

Third, for some jobs, assessing *able-to* competencies also helps predict success or, sometimes, lack of success. These are competencies that predict whether a candidate has the capacity to perform when succeeding is based on physical competencies. While requiring these kinds of competencies is being engineered out of many jobs, utility linemen still need to climb towers and firefighters still need to scale stairs with their gear in tow. Assessing these competencies also often focuses on predicting who might be injured on the job. Here, safety often is the driver of the decision to add *able-to* assessment tools to the hiring process.

Finally, when we move past entry-level jobs, assessment of what might be called *done-that* competencies lead to better prediction of whether a candidate's experience, accomplishments, and prior positions forecast that she'll deliver the performance expected. Here, the focus changes from assessing basic abilities, personality, or physical capabilities and looks to past results.

As we move from simpler to more complex jobs or from lower to higher levels in an organization, the relative importance among *can-do*, *will-do*, *able-to*, and *done-that* competencies changes. So does the way we go about framing the assessment process. Figure 9.2 illustrates how moving from less complex entry-level jobs to technical, professional, and managerial jobs can shift the emphasis on *can-do*, *will-do*, *able-to*, and *done-that* competencies addressed in

Figure 9.2 Different jobs call for a different focus in the candidate assessment process

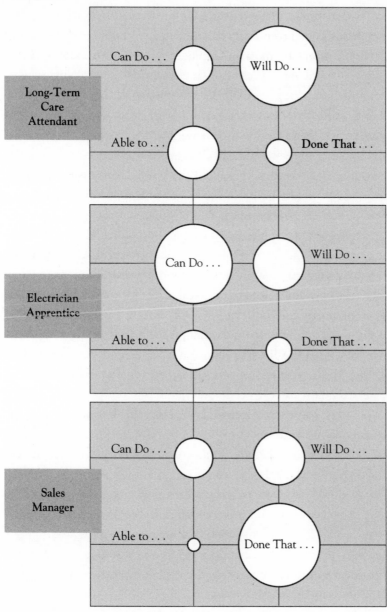

the assessment process. The nature of the job itself dictates the focus too.

For example, the long-term care attendant job in Figure 9.2 poses relatively fewer skill or experience requirements: *can-do* and *done-that* won't be the key targets in assessing candidates to this job. The job demands relatively higher levels of conscientiousness, responsibility, and a willingness to deal with the work environment—all *will-do* competencies. It also requires the *able-to* competencies needed to handle the lifting, pushing, pulling, and carrying tasks that come with the role. The visual depiction of Figure 9.2 illustrates how the thinking about the candidate assessment process for the job might be assembled, and tells us to dig deeper into finding *will-do* assessment tools.

An electrician apprentice job typically requires a four-year training program that draws on a variety of entry-level skills and abilities: math, reading comprehension, spatial visualization, and others. The training also calls for a personal orientation that will carry the apprentice through both on- and off-the-job educational courses. Dexterity, coordination, and other physical abilities are competencies that join the list to produce a broader set of competencies. Clearly the assessment process will differ from that of the long-term care attendant in both scope and detail.

A sales manager job demands experience. Here attention shifts to *done-that* competencies, but the assessment process still needs to look to the *can-do* and *will-do* competencies needed to pull off the higher-level job. It also leads to an interest in assessing *shouldn't-do* aspects of personality—ones that might be derailers of success. The *able-to* domain, though, is of minor importance, even if weekly sales forecasting sessions demand a lot of endurance. Assessment for this job needs to focus on past accomplishment as a primary predictor of future performance, particularly if the candidate has held the same position elsewhere.

Using the *can-do, will-do, able-to, done-that* model helps focus on the competencies hiring departments need for review when it comes time to assess candidates. Recall the competency model building tools introduced in the previous chapter that are posted at www.million-dollarhire.com. Typically tools like these are used to choose the competencies that drive the assessment process for a given job, set of jobs, or major unit of the organization. Matching these competencies to assessment tools is where we turn next.

Different Assessment Tools and How They Work

It's your annual physical exam. The physician spends time looking over last year's results—in essence, reviewing your "health résumé." Then she proceeds to interview you; asks about changes since your last exam; explores what you've done with your diet, exercise, and relationships; and digs into any new conditions or symptoms you've experienced. Every question has a purpose: assessment. Your answers help her identify areas to probe (literally) and help her make predictions about your overall state of health now and in the future.

If it all ended with the interview, followed by suggestions about what to do in the coming year, though, how would you feel? Would you believe the assessment was good enough to predict your future health? What about a urinalysis, blood chemistry workup, cardio test, vision test, and dermatology scan, to name a few? Would you feel the exam was complete without them? And yet we often hire people based on a résumé review and interview: no tests, no assessments, and little probing. We think the assessment was complete enough to make an important prediction about the future.

Like a physical exam, if the objective is to assess the whole candidate, we need to find which "tests" provide a better understanding of a candidate's can-do, will-do, able-to, done-that condition. We should think about assessment tools that target relevant competencies under each of the four broad categories illustrated in Figure 9.3.

As Figure 9.3 suggests, research and practice have shown that certain assessment formats work best in tapping certain competency

Figure 9.3 Different tools tap different candidate competencies

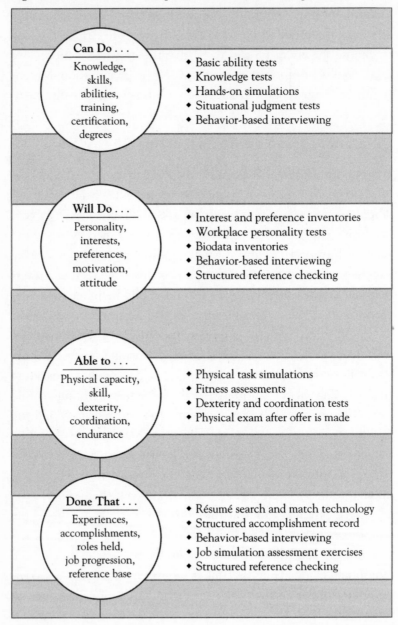

Can Do . . .

Knowledge,
skills,
abilities,
training,
certification,
degrees

- ◆ Basic ability tests
- ◆ Knowledge tests
- ◆ Hands-on simulations
- ◆ Situational judgment tests
- ◆ Behavior-based interviewing

Will Do . . .

Personality,
interests,
preferences,
motivation,
attitude

- ◆ Interest and preference inventories
- ◆ Workplace personality tests
- ◆ Biodata inventories
- ◆ Behavior-based interviewing
- ◆ Structured reference checking

Able to . . .

Physical capacity,
skill,
dexterity,
coordination,
endurance

- ◆ Physical task simulations
- ◆ Fitness assessments
- ◆ Dexterity and coordination tests
- ◆ Physical exam after offer is made

Done That . . .

Experiences,
accomplishments,
roles held,
job progression,
reference base

- ◆ Résumé search and match technology
- ◆ Structured accomplishment record
- ◆ Behavior-based interviewing
- ◆ Job simulation assessment exercises
- ◆ Structured reference checking

areas—among them are ability tests, interview protocols, job sim-ulations, personality inventories, and reference checks. Figure 9.3 offers an inventory of some examples.

As in medicine, too, it pays to stop and look to science for direction about how to make the most accurate, and predictive, assessments of a candidate. Perhaps surprisingly, a great deal of the research has been held to standards much like those that underlie medical assessments: sound experimental design, large group research, and statistical analysis, for example. It helps to look here too because the science of candidate assessment isn't overwhelmed by the noise of the commercial marketplace for assessment tools.

True, I'm back to squeezing research that would fill a book into a few pages, but many of the sources I've cited thus far offer more detail for those interested in digging deeper. Here, the target is to highlight some of the best-established principles and focus on the tools most likely to produce a recruiting and hiring program with payoff.

First, from the 1980s, the work of Frank Schmidt, John Hunter, and other colleagues has shed a growing and generally consistent light on what works and how it works in the field of candidate assessment. Some of the more informative research has involved meta-analysis studies: large-scale, statistically driven reviews that summarize results from hundreds of independent research projects. These studies focus on identifying underlying patterns and conclu-sions that hold across different types of assessment techniques in a variety of settings.[2] Canceling out the quirks that can come with any individual research study, the information they provide helps guide design decisions when candidate assessment programs are assembled.

Most of these studies have asked, among others, a basic ques-tion: What *level of validity* can we expect (see Figures 2.1 and 2.2) when certain kinds of assessment tools are used to predict perfor-mance in training or on the job? As Chapters Two through Five explained, validity is a metric that drives the payoff we can expect to pull from a given assessment tool. *How* we use the tool also drives payoff, but the validity of an assessment tool is the starting point: no validity, no payoff. That's why knowing what to expect about a particular assessment tool's validity is important when laying out the tactics for improving hiring program payoff.

Much of the Schmidt, Hunter, and related research studies compare frequently used categories of assessment techniques in terms of the validity they produce. Using the validity coefficient statistic introduced in Chapters Two and Three, Figure 9.4 shows what one of the major meta-analysis studies of the late 1990s found regarding the validity of different assessment techniques.[3]

Many of the individual studies summarized deal with entry-level jobs. That's not to say the jobs are lower level, just that new hires were expected to undergo training in order to acquire the skills they need to perform the job they entered. The same research, though, shows similar results when the same types of assessment tools are used in making promotional decisions.

In the studies, the assessment techniques that provide candidates a chance to perform an actual work sample, generally assessing a blend of *can-do* and *done-that* competencies, offer the best predictions of future performance. That's not a surprise. The only downside rests in the cost of work sample testing. Such tools take a great deal of time to design, since each job calls for a unique work sample. They also take people resources to administer and interpret them. Deciding how well a candidate has performed can require a great deal of interpretation. The question is how to gain this level of validity without the cost.

Assessment tools targeting general mental abilities—primarily *can-do* competencies—begin to answer the question. These are also among the most valid predictors of future performance, nearly matching the validity of work sample assessments. They help answer the question about drawing the same level of validity without substantial cost. Structured interviewing techniques—often blending a review of *can-do*, *will-do*, and *done-that* competencies—show

Figure 9.4 Average validity for general types of candidate assessment techniques
Source: Schmidt, F. L., & Hunter, J. E. (1998). The validity and utility of selection methods in personnel psychology: Practical and theoretical implications of 85 years of research findings. *Psychological Bulletin, 124,* 265.

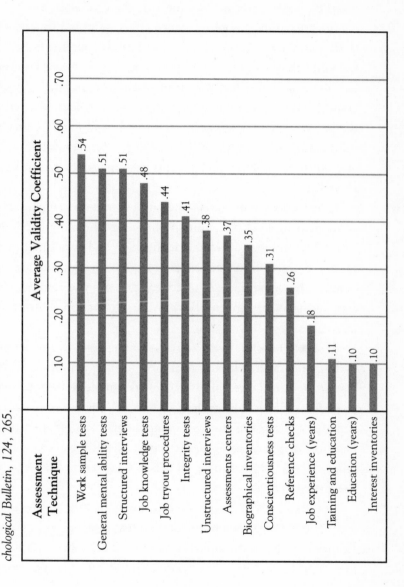

generally equivalent levels of validity, but they also cost more compared to basic ability testing, which can be administered over Web-based platforms prior to even meeting the candidate.

Integrity tests, whose relevance often is limited to jobs where there's concern over theft or other forms of malfeasance, show sound levels of validity in addressing the largely *will-do* competencies that frame the concept of integrity. Next in level of validity come a variety of techniques ranging from unstructured interviewing procedures, to assessment center techniques and biographical information, the last typically measuring a blend of *can-do*, *will-do*, and *done-that* competencies through structured inventories or checklists.

Conscientiousness tests—measures of *will-do* competencies—come next in level of validity, followed by the more experience-focused techniques of reference checking and structured reviews of candidates' training and experience. As shown, candidates' academic achievement, level of education, and the results of their completing interest inventories provide information of little predictive value.

The conclusion is that basic *can-do* competencies predict future performance well, whether measured with general mental ability tests or well-structured interviews, work sample tests, or job tryout procedures. Since validity drives payoff, it's these tools that rise to the top of the list as the best components to populate a tactical plan for candidate assessment to entry-level jobs. These are *the* types of tools the forecasting models in Chapter Five show to bring the greatest payoff.

Results like these, replicated in many meta-analysis reviews, argue for assessing general mental ability, *g*, which is basic intelligence. Studies exploring the reasons that *g* serves as such an important predictor of performance and driver of payoff generally conclude that *g* predicts how quickly individuals are able to acquire job knowledge through training and experience; their level of job knowledge then predicts how well they will perform on the job; and hence, g serves as a sound predictor of their future performance when a noteworthy element of learning is associated with the position.[4]

The research also shows that measures of *will-do* competencies, such as conscientiousness and integrity, predict behavior on the job. Tapped through traditional testing techniques as well as structured interviewing, reference checking, and biographical inventory approaches, these competencies also drive performance in most jobs, and in some, they hold particular payoff. As noted in the payoff illustrations in Chapter Four, best practices cited many cases where assessments of *will-do* characteristics increased the ability to predict employee performance.

There's also evidence in the research that assessment of candidates' *able-to* competencies predicts future success for jobs where physical demands are noteworthy. In many cases, these assessments focus not only on predicting *how well* a candidate is likely to perform the job, but on forecasting his or her likelihood of being injured as a result of poorly matching this person's physical capabilities to the demands of the job.[5]

Not long ago, I reviewed a physical ability assessment technique for positions in a food manufacturing plant. The assessment—actually, a work sample testing approach—required candidates to lift and carry loads similar to those employees handle throughout the work shift. Before introducing the assessment, employees were involved in a work-related injury on average once every 232 work days. After adding the *able-to* assessment to a hiring process that already included mental ability testing, structured interviewing, and an assessment center–type team exercise, injury rates fell to one every approximately 1,535 days, a more than sixfold reduction in injury rates.

What's most important with these assessments, though, is ensuring that they address the specific competencies the job demands and do not verge into areas prohibited by the Americans with Disabilities Act. We'll cover this and other legal compliance matters associated with candidate assessment in Chapter Eleven. For now, though, I underscore the need for care when these types of tools are used. When they're relevant and properly used, they can produce a major payoff, as in the illustration. When they're not, they pose major risk of legal challenge.

Finally, it's important to recognize that the general results of scientific research are just that: general. They summarize the results that different employers have seen in using certain assessment techniques for jobs in various settings, with various pools of candidates. They offer great value in helping choose the types of tools likely to add payoff and reduce the risk of making mistakes in the hiring process. But past results don't guarantee future performance.

Any of the general types of tools I review here must be held to further evaluation before and after they're implemented. Tools that worked well in research settings might pose problems of poor validity, high cost, or legal exposure when they're implemented in the wrong way or in the wrong setting. In addition, if the information they provide is used in the wrong way, their value erodes. In short, the science can point us in the right direction, but we need to check all our own circumstances as we put it to work.

With these cautions, let's look to some examples of how learnings from the science of assessment have been put to work and the payoffs that resulted. All of these examples come from real-world settings and from some of the leading service providers in the business.

Light Industrial Workers

A temporary services company was concerned with the number of worker's compensation claims filed by the light industrial workers it supplied to client organizations.[6] As one part of approaching the problem, the company decided to develop new procedures for assessing candidates who were applying to its pool of temporary employees and engaged an assessment vendor to develop a screening test. A key requirement was to hold the new tool to structured statistical analysis in order to reduce any legal compliance risks that might come with implementation.

You might expect such an assessment to focus on candidates' physical competencies. Assessments of this type, though, can be costly to build and can raise concerns as to whether they conflict with equal employment opportunity and disabilities legislation. Drawing on the science introduced in Figure 9.4, the vendor instead assembled a twenty-minute assessment of *can-do* and *will-do* competencies geared to the entry-level nature of the client's light industrial assignments. Research in recent years has suggested that accidents and injuries, particularly recurrent involvement in such events, can be driven by these characteristics, as well as by *able-to* competencies.[7]

The new tool was implemented and tracked with technology that captured candidates' assessment scores and worker's compensation claims experience for a period of two years. The company tested over three thousand candidates; standards on the test were not made final until the two years of research was ended. In the end, analyses showed that those who performed poorly on the assessment were more than twice as likely to file a worker's compensation claim and were more than four times as likely to file multiple claims.

Importantly, the assessment tool predicted these outcomes without assessing candidates' physical capabilities, an approach that would have been more costly to implement and more likely to bring legal compliance challenges. In short, drawing on the research literature showing that *will-do* competencies predict injury rates resulted in a quick, accurate assessment that predicted an outcome that would be negative for the temporary services firm and its clients.

Electronics and Appliance Retail Sales

A major retailer in the electronics and home appliance sector decided to upgrade its approach to assessing sales associate candidates.[8] The objective was to identify sales associates likely to hit, and then exceed, their monthly sales targets. Because of the large number of employees, the high volume of hiring, and the importance of hitting the sales objective, the assessment process needed to be quick, efficient, and accurate.

The company decided to implement an assessment technique referred to in Figure 9.4 as a biographical inventory, often referred to as a biodata assessment. These tools focus on candidates' background, interests, experiences, accomplishments, and *will-do* characteristics. In this case, the company administered the assessment through a Web-based platform, and candidates' results were available to the employer immediately. As a result of the assessment, the retailer assigned candidates to one of four groups: highly recommended, recommended, marginally recommended, or not recommended.

Here's where it gets interesting. The company advised store managers to interview only the candidates with a recommended or highly recommended outcome on the assessment. In some cases, though, store managers asked for approval to interview, and even hire, candidates who received assessment outcomes of marginally recommended or not recommended. The science summarized in Figure 9.4 would say that was a bad idea. Given the Web-based tracking system underlying the assessment process, the company soon learned just how bad the idea really was.

After a twenty-month follow-up, candidates who had been assessed as not recommended sold 25 percent less than candidates who were assessed as highly recommended. And there was no real need to dip lower into the candidate pool: only 14 percent were assigned to this lowest-scoring group. On average, every exception that a store manager requested cost the company an average of approximately $10,000 in monthly sales when compared to the performance of those who were recommended by the process. Each exception cost the company over $100,000 in annual sales, since there were enough candidates to fill open positions without dipping to this level.

Here the science was right. The well-researched area of biodata assessment had forecast that the tool would predict sales results. Implementing the technique through a Web-based system, with data tracking and follow-up capabilities, fit the cost and operating constraints of the employer. In the end, store managers' requests to override the assessment results actually documented its payoff by setting up the conditions to show, with hard numbers, what happened by hiring those who had failed to pass the recommended standards. The exceptions reinforced the rule: believe the research.

Computer Sales, Customer, and Technical Support

A computer manufacturer decided to design assessment tools to guide hiring around the world for its thousands of frontline telesales, customer care, and technical support roles.[9] The objective was to increase sales closing rates, improve resolution rates in technical service calls, and reduce the percentage of callers who were reporting dissatisfaction with the service they received.

The design effort began with an in-depth review of the competencies underlying effective performance across all of the targeted areas. Because new hires would undergo training in the company's products, services, customer service policies, and all other areas, results identified a range of both *can-do* and *will-do* competencies necessary to learning and performing the roles. Among the *can-do* competencies were quantitative, reasoning, and problem-solving skills, as well as the ability to read, understand, and communicate effectively in English. *Will-do* competencies included a conscientious and responsible work orientation, a willingness to work without close supervision, a willingness to follow rules and procedures, and acceptance of a fast-paced, people-focused work environment.

Assembling assessment procedures to tap the range of competency requirements resulted in drawing on several of the basic approaches listed in Figure 9.4. Along with prescreening questions paralleling a biographical inventory approach, an approximately one-hour battery of Web-delivered tests for *can-do* competencies and *will-do* work orientation served as an initial step in the assessment process.

Next, an approximately one-hour work sample–type assessment, involving a telephone-based role play with a trained assessor, tapped competencies that traditional testing tools can't. Finally, a behavior-based interview was designed to be administered locally. Borrowing from the science summarized in Figure 9.4, the company assembled the process to ensure the major competencies of the jobs would be addressed accurately and cost-effectively.

After tracking the overall program's results, data showed the process made an impact. Individuals who scored among the top one-third of those assessed delivered a sales closing rate more than 10 percent higher than the closing rate of those in the bottom one-third. The rate of unsatisfied customer reports for those falling in the top one-third was nearly 30 percent lower than that of the lowest scoring one-third. Supervisors were twice as likely to rate technical support staff assessed in the top one-third as excellent performers than the bottom one-third. In short, thorough assessment of competencies paid a strong dividend in quality of hire.

Professional Services Firm Account Managers

I recently worked with a large professional services firm specializing in best practice research. The company was restructuring its sales and account management functions. Part of the effort was to create an assessment package to be used during internal staff realignment and in hiring new account managers.

Analysis of the newly defined account manager role highlighted sets of *can-do*, *will-do*, and *done-that* competencies customized from the competency modeling tools shown at www.million-dollarhire .com. The research I reviewed earlier pointed to a number of assessment techniques that could be used to assess both internal and external candidates against the competencies.

We assembled four types of assessment approaches to complement information gained from external candidates' résumés and internal candidates' performance histories. All candidates completed a structured accomplishment record, where they provided examples of specific past accomplishments in specific competency areas. The result was forwarded to interview teams, who integrated the results into a behavior-based interview protocol conducted in a team-based interviewing process.

In addition, candidates completed a workplace personality test exploring what have come to be called the dark side dimensions of workplace personality—tendencies to display arrogance, excitability, skepticism, boldness, and other qualities that research has shown to be derailers of success.[10] Finally, external candidates completed a test measuring tactical reasoning, strategic reasoning, and critical-thinking skills.

Each account manager succeeding in the process and hired was assigned an individual, financially driven set of performance objectives that we tracked and measured on a quarterly basis. During the first quarter after choosing the new account managers, the group of approximately one hundred averaged more than 110 percent of their financial performance targets. Here, assessing the full range of competencies associated with the job contributed to achieving the organization's fundamental financial targets.

When Enough Is Enough

All of the examples showed a payoff. All involved assessing candidates against the job's most important competencies. But when has a candidate been held to enough assessment? When do we hit a point of diminishing return, assessing more but learning little that's new? We can turn again to the science summarized in Figure 9.4. Here, though, I add in the results of additional meta-analysis studies that look at the question of diminishing return.

Figure 9.5 comes from the same major research studies that produced Figure 9.4, but it shows the degree to which an assessment program's validity increases when a second assessment procedure

Figure 9.5 The average validity of combined assessment techniques
Source: Schmidt & Hunter. (1998).

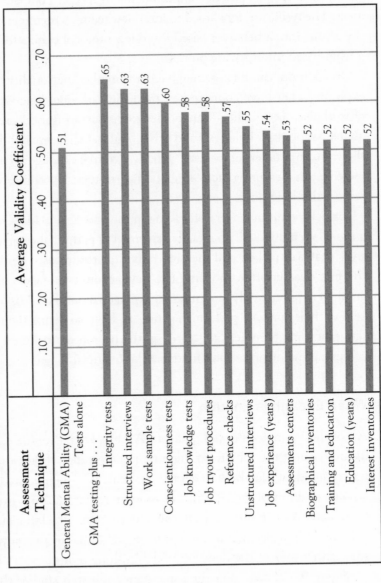

was added to assessment of a candidate's standing on measures of general mental ability.[11]

Of course, the data provide a fairly narrow answer to the original question. First, they begin by using only assessments of general mental ability, valuable as they might be, as the stake in the ground. Then they look to how much the validity of the assessment process is increased by adding a variety of other assessment media. Again, it's important to note that the majority of the jobs on which the data were assembled reflect entry-level positions—not low-level jobs, but ones where training after hiring plays a role in bringing new hires to proficiency.

Assessment techniques involving work samples, structured interviewing, and integrity tests show the greatest increment to the level of validity produced by general mental ability assessments. At a slightly lower level, assessments of conscientiousness, job knowledge, and reference check information also show information with additive payoff.

What's most apparent in Figure 9.5, though, is the finding that the greatest additional payoff comes by widening the view of candidate competencies from *can-do* assessments (general mental ability tests) to techniques that tap *will-do* and *done-that* competencies (interviewing, personality testing, reference checking, and work sample or knowledge tests). The results are quite clear: broader assessment improves the accuracy in predicting candidate performance and the payoff that results. Assess more broadly; extract more value.

Although the data in Figure 9.5 are limited, they lay a foundation in science for the broader principle introduced in Figure 9.1: that candidates differ in a variety of competency areas that, if required by the job, produce the need to assemble different assessment tools in order to make the best prediction about candidate-to-job fit. This in turn comes back to one of the major steps in grounding a hiring strategy in tactics that drive better hiring decisions. Once we know the payoff targets that drive our strategy

Figure 9.6 Thinking through the design of an assessment process

Decide What We Need . . .	Build Pool . . .	Filter the Pool . . .
—Competencies— ranging from broad-based to job-specific capabilities in can-do, will-do, able-to, and done-that areas	—Sourcing and prescreening— targeting the competency profile and refining the pool	—Assessment— holding candidates to the job's key competencies in valid, payoff-oriented ways

(reduced turnover, higher productivity, more sales, fewer accidents or injuries, better customer reviews, or something else), developing a tactical plan really boils down to using the science of assessment to answer three questions.

The first, shown in Figure 9.6, rests in identifying what competencies we need in order to hit hiring objectives. This means identifying the *can-do, will-do, able-to, done-that* competencies that drive performance. There might be broad competencies that cut across many or all of the jobs we hire for. There might be others isolated to particular groups of jobs or even individual positions. Using tools like those reviewed in the previous chapter can give you a handle on the nature of these competencies relatively easily.

Second, we need to find candidates likely to bring at least some of these competencies to the screening process. Here, sourcing, advertising, Internet scraping, and a variety of prescreening techniques can bring the raw material where further review is cost justified.

Finally, the tactical plan needs to choose the types of assessment tools needed to filter candidates in a way that makes the best predictions of future performance. The general types of tools selected to drive assessment—ability tests, biodata or personality tests, interview procedures, work sample or similar assessment exercises, reference checks—can be selected for the competencies targeted by research and best practices information like that summarized here and based on their cost of administration. Specific tools can be selected through vendor reviews or internal build-versus-buy decisions. The point is, there's a great deal of knowledge out there to draw on. The process need not be one-off and need not cost a mint.

Back to Estimating Payoff

Decisions also can be driven by selecting the tactics for a candidate assessment process that maximize the payoff likely to result from the program. Here, we reach back to the payoff estimation formula introduced in Chapter Five. Work underlying the formula extends back more than two decades, with one of its best illustrations being a hypothetical application to projecting the financial payoff if valid assessment tools were used in hiring employees to federal government positions, currently one of the fastest-growing segments of the labor market.[12]

Net dollar value gain for year's hires	=	Increase in program validity	×	Year's no. of new hires	×	Avg. new hire tenure	×	$ Difference in top vs. bottom performance	×	Candidate screening selectivity	−	Year's increased cost of program administration

Rather than government hiring, though, let's say we're building the tactical plan for assessing candidates for an entry-level production assembler job. Say, we employ five hundred operators, hire one hundred every year to cover turnover and growth, and retain new hires for an average of five years before they leave the company or move to other jobs inside the company. Finally, let's say the local labor market typically lets us hire one of every two who apply for the job and that the workforce averages $32,500 in annual compensation. Of course, all of these numbers can be varied if we're in forecasting mode and want to see the impact of making different assumptions.

At the simplest level, we could assess candidates by simply looking at the years of relevant experience they show on their application, anticipating that, on average, one of every two candidates will have sufficient experience. This process will cost us nothing to administer. Drawing on the data presented in Figure 9.4 regarding the validity of job experience as an assessment measure (validity = .10), Table 9.1 shows that the payoff in this approach, compared to hiring at random, would reflect approximately $622,000 in increased productivity over the five years that each year's one hundred new hires are expected to remain in the job—just over $1,200 per new hire, per year, in increased productivity. The return isn't very high, but neither is the validity of job experience as an assessment tool. Then again, using the tool cost us nothing, and the payoff still reflects an increase of nearly 4 percent in productivity: not a bad return on the more than $16 million in compensation that will be spent on the one hundred new hires over the course of their five years' average tenure.

Table 9.1 The Payoff of Assessments with Increasing Levels of Validity

Assessment Approach	One Year's Hiring Payoff over Random Selection	One Year's Hiring Payoff as a Percentage of New Hire Payroll
Hire the most experienced	$622,350	3.83%
Reference-check candidates	1,545,875	9.51
Use abilities tests	3,163,985	19.47
Use ability and conscientiousness tests	3,719,100	22.89
All of the above, but hire the top one of every three	5,113,200	31.46

Note: These figures are for a production assembler job based on 500 in the total workforce, 100 hired annually, with an average annual compensation of $32,500, and an average tenure of five years.

If reference checking, at a cost of, say, $50 per candidate, were used as the assessment tool (validity = .26), the payoff value rises to approximately $1.54 million over five years, nearly 10 percent of the total compensation awarded to the one hundred new hires over the time frame. Reference checking as the primary assessment tool offers more validity and more return on investment.

Shifting to an assessment process that uses a $50-per-candidate mental ability test (validity = .51) to target the competencies required by production operator jobs (basic math skills, reading comprehension, perceptual speed and accuracy, spatial visualization, and others) would be expected to raise the payoff to approximately $3.16 million over five years, now nearly 20 percent of the total compensation paid for the year's one hundred new hires over that time. This improvement might be sufficient to consider whether we could meet the production volume with four hundred rather than five hundred production operators. And all we did was add a basic abilities test to the assessment process.

Adding a conscientiousness assessment to the mental ability tests, at an additional $25 per candidate, according to Figure 9.5, results in validity = .60 for the assessment battery. Under the same one-of-every-two hiring model, the payoff rises to approximately $3.72 million, about 23 percent of the new hires' five-year compensation. This is just about the highest payoff possible under the scientific data reviewed thus far.

As the pitchman says: But wait, there's more! If the local labor market permits, we could increase our selectivity. We might raise the bar and accept only the top one of every three candidates. The payoff shown in Table 9.1 indicates that we can expect to raise the dollar value of improved performance to approximately $5.11 million, now more than 30 percent of payroll costs. All of this comes as the result of implementing a fairly simple assessment platform. And remember: the cost of administering the program is covered in the payoff estimate.

Of course, the estimates summarized in Table 9.1 draw on general research findings. Vendors might provide data more closely matched to jobs and competency requirements. Historical hiring and performance information might help compute the validity levels of past practices. An internal tracking study might assess the validity of different assessment platforms and, over time, be used to add or subtract elements from the process that refine the payoff.

The central point is that *there are* tools and research data available in the marketplace that can help get you get started in framing an assessment process and projecting the economic payoff you can expect to see once it's up and running. This information can be drawn on as an overall strategy and tactics are framed. Then the employer's own internal quality-of-hire reviews can guide decisions about refining the process once data internal to the business begin to emerge.

Buyer Beware

There's a caution, though. As noted in Chapter One, this is a generally unregulated business. There are many very professional, well-staffed, financially secure vendors in the space. The examples summarized throughout these chapters mention some of them, and there are more. The tools these vendors provide can help produce a major payoff in exactly the ways I have illustrated in the examples.

There also are vendors, though, who market tools of little or no value—tools that look good on their face but bring the risk of legal challenge if their use has a disparate impact on groups protected by law. Worse, their tools offer no payoff and no validity; they simply increase the cost of the recruiting and hiring process. From both a legal compliance and a payoff point of view, experience suggests five questions an employer should pose to product vendors in this area:

1. Do you have professional (not sales) staff who can work with us to document the validity of your tool for our organization and help us decide how best to use it? If so, where have you done this before and whom can we contact for reference information?

2. In what other settings similar to ours has this tool been used, and what information can you provide about its equal employment opportunity impact in that setting?

3. Who are your five largest clients similar to our organization who use the tool, and how can we contact them to discuss the payoff they've seen?

4. Has your tool ever been challenged from a legal compliance point of view? If so, what was the outcome? What documentation can you provide to help us understand the matter?

5. Can you provide technical documentation, consistent with the federal agencies' Uniform Guidelines on Employee Selection Procedures showing that the tool you offer is valid and job related?

All of these questions go to the vendor's experience, track record, and capacity to fit its tool into the buyer's overall recruiting and hiring strategy in a way that makes sense from a legal compliance and bottom-line payoff point of view. The questions also provide a way to gauge the vendor's capability of supporting any challenges that come in the future. In short, an assessment vendor should be held to the same level of reference checking and review that's applied to any other product or service. Input from internal or outside labor counsel is a good idea too.

One sales technique to watch for—actually, a scam—involves a vendor that offers to customize and validate its assessment process by administering it to a sample of your best-performing employees. Then, the offer goes, the vendor uses the results to set your new hiring standards so its tool matches candidates to the profile of your top performers. Makes sense, right? Every employer would like to clone its top performers. Setting standards that mirror this group's performance on the screening tool sounds like a solid, data-driven approach.

There's something missing, though. The offer might make sense if the vendor also wanted to evaluate a sample of your poorest-performing employees. Then it could show that its screening tool differentiates between those at the top and bottom of the performance distribution.

I reviewed a sales screening tool for a major insurance company a while back. The "profile your best" pitch had accompanied the tool's implementation several years before, and thousands of candidates had been tested. Many had been hired. On review, we found that the screening tool produced the same profile for the company's poorest-performing sales professionals as for those performing best. It's a nice sales pitch, but there's no payoff. It's just a waste of money.

There are even cases where the vendor offering a solution doesn't really understand the implications of the assessment tool it offers. This might sound unlikely, but with the expansion of technology into the recruiting and hiring arena, a good number of businesses have been formed by people with a great grasp of technology but no understanding of the pitfalls that come with day-to-day recruiting and hiring practices. Some have been formed by individuals with recruiting expertise, but no understanding of the legal compliance challenges that HR departments face and no background in how the smallest error from using their tools can cost millions.

Make sure your assessment vendor is broad-based enough to understand the risks that come with the tools he or she is selling. Make sure that risk-tracking and risk-reduction procedures are built into the product. Many vendors have done a great job assembling professionals with knowledge in technology, recruiting, screening, and legal compliance. Many have the staff and financial horsepower needed if it's necessary to face legal challenge too. But some don't.

Again, It's About Predicting the Future

In assembling a candidate assessment process, you've created a quality control program. You've decided what it takes to perform the job, relying on science, best practices, industry peers, and your own continuous improvement work to be confident that certain competencies lead to success. You've relied on the same science and best practices, along with vendor reviews, to identify tool kits that assess the competencies you need. The tools assess these competencies in ways that are valid and where the payoff from using the tools can be set to numbers.

Once the assessments are in hand, you're ready to make a decision—actually, a prediction—about the candidates you review. Then you can track these decisions to keep the quality control process rolling and adjust how to make future decisions.

We all make mistakes, but perfection is not the objective. Incremental improvement is. For jobs where the volume of hiring is high (retail sales, customer service, production, and operations, for example), substantial payoff will result from even small gains in the validity of the assessment process. Here, assessing a few key competencies and holding the cost of the assessments to low levels can pay off substantially. For jobs where hiring volume is low but impact is high (key technical positions, creative design roles, or senior management) making a mistake carries greater risk. Here, broader, multiple methods of assessment, at greater cost of execution, are necessary. Both cases can be put to the payoff formulas introduced in Chapter Five to help decide on the assessment approach. Now, though, it's time to decide how to use all the information you've pulled from the hiring funnel to make the best million-dollar hire.

CHAPTER TEN

MAKING THE MILLION-DOLLAR DECISION

Once candidates have been assessed against the job's basic qualifications and competencies, it's time to make the million-dollar decision. This chapter reviews how to use the information you collected during prescreening and assessment to make simple pass-versus-fail decisions or to decide which candidates are likely to be the *best* investments, with the lowest risk. It also reviews how to use information not only about candidates' strengths but also about their weaknesses to broaden your thinking. Finally, it points out some of the decision approaches that can decrease or increase the risk of legal challenge and reviews how to mitigate the risk.

Throughout, the focus is on assembling everything you've learned as you moved down the hiring funnel, even if the funnel was filled with only a handful of senior-level candidates. You'll continue to emphasize your overall objective: drawing the best payoff from the hiring decisions you make by using all the information you've paid to collect.

The Key: Valid Data, Correctly Used

By this stage, you've collected the information to guide the hiring decision. Well, almost all. If the prescreening and assessment stages of the hiring funnel were relatively simple, as in the Chapter Seven fast food restaurant example, the decision can be straightforward, even mechanical. If the process is more complex, as in the Chapter Nine account manager and telesales examples, you'll need a more sophisticated process to guide the way you review, combine, and even weight candidate information to drive the best decision.

Regardless of the program's complexity, though, the concept first introduced in Chapter Two deserves another mention: validity, also referred to as job-relatedness. It fuels payoff, and it supports risk management.

Validity is also a concept that needs to be preserved in *the way you use* candidate information to make a final hiring decision. Validity rests not only in the tools you choose that create payoff and risk reduction; it lives in *the way you use them.*[1]

You might have used tools—lists of basic qualifications, tests, interview formats, reference checking methods—that provide information you know is valid. That is, knowing how each candidate performed on the prescreening and assessment tools provides information that you know predicts their performance on the job. When you assembled the tactics of the recruiting and hiring process, you sought out, adopted, or even developed tools with the best evidence of validity because you saw, in Chapter Five and again in Chapter Nine, how validity translates to dollars. More validity equals more payoff in the process.

From choosing basic qualifications items, to selecting tests, interview protocols, work simulations, or reference checking procedures, you've done your best to make sure the tools show evidence of validity, whether based on use in other settings or through your own quality control–oriented analysis of the results they've produced internally.

But using the information the tools produce in the wrong way can actually result in their validity evaporating. So before making the million-dollar decision, think about how to maintain the validity of the tools you assembled as guidance. You need to think about how *not* to let the validity evaporate as a result of what you do with the information. You need to be sure *the way you make decisions* doesn't undermine the validity of the tools assembled to guide the sourcing, prescreening and assessment, and other stages of the process.

Of all the expert witness assignments I've taken, the majority haven't involved defending a given recruiting or hiring tool. Most have focused on how the tool was used. Recall the illustration of the employer who implemented a physical ability assessment tool to screen employees in a food manufacturing plant. The employer found that new hires experienced a sixfold reduction in the frequency of on-the-job injuries after the tool was introduced. Simulating the physical demands of the job, the tool asked candidates to show that they could lift loads of the same weight and carry them the same distance required by the job.

However, the tool was challenged by an outside agency because it resulted in a higher failure rate for female candidates than for males. As part of the jury trial that followed, the plaintiff argued that on the job, employees lift and carry materials at a pace dictated by the automated machines onto which they placed their loads. When the test was administered, though, candidates were instructed to perform the simulation at a pace *comfortable to them*.

Review showed that candidates performed the physical simulation, the assessment tool, at a faster pace than would be required on the job. The result was a weaker link between performing well on the test and performing well on the job, because the two were performed at a different pace. This might seem like a small point, but not to the court.

In the end, the court cited the difference between *how the assessment was performed*, compared to *how the job was performed*, as one reason for ruling against the company. *How the tool was used* became a major issue in the legal action despite the statistical evidence that the tool actually worked.

And it's not just legal challenges that focus attention on how the information you collect on candidates is reviewed and combined to make a final decision. Overweighting or underweighting a given assessment tool, combining the information from different tools in the wrong way, or including information that's unreliable in the final decision, such as recommendations of poorly trained interviewers or reference checkers, can undermine the validity in the final hiring decision. All these potential flaws in how to use the information you collect amount to letting value leak out of the system. That's why you need to make sure the information you learn about candidates through all the recruiting and hiring tools you've assembled is used in a way that drives the best decisions.

Combining Candidate Information: Basic Principles

The steps to making a final million-dollar decision were triggered when you decided who met the job's basic qualifications. That was the first decision in narrowing the hiring funnel. Although fairly mechanical, the decision as to who meets the job's basic qualifications saves the time of dealing with what are in fact noncandidates. For these individuals, this stage of the process *is* the final decision.

From that point forward, though, payoff rests in deciding which of several thinking models to follow in weighing, combining, and using the basic qualifying and assessment information you have collected. Of course, you'll have thought through and decided on the model when you created the strategy and tactics that steer the program. Now the process takes center stage.

One choice is whether to follow what's referred to as a simple, multiple-hurdles approach to processing candidates. The alternative is referred to as a compensatory model. The two approaches take a fundamentally different view about what we seek and about the

Figure 10.1 How a multiple-hurdles hiring decision works

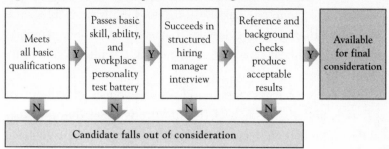

things candidates are capable of doing to balance their strengths and weaknesses as they perform the job. A choice between the two models might seem simple, but the implications are noteworthy. The choice communicates how we think about the demands of the job and the capabilities of people.

For example, taking a multiple-hurdles approach to making final hiring decisions follows a path like that shown in Figure 10.1. In fact, the model doesn't wait to make a final decision; rather, it makes a series of decisions, each one potentially final. In the example, the different assessment tools that hiring professionals used to evaluate candidates defined four hurdles. Candidates' performance against each assessment tool determines which ones survive to face a final hiring decision. Failing to clear any one hurdle means eliminating the candidate from consideration.

The multiple-hurdles model works when the qualifications or competencies reviewed at each stage in the process are relatively independent and when each is so critical to the job that failing to clear any hurdle reflects a likelihood of performing poorly on the job. The logic is that no candidate can make up for a lack of competence in each area even if she or he is highly competent in another.

The multiple-hurdles model sets a tough standard. The model and variations that adopt its main features make sense when the number of candidates is large compared to the number of positions available. It makes sense when low-cost screening tools can be used early to begin the pass-fail process. Finally, it makes sense only when there's clear evidence that lacking the competencies assessed at each stage has a clear impact on the likelihood of success in the job.

When it's a buyer's market and when evidence of validity for the tools underlying each of the hurdles is clear, the multiple-hurdles approach produces payoff by identifying the best-qualified candidates—those who jump each hurdle successively and show no weaknesses. The model's payoff also comes through reducing the cost associated with processing every candidate through the entire system. Money is spent on each step in the process only if a candidate demonstrates that he or she is sufficiently qualified to warrant consideration in the next step.

I've used the multiple-hurdles process in screening new hires for jobs ranging from lower-level labor to manufacturing and skilled technical positions. These days, the labor market offers many candidates in these occupations, particularly in large-scale start-up or expansion efforts, where thousands of candidates often pursue hundreds of jobs. I've also used it in professional hiring, where screening on the basics, and then on specific skills and abilities, eventually proceeds to more costly interviewing or hands-on simulation assessments.

Finally, senior executive hiring literally demands a multiple-hurdles model. Here, those on the board of directors are seldom willing to overlook poor CEO qualifications in one area because of strengths in another. There's little interest among C-level executives in hiring managers who present weaknesses in areas important to the job. The risks are too great.

In summary, the model is simple, produces strong quality-of-hire results, and is cost efficient. It sounds too good to be true. And it can be, as I explain a bit later.

The alternative, a compensatory approach, takes a different view on candidates (Figure 10.2). Although it too requires that

Figure 10.2 How a compensatory hiring decision works

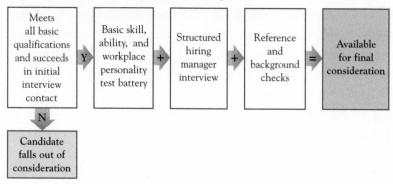

candidates meet the job's basic qualifications, the approach takes all candidates through the full prescreening and assessment process. There are no hurdles. Literally, the process is designed to gain a view of the whole candidate. The logic behind it is that although the competencies assessed are all important, candidates can compensate for weaknesses in one area with strengths in another. Hence, the final hiring decision should roll together a full picture of each candidate as reflected by the overall pattern of performance each displays across all stages of the process.

For jobs where the number of candidates might not be as large and the possibility of balancing weaknesses with strengths has shown itself in the organization's experience, the compensatory model can provide a richer view on each candidate's profile than the multiple-hurdles approach. The multiple-hurdles approach, in a way, doesn't provide a picture of the whole candidate. It offers a series of snapshots, taken up to the point where we don't like what we see. In the compensatory model, though, there are questions: Does the value (that is, the validity) of the additional information collected justify the increased cost in collecting it? And does the concept of compensating competencies really hold?

Hiring often follows this model when legal oversight demands that the employer avoid eliminating certain candidate groups because they fare less well in certain areas. Too, an employer's basic philosophy about the things people are capable of accomplishing, given their individual strengths and weaknesses, can drive a decision to use a compensatory approach. The fact is that if the tools used to collect candidate information are valid, and therefore predictive of future performance, then poorer performance at one hurdle predicts poorer performance on the job. The question, too, is *how much* strength is needed to compensate for a given weakness and whether this offset really happens in the workplace.

There are also hybrid versions of the two basic models. In some settings, assessment of certain competencies might be used as a hurdle, while assessment of other competencies might be treated in a compensatory way. For example, whether candidates possess basic reading and math skills might be a hurdle in hiring skilled trade apprentices. At the same time, measures of candidates' related training, hands-on experience, or job-related hobbies and interests might be handled in a compensatory way because, among these, strong qualifications in one area might offset weaker ones in another.

The nature of the job, the recruiting and hiring tools used, the employer's cost limitations, legal compliance concerns about rejecting candidates for failing at a single step in the process, and the employer's basic philosophy about people all play a role in deciding whether to stress one approach or the other in building a hybrid of the two.

A frequently used hybrid, in fact, is first setting a relatively low hurdle at each step in the process to ensure that those who pass to the next step possess at least a minimum level of the competency measured at that stage; in effect, this is a multiple-hurdles model. Then, given assurance of at least minimum competence and elimination of a relatively small proportion of candidates at each step, those who remain can be viewed from a compensatory point of view. As always, quality-of-hire reviews and internal payoff evaluations can help set the height of the hurdles so the best balance of cost savings and quality-of-hire payoff results.

Setting the Bar

Regardless of whether a multiple-hurdles, compensatory, or hybrid model shapes the decision-making process, there's another choice to make. If you follow a multiple-hurdles approach, how high do you set the bar on each hurdle? If you use a compensatory approach, where do you set the bar after you've combined all the information? If you follow a hybrid approach, with relatively low hurdles at each stage and a final compensatory combination, where do you set *all* these bars?

Setting the bar, or cutoff, as it's often called in the assessment arena, calls on judgment, science, economics, and risk management. Recall Figure 3.4 to explain how validity and payoff link together. Repeated here with some minor additions as Figure 10.3, it shows how increasing the cutoff score, that is, raising the bar, on the candidate qualifications measured by a prescreening or assessment

Figure 10.3 Raising the bar on qualifications raises the level of job performance expected

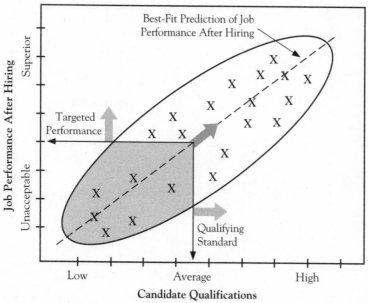

tool links to increasing the level of job performance expected of new hires.

In the illustration, pulling the solid arrow in the center of the figure upward and to the right in effect pulls the bar on the candidate qualifications measure to a higher level (to the right) and, because the two are connected, simultaneously pulls the level of targeted performance upward. In short, if the tool used to prescreen or assess candidate qualifications is valid, then setting a higher candidate qualifications standard as a general rule yields better performance among those hired.

There's another outcome that comes with raising the bar, though. Figure 10.4 repeats the caution that even valid hiring tools produce errors. The illustration shows that setting a candidate qualification cutoff at the point labeled "Qualifying Standard 1" can be expected to produce generally equivalent numbers of false-positive hiring errors (we thought they'd perform up to target per-

Figure 10.4 Raising the bar creates different kinds of errors

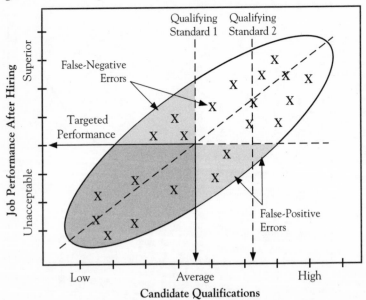

formance levels, but they didn't) and false negative hiring errors (we didn't think they could perform up to targeted performance levels, but we were wrong). If the level of targeted performance we seek in new hires is set as shown in Figure 10.4, then sliding the candidate qualifications bar higher, to "Qualifying Standard 2," changes the mix of errors. Now we make almost no false-positive errors but many more false-negative ones.

If we have surplus candidates and increasing the cutoff has no negative impact from a legal compliance point of view, then raising the bar protects us from false-positive errors, at the expense of rejecting candidates who would have performed to expectations— the false negatives. Of course, if the labor market is tight or if lifting the standard has a negative impact on groups of legal concern, then the increase in false-negative errors also brings the risk of challenge or of not filling the openings at hand. Like everything else, it's a trade-off. While higher might mean better from a performance-based point of view, other factors might set a limit to how far we can go.

Both Figures 10.3 and 10.4 suggest holding the data to make fairly precise decisions about where to set the targeted performance level and, as a result, where to set the bar on measures of candidate qualifications. In many cases, finding hard data to drive this standard isn't easy. The general thinking model that the figures illustrate, though, applies to any qualification measure, whether as basic as years of education or as complex as the judgments produced through a hiring manager interview.

At a technical level, a variety of approaches can help guide the standards-setting process. Readers interested in different ways an employer can go about setting the bar, or cutoff level, can turn to the technical literature,[2] or to more applied advice about rational and statistical approaches available.[3] From a typical practices point of view, though, employers today, particularly those in the private sector, tend to set qualifying standards in ways that boil down research, practice, and vendor studies to a few classic alternatives.

Some alternatives classify candidates in a simple pass-versus-fail manner. Others try to retain more information to drive hiring decisions and seek finer distinctions by grouping candidates into three or four categories. Few approaches rely on literally rank-ordering candidates according to the exact prescreening or assessment results they achieve.

In the public sector, though, civil service rules and merit hiring guidelines often dictate that candidates be rank-ordered on tests, interviews, or other competency measures. In these cases, even tiny differences between candidates can guide the rank-ordering process and the possibility of being hired. It's not unusual, for example, to find twenty thousand candidates taking a test for the job of firefighter or law enforcement officer when only hundreds will be hired. Here, merit hiring rules, designed to keep politics from entering the hiring decision often mean that a one-point difference in test score is the difference between being hired now and waiting until the next test is issued in a few years. As noted, the tools available for assessing candidates typically aren't accurate or reliable enough to make such fine distinctions. As a result, these systems are fraught with challenges, even though they all attempt to do the right thing from a merit-based hiring point of view.

In the private sector, approaches such as a red-yellow-green designation of candidates' assessment results, or even red-green approaches, give prescreening and assessment tools their due. But they avoid decision criteria so finely calibrated that they're unsupportable if challenged or if held to internal reviews as to whether they actually make a difference in quality of hire.

For lower- to midlevel jobs, many employers work to accomplish a simple objective: eliminate candidates whose qualifications predict they *won't* succeed on the job. Recall the Chapter Four example where 20 percent of the employer's truck drivers produced 80 percent of its traffic accidents. That's the concept, and the outcome, targeted in many red-green or red-yellow-green cutoff score strategies: eliminate those whose performance will *cost* the employer, rather than trying to maximize the outcome by hiring only the very best.

The discussion in Chapter Five about high performers' producing more than they're paid to do and low performers' costing an employer to have them around enters the thinking model when setting the bar. At lower levels in the organization, employers typically don't seek perfection by hiring the best. Instead, they work to avoid those who, if hired, will bring downside outcomes to the workplace. The simple illustration shown in Figure 10.5 depicts this approach.

Similar to the models that many of today's assessment vendors follow, Figure 10.5 shows a case where the qualifications bar is set so that approximately 50 percent of candidates are expected to pass the assessment process, having achieved assessments that designate them "green." Another approximately 25 percent, whose assessment results suggest caution in proceeding to a hiring decision, are designated "yellow." Often this group is subject to close review in the

Figure 10.5 A hypothetical approach to "setting the bar" on a qualification standard

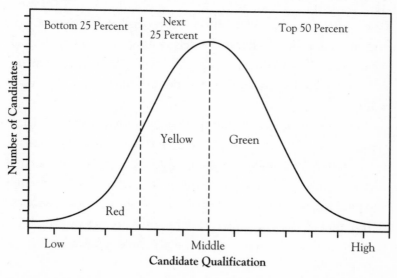

interview, reference, or background checking phases of the process. Finally, approximately 25 percent achieve assessment results that predict unacceptable performance and are "red-lighted" out of the process.

Hiring professionals who are deciding whether those designated as red make up 15, 20, 25, or more percent of the candidate group review the data on which the bar is set, the flow of candidates available, and the risk of legal challenge to the standard from an equal employment opportunity compliance point of view. They follow the same review in determining whether those designated green make up 50, 40, or 30 percent or less of the candidate group.

The point is that drawing payoff from the hiring process need not rely on finely honed use of candidate prescreening and assessment data. Allocating candidates to basic groups and combining the results from multiple tools intelligently is where the payoff rests. And regularly checking the quality of hire that results with tracking and continuous improvement tools remains the touchstone for deciding if the standard needs adjustment.

The Principles at Work

Combining candidate information, setting the bar on qualifications, and creating your own hybrid models all involve thinking through what you really seek in new hires. All involve balancing what you see as the ideal with what you can afford or the level of risk you're willing to take.

Many of the questions that spill out as you think through these topics have been asked before. In fact, assessment specialists' research and field study provide guidance about what works and what to expect. As in any other general guidance from research and practice, though, the ability to generalize to a broader application is tied to the circumstances where the studies on which it's based were done. Hence, the general principles that result are just that: general.

I'll review a few of them here, but I offer the caution that all employers need to look at the circumstances in which they operate to decide whether each generality fits. With that, here are some basics.

First, all else being equal, a multiple-hurdles-like approach produces the best-qualified candidates—those who will perform best in the long run. The approach requires that candidates measure up at every step in the prescreening and assessment process. Here, there's no need to decide on, and possibly make a mistake about, the degree to which a weakness in one competency can be offset by strengths in another. Although it's more mechanical, the approach also introduces a greater degree of quality assurance.

Second, the higher you set the bar on each hurdle, the greater is the payoff in hiring decisions that result. Recall the payoff modeling formula from Chapters Five and Nine. Although the validity of the tools for assessing competencies drives the formula, the *selection ratio*, that is, the percentage of candidates actually hired, also makes a big impact on the result. All else being equal, the higher the bar is set, the lower the ratio of candidates who will be selected, and the higher will be the payoff.

But if the cost of the assessment process that drives decisions is so high it offsets this principle, then you need to reconsider. It typically isn't. Too, the labor market might not permit selectivity beyond a given level. Both possibilities can limit an employer from installing a highly selective approach to candidate screening. Of course, you might turn attention to whether an upward adjustment in compensation levels will produce more candidates who can be screened more selectively and, once hired, will perform at levels that offset the increased compensation costs. After all, it's a system, and there are lots of ways to meet the targeted output.

Third, if you use a compensatory approach, research argues against complex strategies for weighting different categories of information about candidate competencies. I once developed a prescreening and assessment process for hiring automotive design engineers. The client wanted to follow a compensatory model that started by weighting each of the job's competencies in terms of its importance, dividing 100 points among the various competencies. Then precise scores on each assessment tool were multiplied by the weight of the competency each measured. The resulting weighted composites were summed and candidates were rank-ordered on the overall sum of the weighted composite scores.

True, some competencies might be more important to success, and no one should ignore this. Research shows, however, that a relatively simple combination of the information gathered for various competencies predicts future performance as well as more engineered solutions. Highly complex strategies for combining assessment information can offer the illusion of accuracy and reliability, but today's measurement tools typically can't support the illusion.

Fourth, if the tools used are those on which minority or other groups who are protected by equal employment opportunity statutes fare less well, a multiple-hurdles approach has the greatest negative impact on the groups' chances of being hired. In addition, the higher the bar is set at each stage of the process, the greater the negative impact on these groups will be. Hence, if you use screening and assessment tools on which minority or other groups fare less well, the outcome of higher standards will be a higher negative impact on these groups. Enter risk management.

This is why the types of monitoring and self-review steps set out in earlier chapters apply to tracking the way we make final hiring decisions. It's always a balance. Watching the way the process of combining candidate information works, tracking the results it produces, and focusing on equal employment opportunity compliance all play a role in showing that the decision strategy is working as planned or that it needs refinement. This is where applicant tracking technology can offer much benefit. Tracking the results of cutoff levels, viewing their impact on various candidate groups, and exploring what-if scenarios that make alternations in the system's decision rules can pay major benefits from a risk management point of view. They can identify ways to increase the system's payoff as well.

Is There Anything We Missed?

So far, the models I've reviewed here for reaching a final hiring decision have shared a common idea: more is better—or, at a minimum, more is better up to a point. Then enough is enough. More education, training, and experience increase the chances that a candidate can make it over the basic qualifications hurdles. More matches in candidate prescreens that tap the individual's willingness to accept working conditions, compensation, and travel or relocation requirements improve the chance of further consideration. More favorable performance on tests, interviews, or work simulations improves the chance of making it to the final cut. More favorable references, background check results, or internal referral recommendations improve the chance of being hired. At each stage, possessing *more* of the qualities assessed improves the likelihood of winning at the final hiring decision.

There's one area, though, where the more-is-better concept doesn't hold, and it's an area worth attention in making the final hiring decision. In many cases, it's important enough to consider as part of assessing candidates during the screening process. I have touched on it in previous chapters as relevant in the process of trying to fill supervisory and leadership positions, where a noteworthy part of the job rests in building commitment among those who'll report to the new hire. It holds too for positions where creating and managing relationships with others is key to success: jobs in sales, account management, client retention, and other relationship-intense positions.

As I mentioned in Chapter One, research and practice show that some information about a candidate follows a more-is-worse model. More mischievousness, skepticism, excitability, or other counterproductive personality attributes is worse. Making a final hiring decision represents an employer's last chance to look at this information and add greater risk management to the final decision.

First, some background. For years, research has shown that a surprisingly high percentage of those hired to leadership positions fail within a relatively short time after taking the job. The findings cover jobs ranging from first-level supervisors to CEOs. Although the numbers vary, trends indicate that *at least* half of those who take these roles fail within two to three years of assuming the job. Some researchers place the number at two-thirds. Both academic and company-based research support the trend.[4] The reasons for failure include an inability to establish and maintain effective relationships with others, particularly those in subordinate roles.

Related research by one of the world's leading best practices companies, the Corporate Executive Board, shows that employee engagement drives effort, performance, and retention in the workforce.[5] The research shows that engagement depends, among other things, on the way supervisors and higher-level leaders behave when they interact with subordinates and on how they make presentations, make individual decisions about people, and award achievements. These behaviors, particularly those that relate to individual interactions with subordinates, do much to determine engagement among the leader's followers. Often they help write the obituary of the leader as he or she departs the organization.

A wealth of research, writings, and prescriptive advice from leadership coaches addresses the steps employers can take to evaluate their leaders, identify weaknesses, and lay a course for internal development.[6] This work, though, focuses on solving, rather than avoiding, such problems. It deals with ideas for "fixing" leaders who have gone astray, alienated themselves, or failed to live up to expectations in their own performance.

Some of the more interesting writings take an evolutionary view on the topic, hypothesizing that we humans evolved to sometimes expect certain things of our leaders and sometimes not. Some suggest that times of uncertainty, fear, and risk are when followers seek out leaders and accept the direction, assurances, and bad behavior they offer. In good times, we're less likely to seek out leadership and less likely to accept the direction and control that naturally follows. In effect, we become less willing to suffer the behaviors that typically come with leaders.[7]

Here, though, our interest doesn't rest in remediation; it rests in prevention. It involves understanding what we can do in assessing candidates for supervisory, higher-level leadership, or relationship-intense jobs to decide whether they might bring the risk of derailment and the likelihood of building little engagement among those they direct. It rests in seeking tools for exploring the concept that for some attributes, more is worse.

Dotlich and Cairo, in *Why CEOs Fail*, profiled eleven dimensions and associated behaviors that other researchers also have found to define a more-is-worse list of leadership derailers. Although different consultants and assessment specialists use different names to label the attributes, the eleven chapters in the Dotlich and Cairo book capture the ideas well, as shown in Table 10.1.

Wait a minute, you might say, *this sounds like personality*. It is. By most definitions, *personality* amounts to an inclination or tendency to behave in a certain way in certain situations. The attributes listed in Table 10.1, simply put, are dimensions of work-related personality. They describe the ways that leaders—supervisors through CEOs—who *possess more* of each attribute are likely to behave on the job, particularly when faced with stress, uncertainty, or an assignment that's new to them. More of these attributes is *not* better.

These eleven constructs are ways of behaving. They represent behaviors that individuals learn (or get away with) over time. They are things that, with time, become standard ways of dealing with pressure, stress, or even normal day-to-day challenges on the job. Each of the characteristics can be found to a greater or lesser degree in most people. We've all learned, and been reinforced in,

Table 10.1 Dark Side Characteristics

What It's Called	How Those with the Characteristic Behave on the Job
Arrogance	Assumes that he or she is right, and everybody else is wrong
Melodrama	Always grabs the center of attention
Volatility	Has sudden and unpredictable mood shifts
Excessive caution	Rarely willing to make decisions
Habitual distrust	Focuses on the negatives
Aloofness	Disengages and disconnects
Mischievousness	Views rules as only suggestions
Eccentricity	Wants to be different just for the sake of it
Passive resistance	Remains silent, which others misinterpret as agreement
Perfectionism	Gets the little things right while the big things go wrong
Eagerness to please	Wants to win any popularity contest

Source: Dotlich, D. L., & Cairo, P. C. (2003). *Why CEOs fail: The eleven behaviors that can derail your climb to the top—and how to manage them.* San Francisco: Jossey-Bass. Copyright © 2003 Jossey-Bass. Used with permission.

behaviors that help us cope with certain situations. We tend to rely on these scenarios as the default way to behave when we face a challenge.

These strategies define a side of personality—the dark side. Unlike bright side attributes such as conscientiousness, emotional stability, and sociability, where more is better, dark side attributes define the more-is-worse side of personality. A number of tools claim to help in looking at candidates' dark side inclinations. Based on my review and experience using it, I believe the Hogan Development Survey (HDS) offers one of the best-structured approaches to assessing dark side tendencies. I've used it with leadership positions and with jobs where creating and maintaining interpersonal relationships is key.[8] The tool, completed by a candidate in self-report fashion, has been shown to correlate with the views others provide when, for example, given the opportunity to use 360-degree or other feedback mechanisms to evaluate a leader's on-the-job behavior. The HDS uses a titling scheme somewhat different from the Dotlich and Cairo scheme but addresses the same attributes (Table 10.2).

Table 10.2 Equating the Language of Dotlich and Cairo (2003) with That of the Hogan Development Survey

Dotlich and Cairo	How This Behavior Looks on the Job	HDS Terminology
Arrogance	Assumes that he or she is right, and everybody else is wrong	Bold
Melodrama	Always grabs the center of attention	Colorful
Volatility	Has sudden and unpredictable mood shifts	Excitable
Excessive Caution	Rarely willing to make decisions	Cautious
Habitual Distrust	Focuses on the negatives	Skeptical
Aloofness	Disengages and disconnects	Reserved
Mischievousness	Views rules as only suggestions	Mischievous
Eccentricity	Wants to be different just for the sake of it	Imaginative
Passive Resistance	Remains silent, which others misinterpret as agreement	Leisurely
Perfectionism	Gets the little things right while the big things go wrong	Diligent
Eagerness to Please	Wants to win any popularity contest	Dutiful

Source: Dotlich, D. L., & Cairo, P. C. (2003). *Why CEOs fail: The eleven behaviors that can derail your climb to the top—and how to manage them.* San Francisco: Jossey-Bass. Copyright © 2003 Jossey-Bass. Used with permission. Hogan, R., & Hogan, J. (2009). *Hogan development survey manual* (2nd ed.). Tulsa, OK: Hogan Assessment Systems. Used with permission.

I've used the tool, along with two other Hogan Assessment Systems tools, the Hogan Personality Inventory (HPI), a measure of bright side personality factors, and the Hogan Business Reasoning Inventory (HBRI), a measure of strategic and tactical reasoning skills, to produce a model for assessing candidates for supervisory, managerial, and executive positions. Captured in Table 10.3, the

Table 10.3 Model Characteristics for Evaluating Leaders

Intellectual Horsepower[a]	Bright Side Attributes[b]	Dark Side Attributes
Tactical reasoning	Outgoing nature	Excitability
Strategic reasoning	Agreeableness	Skepticism
Critical thinking	Conscientiousness	Cautiousness
Specific knowledge	Emotional stability	Reservation
	Openness to ideas	Leisurely
		Bold
		Mischievousness
		Colorful
		Imaginative
		Diligence
		Dutifulness

[a]Generally straightforward to assess. Not typically the challenge to leadership effectiveness.
[b]A generally high base rate at the leader level. Not typically the challenge.

model looks to both personality and critical-thinking skills and, of course, is supported by information collected through background reviews, interviews, references, and information such as internal 360-degree assessments.

As Table 10.3 shows in the notations for the HBRI and HPI segments of the model, these tools measure attributes that are relatively straightforward to assess. As one climbs the organizational hierarchy to the C-level, these become attributes that most candidates possess at the levels needed, having been screened on them repeatedly as they climbed through progressively higher levels in the organization. It's the HDS-measured attributes—dark side personality dimensions—that often provide the most telling assessment of candidates at these levels and, at times, at supervisory levels.

At progressively higher levels in the organization, individuals have more latitude, and they often get away with the kinds of behaviors the HDS predicts. Their position power permits it. In assessing management groups as small as fifteen to twenty people, I've often found individuals' HDS profiles ranging from the absolute bottom to the very top on each dimension. In short, little appears to have been done to screen out individuals with exceptionally high-risk profiles on these measures. Perhaps that helps explain the 50 percent failure rate of executives.

It's the folding in of candidate information from tools like the HDS that can add information to the final decision from a new, more-is-worse perspective. This information can help expand the picture of a candidate who is otherwise highly qualified but brings the risk of being a leader whose day-to-day behavior is likely to derail him or her. Whether these types of tools are placed at this final stage in the hiring process or integrated with other tools as part of all candidates' assessments, hiring decisions can take into account this additional perspective in ways that reduce risk.

The fast-emerging use of these tools in leadership assessment certainly will produce more data to help decide their true value. For example, the leadership candidate profiled in Figure 10.6 is

Figure 10.6 An HDS profile with dark side risks

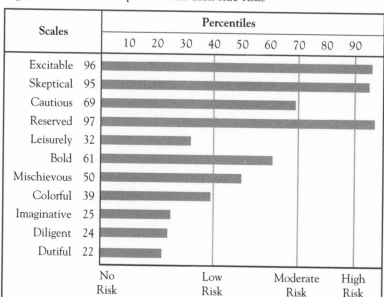

unlikely to build engagement among those on whom *her* success depends.

Well above the cutoffs recommended as evidence of high risk by the HDS for the dark side dimensions of excitable (volatility), skeptical (habitual distrust), and reserved (aloofness), the profile indicates a candidate whose inclinations are to work against rather than with those who report to her. The risk of derailment reflected in these scores can help inform a final hiring decision by calling for a deeper level of reference checking, a request for 360-degree feedback information from the candidate's previous jobs if available, and a deeper level of one-on-one interviewing. After all, this can be the last chance to make the right decision and reduce risk. The higher level the job is, the more the investment of time and energy is warranted when a profile similar to the example is found.

Of all the areas in the field of assessment and candidate screening, this is the newest and most intriguing. We've known for many years that intellect and personality are relatively independent. Smart people aren't necessarily personable, and personally unappealing people aren't necessarily dumb. Exploration of dark side dimensions, particularly in a hiring context, though, is fast evolving and showing evidence of adding to the validity of hiring systems that have heretofore ignored these traits.

The Value in Consistency

The final hiring decision is driven by where we set the bars on all the information and assessments we collect, from prescreening on basic qualifications to final reference checking or dark side reviews. It's also driven by how we combine the information we collect, by whether we adopt a straightforward multiple-hurdles model, a compensatory one or a hybrid approach. Finally, once all the data are in hand, the decision is also driven by the considerations reviewed in the next chapter: legal ones.

As a bridge to legal considerations in how to make hiring decisions, one factor is tied closely to the topics reviewed in this chapter. It's the matter of how to build consistency into hiring decisions. I've introduced various decision-making models in the abstract to illustrate the thinking that they reflect. A survey would likely show that most employers don't follow any of the strategies in their purest forms. The models I review in this book help guide how to think about making decisions and how to help guide all the hiring managers who participate in the process. But they don't dictate. Individual circumstances in each hiring assignment influence how decisions are made too.

It's important to think about the topic of cutoffs, information-combining models, and final decision criteria from a consistency point of view. Many of the legal actions I've been involved in had nothing to do with the tools, standards, or decision criteria on the table. The questions driving the legal review were: Why was the process used *inconsistently*? Why were different candidates treated *differently*?

Consistency is central in risk reduction. For example, if we set a cutoff on a competency assessment or basic qualification and later lower it for a given candidate, *the new cutoff* is now the level associated with that exception. If we follow a multiple-hurdles model but make an exception on one of the hurdles for a given candidate, then the exception defines *our new practice*. As we'll see in the next chapter, disparate treatment, that is, treating people differently, is a pathway to problems.

Of course, there are special circumstances. Things happen in the hiring process that couldn't have been predicted in advance. The caution, though, rests in having a clear set of tactics in mind at the outset, sticking to them in making final decisions, and, when absolutely necessary, documenting the hell out of any exceptions you are forced to make. Inconsistency is the Achilles heel in hiring. The next chapter makes this abundantly clear. In fact, be sure to review it before making that final million-dollar decision.

CHAPTER ELEVEN

NAVIGATING THE LEGAL PITFALLS

'm not an attorney. But I've been an expert witness in matters dealing with claims of ethnic, gender, and even reverse discrimination in recruiting and hiring practices for about two decades. Working with both plaintiffs and defendants, on the side of both federal agencies and private employers, I've seen challenges to virtually every aspect of a recruiting and hiring program. Some of the cases have involved tens of thousands of candidates and tens of millions of dollars in claims.

In writing this chapter, though, I've drawn on the big brain and experience of a senior attorney in labor and employment law, Jeffrey Ross. Jeff is a Partner with Seyfarth Shaw LLP, a firm with one of the most respected employment law practices in the United States. A few years back, we developed HireCompliance, an employment practices auditing tool used to guide those engaged in risk-reduction planning when creating or reviewing an organization's hiring strategy, tactics, and day-to-day practices. In the process, I experienced firsthand Jeff's knowledge about what can go wrong in choosing between the people we hire and those we don't.

Jeff helped create this straightforward, practical review of the legal compliance concerns employers face in their recruiting and hiring programs.

Dealing with the risks reviewed in this chapter can be tough. The main thing is to approach employment risk in the same way you do risk in every other area of the enterprise. Having worked with many companies under legal scrutiny, I've learned to blend risk reduction with fear reduction.

Some Background on the Legal Risks

Making mistakes in a recruiting and hiring program can result in costs to defend the challenge, judgments if you lose, bad press, and maybe even the loss of business. These all are things a CEO doesn't want to happen.

Nearly ten years ago, Jim Sharf and I authored a chapter, "Employment Risk Management," in which we covered a good deal of the legislative history, enforcement mechanisms, and court decisions underlying the legal side of recruiting and hiring.[1] We also profiled some of the most noteworthy actions taken against employers by either federal agencies or private plaintiffs and pointed out the level of financial consequences associated with adverse court decisions or company settlements. I'll note here some of the basic history that's necessary for those uninitiated into the field but won't repeat the details of the previous work.

As Jim and I noted in 2000, in recruiting and hiring, the most typical legal risks are those that come in the context of equal employment opportunity. Federal and state laws, reporting requirements, and a variety of government agencies all oversee the way organizations hire people. In fact, most employers are called on to report their hiring actions in regular updates to federal and state agencies. The government also oversees businesses that hold government contracts and face additional regulation and reporting requirements.

Let me be clear: the purpose of recruiting and hiring is to discriminate—discriminate between candidates who *can do* the job and those who *can't* and between those who *will do* the job and those who *won't*. The purpose is to discriminate among candidates in a way that captures the talent the business needs, builds the performance that keeps it competitive, and produces the payoff required to remain stable and secure as an organization.

But the purpose of a recruiting and hiring program is not to discriminate among candidates on characteristics that have nothing to do with how they'll perform the job. Certainly the purpose is not to discriminate on attributes where the laws of our country draw the line: race, color, religion, gender, age, national origin, disability, veteran status, and other factors cited in federal laws and executive orders, state laws, and local statutes.

The world of recruiting and hiring is complex from the very beginning. For example, illegal discrimination might result from actions taken intentionally, but it can happen unintentionally too. And even if it is unintentional, it can bring major consequences, financial and otherwise. The laws dealing with equal employment opportunity spell out the groups of candidates protected by specific statutes.

For example, Title VII of the Civil Rights Act of 1964 prohibits employment discrimination on the basis of race, color, religion, gender, and national origin. As shorthand, we often refer to candidate groups referenced by these statutes as "protected groups." With challenges also taking on claims of reverse discrimination, though, the concept of protection is not unique to minorities, women, or those of certain national origins. This, when paired with the difference between discriminating legally versus illegally among candidates, is what brings complexity to the process.

The sources of a challenge can be complex too. Employers face the risk that candidates will claim that they were treated differently from other individuals when they sought a job—that they suffered what's referred to as *disparate treatment*.

Consider an employer who interviews candidates as part of the screening process, but in a way where the format, content, or overall approach to the interview is unstructured. In such a system, it's not difficult for a candidate to claim that he was treated differently from other candidates because the interviewer followed a series of questions that were not documented, potentially not related to the job, and resulted in the candidate's being rejected, at least in the challenge, because he suffered disparate treatment. The candidate may claim that the different treatment was a result of his (fill in the blank) status.

There's also risk that *groups* of candidates will claim they've been affected differently in the hiring process from other groups and that they've suffered disparate impact sometimes referred to as *adverse impact*.[2] In the latter case, employers can face class action lawsuits, with potentially thousands of candidates assembled into a plaintiff group, or class.

I noted in Chapter Two that many of the statutes, regulations, and enforcement agencies dealing with recruitment and hiring practices are connected to Title VII of the Civil Rights Act of 1964, amended in 1991.[3] Some also are linked to the Americans with Disabilities Act (ADA) of 1990, amended in 2008 (the ADAA),[4] and the Age Discrimination in Employment Act.[5] Through executive order 11246, issued in 1965, the U.S. Department of Labor also has the authority to review the employment practices of federal contractors and those who do business with federal contractors.[6] Other federal, state, and local statutes also can bring challenges, but the ones cited here cover most of the issues that employers face.

Very few organizations fall outside the coverage of these statutes. For example, oversight rests with the U.S. Department of Justice if the employer is a unit of government, the Equal Employment Opportunity Commission (EEOC) if the employer is in the private sector with more than fifteen employees, and the U.S. Department of Labor's Office of Federal Contract Compliance Programs (OFCCP) if the employer is a federal contractor holding a contract of $10,000 or more or does business with a company that does.

During federal fiscal year 2007, for example, the EEOC reported over eighty-three thousand charges filed against private sector employers, the highest number since 1992. During the same year, the agency collected monetary relief from employers amounting to $345 million, up over 25 percent from the previous year.[7]

In March 2008, the OFCCP issued approximately five thousand corporate scheduling announcement letters. These are notices that the employer can expect a review of its employment practices by the agency. They kick off new compliance evaluations for companies with government contracts. During federal fiscal year 2008, the OFCCP completed over four thousand compliance evaluations and collected over $67 million in remedies from employers; this was up more than 30 percent from the approximately $50 million in remedies of the two preceding years.[8]

But contrary to what many believe, the risk of a challenge to recruiting or hiring practices is far more likely to come from a private plaintiff than a government agency. As Jim Sharf and I pointed out in 2000, employers were four hundred times more likely to be sued by private plaintiffs' attorneys than by the EEOC when one reviewed the real trends in employment litigation.[9]

In private plaintiff litigation everything changes. Different statutes are involved than in matters brought by governmental agencies; statutes such as the Civil Rights Act of 1866. In addition, private lawsuits are brought where the predominant numbers of claims are made under common law tort theories rather than under federal equal employment opportunity statutes. And in many of these cases, private plaintiff counsel can present the case to a jury, seek uncapped compensatory and punitive damages, and even get attorneys' fees for bringing the case.

Fortunately, the decades of agency challenges, private litigation, and courtroom decisions have laid out road maps to help reduce the risks of legal challenge. As I noted in Chapter Seven, the best time to begin covering the risk is when you are framing an overall recruiting and hiring strategy and assembling the package used in implementing the strategy. It's Risk Reduction 101: reviewing best practices, planning, monitoring, and pursuing continuous improvement. But things still can go wrong.

Where Things Can Go Wrong

I've seen things go wrong in recruiting and hiring programs in four major ways: in what those recruiting and hiring use to guide employment practices, how they use it, the results produced, and what they might have done. I'll review each general area and provide some examples of techniques likely to reduce the risk profile.

First, challenges to what recruiters use in executing a recruiting and hiring process are broad. They can involve the types of candidate information collected, as well as the tools, standards, and day-to-day practices applied in deciding which candidates to hire. Here are some of challenges I've encountered:

- Sourcing failed to reach out to minority candidates.

- Experience and education standards were set too high.

- Prescreening interviewers were inconsistent in standards.

- Résumé reviews were inconsistent and biased.

- Tests measured abilities unrelated to the job.

- Interviewers rejected candidates for skills that they would learn in training after they were hired.

- Physical ability assessment set standards too demanding.

- Reference checking was inconsistent and subjective.

- Personality tests were used as ADA-prohibited assessments.

- Background checks covered facts unrelated to the job.

Challenges can deal with the techniques for recruiting and sourcing candidates, the timing of the information collection, and the platforms used to frame the recruiting process. They can reach into the nature of job posting platforms used to get the word out, prescreening questionnaires used to capture information from those interested in a position, tests or interview protocols used, or even techniques used to execute and store keyword or conceptual search routines on a set of candidate résumés. It's a broad category.

Preparing for and limiting challenges to what you use involves showing that the practices are *job related*. Think about the figures used in Chapter Two to illustrate the concept of validity. Validity, in effect, is what job relatedness means. If an employer can show that the tools, techniques, and practices it uses are effective in forecasting who will be the better and poorer performers on the job, then the standard of job relatedness is met. A variety of governmental and professional guidelines will help employers show that their recruiting and hiring tactics meet this requirement.[10]

Importantly, making sure what you use is job related not only reduces the risk of legal challenge; it's the formula for gaining a payoff as well. Use a valid set of tactics, and the risk goes down while the payoff goes up. If there's one important message in this chapter, there it is.

A second source of challenge can come from how you use the information that the recruiting and hiring program produces. Here are some examples of challenges to how programs are used:

- Qualifying standards set above the level of current employees

- A single qualification of minor importance used to exclude candidates

- Cutoff scores on tests indexed to unknown standards

- No opportunity for candidates to retest

- Work sample assessment based on tasks not performed on the job

- No accommodation permitted for candidates with disabilities

- Interviewers untrained and no structure provided

- Candidates rank-ordered with no showing of validity

The examples deal with choices employers make in setting up the tactics of a program. How qualifying standards are set; how different pieces of candidate qualifying information are weighted and combined; whether candidates are required to pass a series of qualifying steps, with some rejected at each successive stage in the process (a multiple hurdles approach) versus having an opportunity to compete in all stages of the process (a compensatory approach): all can result in a challenge that how the information was used produced illegal discrimination.

In addition, if candidates are evaluated on several screening devices, are they rank-ordered from highest to lowest in some fashion, or is a single pass-fail standard applied, with everyone above the standard considered qualified? Is the process highly mathematically driven, or does judgment play the major role? All of these method-of-use tactics are potential points of challenge.

Reducing risk in *how* you use the information produced by *what* you use also rests in the job relatedness of each step in the process. The more you can show with outcome-related data that using a given practice, in a given way, identifies better-performing employees, the lower the risk is of a successful challenge to the practice.

Also, the broader the range of training, past experience, skill, ability, and other information that's used to guide hiring decisions, the lower the risk is. In effect, the better the demonstration that all of the job's important requirements were considered, with valid tools, the better the job-relatedness argument is that your company can put forward to answer a challenge.

The more a how-you-use-it strategy acknowledges that no single piece of candidate information is perfect, and the closer the how-you-use-it strategy comes to evaluating the whole candidate, the lower the risk is that your company will be challenged for having relied too heavily on a single piece of information. Like an investment decision, ask yourself: Does the information I have in hand really support the kind of decision I'm about to make? Have I assembled enough information to be confident I've seen the whole candidate?

A third source of challenge relates to the results produced by what you use and how you use it. In fact, this is a major issue where challenges from groups of candidates—ones of disparate impact—typically begin. Here, attention shifts from what you use and how you use it, to the results the practice actually produces from an equal employment opportunity point of view. Attention turns to whether the practices result in considering further, or in hiring, proportionately fewer candidates of a particular group (women, African Americans, Hispanics, and so on) than is the case for other groups.

The question is whether a given practice passes a given protected group on to further stages in the recruiting and hiring process at a lower rate than the rate at which the group applied; whether it results in making employment offers at a lower rate; or whether it results in hiring proportionately fewer candidates than the group's representation in the labor market or candidate pool would lead one to expect. That's a mouthful, but each part of the sentence is a potential source of challenge. Here, challenges typically are couched in numbers: percentages, proportions, expected hiring rates, and shortfalls, for example.

A challenge can begin when the percentage of those from a given candidate group who qualify at various steps in the hiring process or are ultimately hired is compared to the group's relative representation in the relevant labor market, whether local, regional, or national. It also might spring from the number of the group who entered the overall recruiting and hiring process if the number of candidates considered is relatively large—say, dozens or more. Such comparisons might be made for a given hiring event. They also might be made for a given period of time, like quarterly or annually, or they might be made for a given unit of the organization.

Employers, compliance agencies, and private plaintiff attorneys track results using a variety of statistical ways to evaluate whether a given practice has produced a problem. One frequently used approach, titled the 80 percent rule in federal agencies' Uniform Guidelines on Employee Selection Procedures, compares the success rate of a given protected group (say, female candidates) to the success rate of the contrasting group (male candidates).[11] Success might mean "passing" a résumé screen, succeeding in a prescreening interview, meeting standards in a background questionnaire, or performing acceptably on an employment test, interview, or reference check.

If the rate at which the protected group succeeds is less than 80 percent of the rate at which the comparison group succeeds, then there is said to be evidence that the practice has produced an adverse (or disparate) impact on the protected group. For example, if 80 percent of male candidates but only 60 percent of female candidates pass a résumé review pass, then an adverse impact ratio of 60 divided by 80, or .75, shows that the success rate for females is less than 80 percent that of males. The result can be considered as reflecting prima facie evidence of discrimination against female candidates through either *what you used* or *how you used it*. There are other statistical approaches, but they all operate on the same kind of thinking: a lower rate of success for a protected group raises alarms, and a significantly lower rate means trouble unless a good reason—job relatedness—can be offered to explain the outcome.[12]

If the outcome of a recruiting and hiring practice produces adverse impact, it's critical to track down the source. So monitoring every part of the process for evidence of adverse impact is important. In 1982, the U.S. Supreme Court made it clear in its *Connecticut* v. *Teal* decision that concerns about adverse impact rest not only with the question of who is hired versus rejected.[13] They rest with whether any given step in the overall recruiting and hiring process has had a disparate impact on a group protected by statute. If it has, then the employer is obligated to show that the step is job related and defensible in light of the job's requirements.

For example, even if, say, male and female candidates are ultimately hired at similar rates, the fact that females were rejected at rates producing an 80 percent rule problem at one stage in the hiring process can be the source of a challenge. In short, hitting the bottom line from a compliance point of view is not enough if one step in the process produces an adverse impact that can't be supported as job related.

Fourth in the list of potential sources of challenge, and related to all three of the preceding ones, is the possibility that although an employer has paid close attention to job relatedness and its method of using a given practice, there might be a challenge that *an equally valid but less adverse alternative* exists that could have produced less adverse impact on protected groups while still producing sound hiring decisions.

These challenges can be tough to rebut. Obviously there might be many alternatives to what the employer has done, each differing from the employer's practices in many ways. How is an employer supposed to examine all possible alternatives and identify the one that is both job related and produces the least adverse impact? It sounds like an impossible mission.

Fortunately, it's the challenging party who needs to pose the alternative practice, along with evidence that it's equally valid and less adverse in its impact on the challenging group. It's also fortunate that much has been learned over the past several decades about the kinds of practices that produce various levels of adverse impact and different levels of validity. Chapters Eight through Ten covered a good deal of this learning and discussed how different recruiting and hiring practices affect payoff. They also underscored the need to build these ideas into the strategy and tactics that guide hiring in a given setting.

Of course, the four general sources for a challenge are interconnected. It's not unusual for a challenge under Title VII of the Civil Rights Act to follow a model of shifting burden, as shown in Figure 11.1. The figure shows a recruiting or hiring program, made

Figure 11.1 The shifting burden in defending a Title VII legal challenge to recruiting or hiring practices

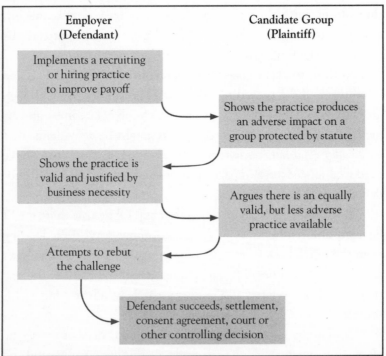

up of a variety of individual tactics, that the employer implemented to guide the overall hiring process. On review, though, perhaps because a candidate filed a complaint, an audit by the OFCCP, an investigation by the DOJ, or a private plaintiff charge, one or more of the practices is found to produce an adverse impact on a given group of candidates.

If so, the burden bounces back to the employer to rebut the evidence of adverse impact by arguing that it's not sufficiently noteworthy to make a prima facie case of discrimination or that the recruiting and hiring practice that produced it is job related. The more this rebuttal is driven by hard data, the better. Sometimes data are available to show the practice's job relatedness for the employer. Sometimes an argument can be made that the same practice has shown validity in a similar employment setting. Sometimes an argument can be made that much research has shown the practice to provide evidence of job relatedness that generalizes across many settings.

Finally, it might be argued that so few candidates have been screened that it's not even feasible to review the practice's job relatedness, but that such a study is under way. There are many bases on which to argue in support of, or to challenge, the job relatedness of a given practice, but such a showing is necessary to justify the fact that the practice has produced an adverse impact on a group protected by statute.

If evidence of job relatedness can be demonstrated, the employer may continue to use the practice. The adverse impact produced by the practice is not in itself illegal. The courts have held that evidence of job relatedness results in the employer's being found to comply with the law. If not, the employer might be found to have violated the statute under which the challenge was brought, and that decision can carry a host of results, ranging from financial penalties, to mandates to hire specific numbers of the protected group, to multiyear oversight of the employer's practices by the court or an outside agent. I was involved as an outside expert in monitoring an employer's hiring practices for more than fifteen years following such a finding. Then the job was taken over by yet another expert when I decided to move on.

If the challenging party can show, despite the fact that the employer's practices are job related, that its what-you-do or how-you-do-it tactics have produced a greater level of adverse impact than necessary, the practice still can be found at fault (see Figure 11.1). This takes us to the realm of expert witnesses, technical studies, and negotiation. This possibility underscores the need to think about legal compliance at the time a recruiting and hiring strategy is formed and when the tactics for implementing it are being assembled. It underscores the need to stay aware of approaches, tools, oversight agency initiatives, and court decisions that help define the level of risk in any initiative.

If this challenge can be rebutted, then Figure 11.1 shows that the employer has survived the challenge. If the employer was unsuccessful at this or earlier stages in the shifting-burden process, the consequences previously discussed are likely to follow.

We can overlay these four major areas of challenge on the recruiting and hiring funnel navigated through the previous chapters. At each stage, there can be challenges. The conversation can quickly explode into hundreds of "yes, but what if" possibilities. That's why I next take a very telegraphic approach to communicate the best guidance I can give in executing each stage in the hiring funnel. The purpose isn't to answer every question; it's to trigger the most important elements of risk-reduction thinking. (For those interested in more detail, visit www.million-dollarhire.com and scan the HireCompliance guidelines Jeff Ross and I created to help guide employers in each of the following areas.)

Reducing Risk at the Sourcing and Prescreening Stages

From a payoff point of view, the major objectives at this initial stage in the process are to make sure sufficient numbers of qualified candidates are attracted and that clearly unqualified individuals don't consume time and resources. From a compliance point of view, this stage involves avoiding practices that might fail to attract, or that eliminate prematurely, protected group members from joining the candidate pool or being minimally qualified so as to join the applicant pool. Practices here should work to ensure the following:

- Information used to communicate the employment opportunity should present an accurate picture of the job, its requirements, and the qualifications that candidates are expected to bring to the process.

- Any minimum qualifications necessary in order for a candidate to be considered an applicant should be linked to the position description for the job and reflect qualifications possessed by those currently holding and performing the job successfully.

- Advertising, job board posting, social media searching, and related candidate sourcing activities should tap venues that offer a diverse group of candidates; employer linkages with targeted minority, gender, disability, or other recruiting agents should be pursued.

- Procedural requirements associated with candidate submissions should be noted, such as time limits or employer policies on accepting general expressions of interest versus submissions for a specific job opening.

- Policies regarding the retention of candidate résumés, applications, and other material should be explained clearly.

- Use of résumé data extraction tools and résumé search technologies should be driven by information supportable as basic job qualifications, and résumé search tools should archive the parameters of each search.

- Screening of résumés or other candidate submissions against basic qualifications in order to identify those who will be considered applicants for the opening should be based on criteria that are clearly job related.

- The makeup of the candidate group should be compared to the company's affirmative action hiring plan (if one exists) and any significant shortfalls reviewed to determine whether possible additional recruiting efforts are needed.

- Candidate tracking tools should be used to analyze any potential adverse impact resulting from basic qualification requirements and prescreening tools, and a decision regarding the need to further supplement the candidate group might be made.

- Any follow-up inquiries or telephone-based prescreening interviews of those expressing interest in the opening should be tracked to document lack of response.

Important in evaluating the results at this initial step in the process are analyses that compare the applicant pool moving forward in the hiring process to the pool of candidates who expressed interest or the relevant labor market ethnic, gender, race, and other makeup. If recruiting extends beyond the local area, broader comparisons, as well as comparisons to goals in the company's affirmative action plan, also are important. If adverse impact is noted, the factors producing it need to be isolated and decisions about their job relatedness made. Reaching out in a targeted manner for additional candidates to avoid adverse impact at this initial stage is not out of the question and helps lay a record of interest in affirmative efforts.

Reducing Risk at the Assessment Stage

Once a preliminary pool of applicants is assembled and screened, attention turns to gaining a deeper view of individual applicants' qualifications. From a payoff point of view, building quality of hire into the process is the objective at this stage. From a compliance point of view, avoiding unwarranted adverse impact is the goal. Practices here should work to ensure that

- Those who participate in the screening process (HR staff, hiring managers, recruitment process outsourcing providers, and others) are trained in the roles they play and aware of actions that might produce potential legal challenge.

- Clear policies and procedures are available to guide answers to applicant questions or complaints about their treatment in the screening process.

- The tools used to evaluate applicant qualifications are grounded in job relatedness and administered in a way that reduces the likelihood of applicant challenge.

- The relative sequencing and weight given to each of the screening tools is reasonable in light of the qualifications that the tool assesses and their relative importance in learning and performing the job.

- Clear criteria are established for any sequential pass-fail decisions made in the screening process.

- Guidance is provided to non-HR staff involved in the screening process in how to avoid events that might subsequently lead to a challenge of disparate treatment or disparate impact.

- The overall set of applicant assessment practices is monitored to determine whether certain aspects of the process appear to produce an unexpected negative effect on protected group members.

- Opportunities are given to applicants who justifiably claim that circumstances such as illness, misunderstood directions, or the absence of appropriate instructions resulted in their not presenting a true picture of their qualifications, along with an opportunity to complete the assessment cycle again.

- All information collected on applicants is captured and tracked, so that any adverse impact associated with the hiring process can be identified and isolated.

- Follow-up steps are taken to monitor aspects of the screening process that, with minor adjustment, might continue to provide value in applicant screening but less adverse impact on protected groups.

Just as in the preceding step, it's important to track and identify any sources of adverse impact that emerge in this stage of the process. Was it a test, interview process, work sample task, reference check, background check, or some other practice that produced an impact? Is sound evidence of the procedure's job relatedness available? Was any adverse impact isolated to a single tool, or was it spread across all the different evaluation tools used in screening candidates? If you used a single tool, are you confident it could withstand a challenge to its job relatedness and to the way it was scored or interpreted? If not, a change is needed.

Reducing Risk at the Decision Stage

Once applicant information is in hand, building a payoff rests in minimizing both false-positive mistakes (hiring candidates who will not succeed) and false-negative mistakes (rejecting candidates who would have been successful). The former bring costs related to poor performance, and the latter produce wasted effort and lost opportunity. The goal is to maximize the number of candidates who will succeed once hired. From a legal compliance point of view, the objective is to avoid practices where the decision-making strategy itself introduces unwarranted adverse impact. Practices here should seek to

- Lay out clear guidelines regarding how information collected during the screening process will be combined, including clarity about any quantitative cutoff scores and data-combining strategies.

- Avoid overweighting any component of the process so that a qualification of relatively minor importance does not carry major decision-making weight.

- Assign weight to those aspects of the screening process where evidence of job relatedness is strongest.

- Determine whether minor changes in qualifying standards might produce noteworthy differences in the adverse impact produced by the process.

- Evaluate the potential for reframing hiring practices in ways that will produce equal validity (payoff) with a lesser degree of adverse impact on protected groups.

- Document the basis for any exceptions made to the standard decision-making strategy.

- Capture and track all screening and decision-making data for use in subsequent payoff analyses and efforts to both improve payoff and reduce any adverse impact.

Rigidity in how hiring decisions are made is not the goal. In fact, using basic quality control approaches to evaluating hiring and rejection decisions against subsequent job performance, along with equal employment opportunity tracking, can point out how relatively minor fine-tuning might help lower the risk of legal challenge and potentially improve payoff.

The key is to avoid locking down a decision strategy and believing that any change is an admission that it was wrong. In fact, the agencies that monitor equal employment opportunity compliance encourage ongoing self-evaluations and adjustments. Fine-tuned improvements are viewed with favor. Such changes theoretically run the potential risk of causing rejected applicants to become claimants, but good-faith changes can minimize the risk of punitive damages and cut off future liability.

It Comes Down to Four Things

All the suggestions covered thus far really boil down to four basic risk-reduction principles:

1. Deal with risk reduction as part of creating the initial strategy and tactics that drive the recruiting and hiring process. If strategy and tactics already are in place, audit them as though you're starting from scratch, identify high-risk elements, and replace them.

2. Focus on the concept embodied in both compliance agency and professional standards and in court decisions: job relatedness. Hold every step in the recruiting and hiring process to the question, Does this step produce candidates, or information about candidates, that results in hiring individuals who perform well on the job? Can I show that this is true?

3. Track outcomes produced by the process in terms of who gets hired and how they perform. In effect, take a quality control and quality improvement perspective that provides information about the *validity* of the overall system. Also, track the system's

results with respect to groups protected by the various legal statutes reviewed.

4. Adjust the system when needed. Risk reduction requires altering the overall recruiting and hiring system to balance risk with payoff. A hiring system that brings substantial adverse impact against groups protected by law carries risk, even if job relatedness can be documented. Steps can be taken to explore how to retain its payoff but reduce its adverse impact. Finally, developing a system that produces no adverse impact but shows no evidence of validity or payoff is a problem too. It's a waste. At a minimum, stop spending money to administer it.

Every other area in an enterprise balances risk and payoff. Recruiting and hiring are no different, and no single approach is bullet-proof. Drawing on employment law expertise in reviewing a new or ongoing program comes at a cost, but so does paying for an annual financial audit. Gaining a professional review or audit from an individual experienced in employment law can lower risk. If you're of a technical bent, the costs can be plugged into the payoff model shown in Chapter Five, and the model can be used to determine how quickly the costs will amortize themselves as new, better-performing employees join the organization.

You Can Do It Without Being Afraid

Maybe you're tempted to throw up your hands and decide you don't want to deal with all the risks of legal challenge reviewed in this chapter. Your thinking might be to keep it simple, avoid complexity, not review candidates too closely, and always err on the side of caution.

But even this approach doesn't guarantee you won't be challenged. I recently reviewed a matter where the employer used practices that produced an adverse impact ratio of .95. There was no evidence of adverse impact by the 80 percent rule and no prima facie case of discrimination. On review, the validation evidence was sound, and the candidate lodging the complaint had actually passed the step that fell under legal compliance review by outside parties. The outside party challenge continues. An employer can draw numbers out of a hat and still be challenged.

You will be better off to lay out a strategy, do your homework, learn from others, and track your results. In the process, the level of payoff I reviewed in earlier chapters will pay many times over for the periodic challenge and the regular review and audit of the practices. It's no different from the level of risk management taken in the audit and finance area, the IT area, or, if you're a public company, the investor relations department. And the payoff from making better million-dollar decisions will match the contributions of any of these units.

The key is planning for risk reduction *while* pursuing a payoff. If you want to evaluate whether it's truly worth it, choose reasonable risk-reduction cost estimates, plug them into the payoff formula reviewed in Chapter Five, and see just how big a problem you would need to encounter to cancel out the payoff from better recruiting and hiring. I've never seen a reasonable analysis where the payoff was offset, particularly when continuous improvement was the target, as it is in the next chapter.

CHAPTER TWELVE

HOLDING AND GROWING THE INVESTMENT

We know there's risk when an individual makes a transition from one job to another. It's more like an arranged marriage than a first date: neither party knows all that much about the other, but both sides have made a commitment.

This is the time when predictions about future performance driven by facts learned during the hiring process can prove woefully incorrect. It's also the time when the first handshake with the new supervisor sets the tone for the future, for better or worse. The evidence is clear: new hires don't leave jobs, they leave bosses, and the initial transition weeks are when that process can begin. This is the time when a solid onboarding process can cement new hires to the company.

This chapter looks to the seeds of unwanted turnover, which are planted when this transition period is managed poorly. It also looks at how to begin tracking the performance of those you hired and begin determining whether you've really made the best million-dollar hires. I'll review techniques for gathering short-term information about the new hires' performance and integrating it with data collected during the hiring process.

The focus is on analyzing any hiring mistakes made and determining how to avoid them in the future. And the message is that even a well-designed program will produce mistakes. The challenge rests in catching the mistakes, isolating what went wrong and why, and making adjustments.

When a company installs programs in any other part of a business—manufacturing, sales, service, customer relations—its leaders don't just call it done and move on. They monitor results, look for opportunities to fine-tune the process, and continually seek better cost or quality results. Drawing a financial payoff from a recruiting and hiring program calls for the same approach: a continuous improvement mind-set and using the tools that support it. We'll look to examples of how this mind-set can be embedded in the strategy and tactics of a hiring program.

After the Million-Dollar Decision

All along, the focus in this book has been on making recruiting and hiring decisions—million-dollar decisions—that pay the best return. I raise the topic of onboarding because the job is far from over when a million-dollar decision is made. In a way, hiring doesn't end with the hiring decision. Now the focus turns from attracting, screening, and assessing to engaging, committing, and retaining this investment.

A hiring decision should represent good news for everyone. The way events unfold after hiring depends on the level of the job and the uniqueness of the role, but this should be a time of celebration. The employer filled a job where it needs help. The new hire found the job he's seeking or at least one worth accepting. The HR department can turn to servicing other hiring objectives, and the hiring manager can begin the job of orientation and training.

Recruiters reviewed the new hire's information and produced a picture that satisfied them. In the process, they decided she represented a good investment. They came to terms in an employment agreement acceptable to both parties, whether through a simple report-to-work call or negotiation of a complex contract. All of this reflected good news. But there's another way to look at the time immediately after the hiring decision: a time of uncertainty, stress, and setting out on uncharted waters.

On day 1, the new hire's world can be a pretty ambiguous place. What do fellow employees really know about her? What does she really know about them? What happens the first time a problem comes up? Will she take it in stride, solve the problem in a way that meets expectations, or revert to dark side coping behavior she learned in the past? Will the asset that cost money to find and land become a liability when the transitional stress of starting a new job, in a new organization, and with a new supervisor unfolds?

We've clearly stepped beyond looking at recruiting and hiring tactics and moved into the arena of workforce onboarding, retention, and employee development. These too are topics for a book, not a chapter, but they need at least a few pages here. (Readers interested in pursuing them in greater depth will find additional information in the material cited in the Notes.) These topics deserve coverage because one of the payoff goals rested in risk reduction. Here, as a new hire enters an unknown setting, risk is highest.

Early in my career, a colleague on the executive search side of the business spent months finding a new chief operating officer (COO) for one of the major soft drink bottlers. Finally, a candidate survived screening, assessment, reference checking, interviews with the CEO and board, and negotiation of an employment agreement. The (many) million-dollar decision was made.

On the Monday morning the COO was scheduled to report, the executive search consultant received a call from the company's CEO: "Where's our man?" After some panicked searching, we learned he had thought about the job and changed his mind. Although he and the company had made a commitment, risk won out. The executive search began again.

There's an entire discipline today referred to as onboarding that deals with risk reduction. Not long ago, it amounted to supplying new hires with tools to enroll in the benefits program, set up tax and withholding arrangements, commit to the employer's 401k or other retirement deposits, and find the coffee bar and ladies' room. It also involved clarifying things such as vacation schedules, time-off rules, expense reporting, and travel policies. In the old days, this was the paperwork part of the hiring process.

Today the concept has expanded, with much of the focus now on risk reduction in a variety of areas. It's also on building positive payoff through employee engagement. Faced with the need to lower employee turnover during the last employment bubble and to deal with a new definition of workplace loyalty that comes with Generation Y and the millennials, onboarding has grown to mean much more. Today the onboarding process of many employers includes information-transmission and engagement-building events that extend over as much as the first year of employment.

These new philosophies and techniques in onboarding look to research and best practices in workforce engagement, commitment, and performance building too. There are volumes on the topic, summarized best in much of the work published by the Corporate Executive Board.[1] This work is guided by some pretty straightforward principles.

I came across the basics a while back when I worked with one of the largest insurance and financial services companies in the United States to reduce employee turnover during the first few years after joining the organization. In seeking a way to analyze the problem, we found the company conducted annual employee opinion surveys. We decided to explore statistically whether information collected in several years of survey data might forecast the turnover of employees who had given their views during the survey process before they left.

After tons of statistical work, we found five items on the employee opinion survey where employees' answers predicted their likelihood of turning over in the short term. All focused on the employee's immediate supervisor. The items dealt with whether employees thought their supervisor (1) was available when they needed him or her, (2) communicated with them sufficiently, (3) cared about their well-being, (4) paid attention to their development, and (5) told them the truth. That's all. Low evaluations on the five survey items correlated highly with leaving the company.

Today these concepts and a few others are central to the onboarding programs created to engage new hires, develop commitment, and raise the level of effort and performance they produce. They also are central to the tools that drive today's onboarding programs. The goal of these programs is to make joining the organization a positive experience. As a result, onboarding today is not a single event but an ongoing series of experiences meant to build a bond between the employer and the investment it just made.

As noted, much of the attention to onboarding springs from a great deal of research in how to engage and develop the existing workforce. In onboarding, though, the workforce consists of those just entering the fray. As an illustration of how the concepts link with new hires, the Internet job site www.careerbuilder.com recently posted The Ten Commandments of Employee Onboarding.[2] Included are actions ranging from making sure the new hire's role is defined clearly, to introducing the new hire to colleagues, making sure tools and resources are ready when the new hire arrives, and making sure one-on-one time with the new supervisor is available from day 1.

Not surprisingly, technology has stepped in too. For example, using onboarding portals available over the Internet, employers today expose new hires to resources ranging from a CEO welcome;

to information about the organization's mission, vision, and values; and to employee development opportunities, training programs, and performance management practices, among others. The programs extend the employment branding that new hires first encountered during the recruiting and sourcing phase of the hiring process. In some cases, they even survey the new hire's reaction to the hiring process in order to review any difficulties in the process that might potentially chase other candidates away.

Software companies that set the trend in applicant tracking system (ATS) design and quality-of-hire automation have moved to automating employee onboarding. One of the more interesting tools some vendors offer is a survey-guided process, where new hires answer questions similar to those used in regular employee satisfaction surveys. These, however, are aimed at gaining clarity on how the new hire prefers receiving assignments, being coached, getting feedback, having interaction with the immediate supervisor, or developing skills that permit movement to higher-level jobs.[3]

These tools produce individualized onboarding reports, shared with the new hire's supervisor, to create an opening "handshake." They help clarify how the supervisor might tailor a way to interact with the new hire to form a productive relationship. The same tools sometimes guide supervisors to automated training aids that help them understand and deal with the profile they receive for a given new hire or guide them in dealing with the trends that Generation Y and millennial employees bring to the workplace.

So what's the payoff in all this attention to new hires? The www.careerbuilder.com site references a recent study by IDC, indicating it costs U.S. and U.K. employers about $37 billion each year to deal with new hires' misunderstanding of the expectations associated with their new job, their misinterpretation of company policies, their failure to understand the specific duties of their job, or a combination of all three.[4] All are typically targets of information included in today's onboarding efforts.

One of the leaders in talent management, Taleo, estimates a return on investment of about $1,200 per new hire resulting from even simple, automated approaches to onboarding.[5] One of the specialists in new hire retention, TalentKeepers, provides a host of studies showing reduced turnover, and costs when technology is used to cement the handshake between new hires and their supervisors.

Most of this research and practice offers three primary points about how to introduce a million-dollar hire to the organization. First, automation can help make the process more available to every new hire and expand access to information about what the new hire and organization expect of one another. Second, although onboarding emphasizes the overall organization's interest in the new hire, the key step rests in using the process to form the most important link: that between the employee and immediate supervisor. The idea that employees leave bosses, not jobs, is the centerpiece in these components in an onboarding program.

Finally, onboarding affects both elements of the return-on-investment model. By bringing new hires information about what's expected, how their performance will be measured and rewarded, and developing workforce engagement (the results of which are increased effort and productivity), onboarding also drives payoff. By lowering short-term turnover, it reduces the cost of recruiting. It also lowers the risk that disgruntled new hires will sabotage the company's brand in the marketplace.

Following Up on New Hires

The work we do after the million-dollar hire is about more than creating a positive experience for new employees. With a hiring decision made and onboarding under way, there's sometimes a tendency to declare, "Mission accomplished!" In many cases it's left to the supervisor in the employee's new job to proceed with the process of day-to-day supervision and longer-term development.

Some HR departments, though, look at the new hire as "a product" of their creation. And they track their product to learn whether the hiring process produced the best quality of hire.

When paper ruled, there was a clear separation between an employer's applicant files and personnel files. Today, too, a candidate typically is tracked in the architecture of the employer's ATS. Everything learned about the candidate—from the copy of her résumé to her results on prescreening inventories, tests, interviews, reference checks, and other measures—is held inside the ATS. The human resource department routinely reviews this candidate information, reports are generated, and improvements on metrics such as time-to-hire, cost-per-hire, and quality-of-hire on assessment tools are produced by analyzing and interpreting all the data in the ATS.

Once the company hires an individual, the onboarding process typically moves information on him or her from the ATS platform to the employer's HR information system (HRIS), where information about such matters as compensation, benefits, taxes, and ongoing training and development is maintained for the long term. It's these systems that typically hold information on employee performance, driven by whatever performance management process the employer follows.

Although ATS and HRIS data are integrated in today's larger, installed software solutions, point solutions (for example, ATS-only offerings) that some employers use don't bring this integration. And even installed solutions typically don't offer easy functionality for linking and analyzing information that crosses between candidate status and employee status types of information. It's often difficult to ask, for example: How are the new hires who were rated in the top half of our interview assessments performing during their first six months on the job? The data reside in two places, and it's too much trouble to load them together to answer the question.

Some tools are beginning to focus on integrating data produced along the process from candidate, to new hire, to employee transition. These are beginning to link candidate information (for example, scores on an employment test or interview ratings) with information about the initial performance of new hires as they progress through training and into their new roles. The tools are straightforward. Their purpose is to view each hiring decision as a subject worth analyzing.

Looking for Weak Spots and Improvement Opportunities

Figure 12.1 shows a tool from an ATS that shoots a brief performance checklist to the new hire's supervisor a preset period of time

Figure 12.1 An automated performance check-up example for new hires

New Hire Performance Check-Up

In order to continuously improve our recruiting and hiring process, we are asking for your feedback on an employee hired into your department. The information you provide *will not* be shared with the employee. The employee's regular performance review, salary review, and other progress with the company *will not* be affected by the feedback you provide through this process. We are collecting this information strictly to assess our recruiting and hiring processes and will use it for no other reasons.

Section 1 — Employee Information

Employee Name: John Doe

Date of Hire: May 23, 2011

Position: Manufacturing Technician

Status: Are you currently this employee's supervisor?

☐ Yes. (If you check this option, please proceed to Section 2.)
☐ No. (If you checked this option, what is the reason you are no longer his or her supervisor?)

   ☐ He or she has been moved to another job, department, or location.
   ☐ He or she is no longer an employee. If so, note why:

      ☐ Voluntary resignation
      ☐ Involuntary termination
      ☐ Layoff, reduction, or similar company action
      Effective date of separation (mm/yy): _____

If this employee is no longer with the company, please answer the following questions as of the employee's last effective date of employment.

(Continued)

Figure 12.1 (*Continued*)

Section 2 — General Performance Evaluation Areas

1. Compared to other employees hired in the past, how did this employee perform during initial training?
   - ☐ Clearly superior
   - ☐ Better than most
   - ☐ About the same
   - ☐ Poorer than most
   - ☐ Clearly poorer

2. How would you compare this employee's performance today to that of others hired in the past?
   - ☐ Clearly superior
   - ☐ Better than most
   - ☐ About the same
   - ☐ Poorer than most
   - ☐ Clearly poorer

3. Does this employee have potential to move to higher-level responsibilities in the future?
   - ☐ Definitely yes
   - ☐ Probably yes
   - ☐ Not sure at this time
   - ☐ Probably no
   - ☐ Definitely no

4. Check all areas that you believe describe this employee's *strengths:*
   - ☐ Learning and applying job knowledge
   - ☐ Following policies and procedures
   - ☐ Meeting quality standards
   - ☐ Recognizing and solving problems
   - ☐ Working effectively with others
   - ☐ Demonstrating positive work habits
   - ☐ Pursuing improvement opportunities

5. Check all areas that you believe describe this employee's *weaknesses:*
   - ☐ Learning and applying job knowledge
   - ☐ Following policies and procedures
   - ☐ Meeting quality standards
   - ☐ Recognizing and solving problems
   - ☐ Working effectively with others
   - ☐ Demonstrating positive work habits
   - ☐ Pursuing improvement opportunities

6. Choose the ONE item that best accounts, positively or negatively, for this employee's current performance:
   - ☐ Experience in the job before joining us
   - ☐ Training gained here
   - ☐ Ability to learn and adapt quickly
   - ☐ Work attitude and conscientiousness
   - ☐ Responsiveness to feedback
   - ☐ Skill in working with others

7. If given the choice, would you hire this employee again?
   - ☐ Definitely yes
   - ☐ Probably yes
   - ☐ Not sure at this time
   - ☐ Probably no
   - ☐ Definitely no

after the hiring decision is made and the new hire is onboarded. Triggered from the employer's ATS through the internal e-mail system, the tool asks the immediate supervisor to fill in a few blanks, check a few multiple-choice items, and send the result back to the ATS, where it's integrated with data learned during the hiring process. This initial performance review captures information ranging from initial turnover or reassignment events, to the supervisor's judgments about the new hire's success in training and on the job. It also asks about strengths and weaknesses the supervisor sees on the job, along with views regarding reasons for any failure to meet expectations. Finally, there's often a bottom-line question: "Would you hire this person again?"

The specifics of Figure 12.1 are not the point. It's the fact that such information can be collected in a preprogrammed way, obtained quickly, integrated with data collected when the employee was a candidate, and used for follow-up reviews. In particular, the information can explore hiring decisions that appear to have been less than optimal—the false positives mentioned in Chapter Ten.

The data don't reflect a full-scale performance evaluation and aren't typically fed back to the new hire. Their purpose is purely to help HR assemble information to drive continuous improvement analyses. Obviously the length of time the new hire has been on the job before the e-mail is sent to the supervisor can be preset for individual jobs. A probationary review for telemarketers might come at the end of ninety days, while the review for a sales professional might require six months or more to provide a solid basis for evaluation.

I recently used the tool to review the end-of-probation results for a group of 118 manufacturing employees hired under a newly designed process. The company followed a temporary-to-permanent approach to final hiring decisions and was willing to fire new hires who showed unacceptable performance during the probationary period. The new program was straightforward: basic skills testing and a hiring manager interview. It replaced a similar test-and-interview platform in which management had lost confidence.

The goal was to answer these questions:

- Did the new program improve on the previous one's quality-of hire in a way visible to supervisors?

- Did false positives make it through the process, resulting in firing new hires before the end of probation?

- For any such mistakes, what shortcomings in the process had permitted them to slip through?

The results for an initial wave of new hires provided an interesting snapshot on this simple approach to follow-up after hiring (Figure 12.1). As shown in Figure 12.2, sixteen of the new hires, about 14 percent, were considered mistakes and terminated during the probationary period. Supervisors described about one-quarter of the group as learning and performing the job *about the same* as those hired under the predecessor program. Of the 118 hired, though, 58 percent were evaluated as performing *better* in training and 55 percent were evaluated as performing *better* once on the job than employees who had been hired under the prior system. Finally, 75 percent were rated as definitely worthy of rehiring again.

So what was learned? First, the probationary termination rate of 14 percent compared to the earlier program's rate of more than 25 percent, for a reduction of nearly one-half in hiring mistakes—not bad for a change that amounted to simply replacing the prior tool kit. Second, the new program showed a quality-of-hire payoff. Costing no more to administer than the predecessor program, it yielded a group in which more than half of the new hires were viewed as performing at a level superior to previous hires.

But the program continued to make mistakes too, albeit at about half the prior rate. That was no surprise. Recall the discussion in

Figure 12.2 An example of a follow-up evaluation for a group of new hires

Supervisor's Performance Review Results	Passed Probation (102)	Failed Probation (16)
Compared to employees hired in the past, how did this employee perform during initial training?		
5 – Clearly superior	15%	
4 – Better than most	43%	14%
3 – About the same	26%	
2 – Poorer than most	2%	
1 – Clearly poorer	—	
How would you compare this employee's performance today to that of others hired in the past?		
5 – Clearly superior	14%	
4 – Better than most	41%	14%
3 – About the same	29%	
2 – Poorer than most	3%	
1 – Clearly poorer	—	
Given the choice, would you hire this employee again?		
5 – Definitely yes	48%	
4 – Probably yes	27%	14%
3 – Not sure at this time	8%	
2 – Probably no	4%	
1 – Definitely no		

Chapter Three on increasing the odds of being right. We'll always make mistakes in hiring decisions. The target is fewer mistakes. The follow-up also shed light on how potentially to reduce the number of mistakes even further. Additional ratings of the new hires' competencies showed that those terminated were rated as lacking basic work habits and conscientiousness. They were viewed as uninterested, unmotivated, and unwilling to take on the job. None of the supervisors indicated the group lacked the skills needed to perform the job, just the motivation.

In short, the new skills tests had found new hires who *could do* the job. Enter continuous improvement and a recommendation to add a basic workplace personality test to the battery: one focusing on conscientiousness and a positive work orientation. The target was improving accuracy in finding those who *would do* the job.

Although the example is a small-scale one, the basic quality improvement principles and technology it illustrates are easily scalable. It illustrates that the level of detail pursued in performance reviews of new employees need not be high—just high enough to clarify whether the hiring program is hitting its targets and reducing the rate of hiring errors. As important as the numbers produced is the anecdotal input from immediate supervisors about what the new program was missing.

Too, the capability provides a way for HR to launch a "what-if" review. What if we had demanded higher standards on the basic qualifications for the job? Would some of the mistakes have been avoided? What if the bar had been set higher on the test battery? Would mistakes have been avoided? What if we had followed a stricter multiple-hurdles approach to making decisions? Would mistakes have been avoided?

All of these questions reflect quality control–oriented ways to follow up on hiring decisions, look for improvements in payoff, and develop a plan for refining the system. Sure, it's necessary to assemble a sufficient number of new hires to be able to draw sound, stable conclusions about what's going on; making changes based on small numbers of hires makes no sense. Logging results, looking for overall patterns, and letting results accumulate over time, though, frames the right approach. Again, it's an illustration of classic continuous improvement thinking at work.

Validating Your Hiring Process

The idea isn't new. Beginning in the late 1980s, quality engineering professionals at Motorola began developing an approach to manufacturing quality control that became known as Six Sigma. Driving the concept were the questions: How much quality is enough quality? How many defects are too many? At the time, U.S. manufacturing was facing challenges from offshore companies, particularly those on the Pacific Rim. Many initiatives focused on improving product quality, introducing more sophisticated manufacturing technologies, and operating at reduced costs. Motorola's focus was on setting clear standards for improving quality and efficiency in all its operations and on keeping them in the United States.

Six Sigma set the quality standard at six standard deviations above the mean—essentially, no errors. As the concept caught on and consulting enterprises began selling Six Sigma training, programs carried the concept outside the manufacturing arena and into service-oriented organizations. The ideas also migrated into the administrative areas of organizations, like the HR department. Programs to train employees in the principles and practices of Six Sigma even created different levels of certification, with the highest level bringing Six Sigma Black Belt status.

A literal Six Sigma standard for measuring the quality of hiring decisions is not a realistic goal. We can predict performance, but not that well. Too much happens after a person is hired to expect this level of success. The general model, though, drives how to review the results of a new hiring program over time and how well it actually controls the quality of HR's product: new hires. In Chapter Three, I referred to this as validating the hiring process and its various pieces.

In working to reduce risk and comply with equal employment opportunity regulations, many employers try to validate their hiring programs with models that call for collecting information to prove out the new process *before* the program is implemented. I've completed many projects where single employers, or consortia made up of dozens of companies in a given industry, analyze the qualifications and competencies their jobs require, create new pre-screening and assessment tools, and then validate the new tools before they're implemented.

In these settings, the process typically involves research that applies the new hiring tools to current employees as though they were candidates applying to the jobs they already hold. A new screening test might be administered to a group of employees currently on the job to find how the group scores. Then information about the same employees' performance on the job is collected, and the two sets of data—test scores and performance data—are plumbed to find patterns of relationships like those illustrated in the Chapter Three discussion of validity. When the reviews show that the way employees perform on the hiring tools correlates to their performance on the job, the new tools are said to be validated.

It's a good way to try out new tools: see how they work, use employee information to set qualifying bars that have a known connection with performance, and work through the details of administering the process. On the downside, it takes time and money to complete, and is subject to the limitations of trying it out on already performing employees rather than real candidates. Technical complexities aside, though, it's a sound approach and shares some of the basic quality control outlook of Six Sigma.

With today's technology, the kind of quality review after hiring cited in the small-scale manufacturing illustration comes much closer to true Six Sigma. It's built on live data gained from the real target of the program: new hires. And rather than holding the new process to what amounts to "postdicting" the success of current employees, it provides a true predictive evaluation of the tools. It's but one example of how a Six Sigma approach to hiring can accomplish two major objectives: monitoring and gauging the true payoff in each piece of a recruiting and hiring program and meeting legal requirements to validate the process.

Improvement Never Ends

Although I mixed two different topics in this chapter, the approach to both shares a common principle: you can drive decisions with data and can rely on data to improve the decisions. The discussion of onboarding emphasized creating a positive experience for new hires on day 1—and actually before that. The discussion quickly moved to reviewing how collecting, analyzing, and using data about the preferences and attitudes of new hires can help create a hand-shake that engages them and sets up the conditions that maximize their commitment, effort, and performance.

Although a positive experience is unfolding, there's no "mission accomplished" to the hiring process. As soon as new hires join a company, it makes sense to begin tracking their performance, finding whether recruiters have predicted correctly, and learning from their mistakes. Just as a company's revenue targets and profitability goals increase each year, the targets and payoff goals of its recruiting and hiring program can be raised continuously. The days when "if it's not broken, don't fix it" are gone. The competition has good programs too. Leaders refine their programs whenever they have a chance. That's what keeps them in the lead.

CHAPTER THIRTEEN

IT'S YOUR MONEY

When a business hires, it commits a great deal of money. Accounting rules don't view the results of hiring decisions as liabilities or assets, but they are. Sure, the company can withdraw a hiring decision any time it wishes, but typically it doesn't. The decision stands, and the financial investment continues. The money invested, your organization's money, adds up.

It doesn't take hiring a CEO to represent a million-dollar decision. Add up the consequences of a hiring decision, including the tenure expected of new hires, and a teacher, police officer, skilled tradesperson, sales professional, engineer, first-level supervisor, and hundreds of others easily represent a million-dollar hire.

As the example of the steps followed in hiring an accountant versus purchasing accounting software underscored, we typically spend a lot of time deliberating before we spend a million dollars on hard assets. Often, though, we spend less time, and take a much greater risk, when it's a new hire being acquired rather than some other business asset.

Through the chapters, the focus has been on elevating the hiring process from an administrative function to one that drives the financial success of the business. You saw how large the gain can be when today's best recruiting and hiring practices are put to work in productivity improvement, cost reduction, and bottom-line payoff. In the process, you saw that gaining a financial return doesn't require a great deal of research, hiring expensive expertise, or spending great sums to acquire technology. All the systems, tools, and capabilities reviewed in this book are within reach of small to midsize companies.

Building on the examples and illustrations I reviewed and the many resources cited, any employer can begin making better million-dollar decisions with its very next hire.

Key Steps in Making Better Million-Dollar Hires

This book has covered a lot. I'll close by boiling it down to steps that summarize the simplest, and most important, ideas I have tried to communicate.

Step One: Accept the Facts

People are different, the differences are many, and the differences can be measured. And these differences follow people into the workplace, affecting how they perform. What companies do to make better million-dollar hires stems from these essential facts. Given these, we can predict which candidates are more likely to succeed and to what degree. The accuracy with which we can make these predictions is surprisingly high, and the payoff is substantial.

Yes, training and development work. People develop skills and talents and become more effective once they are on the job. But the fact remains that some people achieve more than others in training *and* on the job. When we predict accurately which candidates are likely to perform better than others and cost less, we make better million-dollar decisions.

But if we reject these facts and ignore the research that proves them true, then our focus needs to shift. If we believe all candidates can do the job if given a chance, then we need to take a developmental approach. If we do, our investments must go to training, development, and helping everyone succeed. That's one approach. In more than thirty years, though, I've never seen it work as well as beginning with the best talent in the first place.

Step Two: Have a Plan

Different recruiting and hiring tools measure different things, and predict different outcomes. So, the first question is, What do we want to predict in recruiting and hiring new talent: the ability to learn the job quickly, skill in selling, the capacity to manage others, future promotability, less likelihood of turning over soon after hire, or some other outcome? Answering this question, and developing the overall strategy and tactics to hit the target, demands a clear plan.

Developing strategy and tactics involves drawing from the research summarized in this book in order to understand what outcomes are predictable, how they're best predicted, and what risk comes in making the predictions. It also involves setting up an infrastructure or, these days, renting it on demand. And it involves using the payoff estimation tools reviewed to execute a "what if" of the outcomes expected in using different tools, different levels of selectivity, or different cost structures for executing the process, whether internally or through outside resources.

If we accept the idea that better recruiting and hiring hold payoff equal to or greater than that available in any other area of the business, then our strategy and tactics need to be vetted with senior management, memorialized, and tracked, just as we track and measure the success of a new business venture, a new product, or a strategic acquisition. The plan should inform management at regular intervals not only about what we plan to do but what we expect to produce, and how well we've done.

Step Three: Demand Validity

A recruiting process must seek information about candidates that is valid and job related. Only such information predicts the future. Only tools that measure qualifications and competencies related to performing the job predict future performance. Every hurdle presented to a candidate, and every tool used in screening, assessing, and decision making, must be held to two questions: What information does this tool provide that predicts an outcome that we care about? Is there a more accurate way to gain such information or a better way to use it?

The concept of validity has engaged measurement specialists for decades. Studying how to achieve it, document it, or improve it has created professions and populated libraries. In truth, though, making sure a recruiting or hiring practice is valid involves much the same exercise that manufacturing organizations have used to guide quality control, Six Sigma, lean manufacturing, and similar approaches for decades.

Today software systems that track applicants, new hires, and employees in the enterprise provide the means to hold every element of a recruiting and hiring program to validity (that is, quality control) evaluation. In fact, those who are running a recruiting and hiring program today can benefit from reaching into the quality control area of the organization and gaining help from those who guide continuous improvement efforts in other parts of the business.

Step Four: Inject Technology

Technology does wonderful things. Imagine a decade ago, asking a recruiter to find ten thousand résumés that match a job requisition, compare each to the job's basic qualifications, and rank-order them in terms of their fit to the job. Imagine popping into the HR office and asking for an analysis of last year's candidate flow for all ten thousand candidates screened, organizing it according to business unit, ethnicity, and gender. Then ask for a breakdown regarding the stage in the hiring process reached by each group, along with adverse impact analyses, all before lunch.

Faster-better-cheaper comes by taking advantage of recruiting software solutions, whether installed or on demand. These solutions help define what to look for, how to find candidates and screen and assess them, track them once hired, and tally results when the time comes to look for continuous improvement opportunities. Today, any recruiting and hiring program without a major dose of technology is wasting time.

A caution, though, rests in making sure that technology is not simply driving more, and faster, mistakes. Just because a tool comes on a technology platform doesn't mean it works, adds value, or lowers risk. As technology is incorporated into a strategic hiring plan and as technology-based tools are added to tactics, the overriding concept of validity needs to be stressed.

Every vendor product needs to be vetted for evidence that it works. Every work flow step we add to the process must be held to quality-of-hire, risk-reduction, and cost-reduction standards. In short, we need to monitor the chosen technology solutions to make sure they're not actually producing faster-poorer-riskier results.

Step Five: Source Broadly, Screen Accurately

Technology has reinvented the candidate sourcing process. Although job boards got the ball rolling, social networking has taken sourcing to a new level. Today a recruiter can spider social network sites, pull down profiles of people who appear to have what the recruiter is looking for, and reach out to explore their interest. The recruiting process has been opened to numbers beyond belief, and technology solutions make it possible to deal with these numbers with tools that read, evaluate, and even rank the results.

Still, the process of finding candidates needs to begin by defining what we seek—what basic qualifications and competencies define the need. And the process needs to ensure the things we seek with technology are relevant to the job, sought out in ways that reduce legal risk, and are regularly examined for what they produce. We need to use what we know about the validity that rests in basic qualifying information—education, experience, a history in similar jobs—to begin screening potential candidates in ways that reduce the cost of later steps in the hiring process and improve the quality of candidate flow.

If you're new to this world of sourcing techniques, be sure the ways you're setting up processes don't inadvertently bring the risk of legal compliance challenges. Here, the tools and techniques are new enough that legal challenges have not gotten traction yet, but they will. This is where you will need to balance what's possible with what's too risky.

Step Six: Assess Thoroughly

Candidate assessment has been with us for decades. One advance in the past decade has been the movement from gathering candidate information manually to using tools driven by software solutions. Whether manual or technology based, though, the goal remains the same: gain a view of the whole candidate before making a million-dollar decision.

While assessment has always sought information about candidates' knowledge, skills, abilities, and experience, the past decade has seen an increase in the attention given to workplace personality factors. Research is showing that measures of personality are not easily faked, don't necessarily extend into the realm of prohibited "mental evaluations" before hiring, and add to predicting candidates' future behavior on the job. The discussion of dark side personality factors has become particularly interesting in hiring leaders and others whose positions call for creating solid, engaging relationships with others.

A caution in the area of assessment comes from the unregulated nature of the business. Vendor products need to be held to the same quality control (validity) audits a business applies to any other product or service it purchases. This kind of review was once a challenge because of the time, staff resources, and expertise required. Now the tracking and data analytical tools in recruiting and hiring systems make it much more feasible. Just as a business should drop one supplier when one with a superior, lower-cost offering arrives, changing assessment techniques for better solutions should always be on the table.

Step Seven: Manage the Risk

The modeling tools reviewed here underscore the payoff in better sourcing, broader assessment, and continuous improvement. Anything that sounds so good must have a hidden cost. In recruiting and hiring, the hidden costs are primarily within the risk of legal challenge and the need to manage it. And most of *this* risk comes from cases where the process followed, or its outcome, has an impact on the concept of equal employment opportunity.

Risk management begins when strategy and tactics are framed and when the tools and technology that drive them are selected. Yes, it adds cost, but a preimplementation overview of strategy and tactics by employment counsel can help avoid any pitfalls that might be taking shape in upcoming regulations or court actions not yet broadly known. Such review also can make sure that no one has overlooked the many rules and regulations already in place.

Fortunately, the rules are fairly clear: ensure the process is based on the concept of job relatedness, document its results with quality control–oriented data, track results, be consistent, and evaluate ways to reduce any adverse impact the system produces. And make sure vendors who contribute to the system bring sufficient expertise in the legal side of hiring to help avoid risk rather than create it.

Step Eight: Improve Continuously

The idea of continuous improvement might seem a gratuitous add-on. To me, though, it's the most important point on the checklist. If we're going to invest in a payoff-oriented strategy; assemble tactics, tools, and technology; set up tracking systems; and cover legal risks, shouldn't we be interested in checking ourselves? Don't we want to know whether, and how well, the process works at the end of its first year? The sales, marketing, finance, and other areas of the business are expected to show numbers that reflect on their performance. So should the recruiting and hiring function. The strategic plan produced at the outset lays out both the metrics we intended to pursue and the targets we hope to hit.

Continuous improvement techniques tell us whether we're hitting the targets. They also show where we're wasting time, so we can refine the process. They build a record of defensibility for use in answering legal challenges. And they document the return on investment gained from vendor products. Finally, they help present the true importance of recruiting and hiring practices to senior management in terms that everyone grasps: financial ones. Without an emphasis on continuous improvement and the metrics that come with it, it really boils down to, "Trust us, it works."

You Recoup the Investment with the First Million-Dollar Hire

That's the essence of it. If the objective is to bring a payoff to the organization through better recruiting and hiring, then the first question is whether, and how long, it will take to gain a payoff. The answer is driven by volume, how much the current program can be improved, and what the redesign costs in terms of outside services, vendor products, and, potentially, individuals needed to staff the new approach.

The payoff models in Chapter Five can help get the ball rolling. Filling in estimates of current and new program validity, selection ratios, costs per head, and amortized costs of initial program updates can help determine when the improvement in quality of hire will offset the costs of bringing the new program to operation. In my experience, scoping out the costs and payback parameters also needs to factor in how much work can be accomplished when technology is introduced to replace manual approaches and how the corresponding reductions in staffing levels can produce a faster payback.

In addition, the overall review of current practices that comes in modeling a new system often identifies costs being paid to vendors that need not be carried forward because the new system brings bundles of services formerly purchased from a number of different vendors. Too, the ever-present expansion of technology solutions is driving down the costs associated with most of the outside services needed to support the overall process.

In short, the more manually driven the current process is, the more likely that new tactics will reduce the cost of operations. If you believe the payoff estimates produced by the Chapter Five models, I've not yet seen a system redesign that didn't pay for itself in the first year of operation, even in settings where volume is low.

The key is to make sure the new program is watched, tracked, and held to continuous improvement. Sometimes this means adding staff with grounding in quality control techniques or at least basic statistics. In other cases, the software platforms that power the process offer the basic analytical engines, and user training is sufficient to build these skills.

Keeping the Ideas Flowing

Now you know what I know, or at least the important parts. Ideally, the topics I've covered will help you make better million-dollar hires. If your organization is a business where revenue and profit are the fuel, then what we've covered can help find the talent to grow the revenue line. At the same time, the approaches highlighted should help cut the cost of making each decision. The net of it is building the bottom line, one new hire at a time.

If your organization is a nonprofit or a unit of government, then it's not increasing the revenue line that dominates discussion. What's important is providing the best service, operating within budget, and building talent to drive tomorrow's success. Here productivity improvement doesn't mean manufacturing more units or selling more services. It means delivering more value, serving clients or the public more effectively, and having a greater impact on those served by the organization. Controlling costs so the funds available are directed to better service rather than overhead offers a different focus but the same objective: finding better talent.

If you invest in businesses, then it's a return on investment that matters. A recruiting and hiring system that finds the best talent, controls cost, and lowers risk is what you seek. If your investments are early stage, then this will help the enterprise grow and ensure that its management is capable of finding and engaging key talent.

In my experience, this is where attention to the dark side is essential. The idea certainly holds in other business and nonprofit settings, where the dark side can steer any leader off the rails. But many early-stage ventures fail because the founder and his or her team bring a surplus of the dark side to the business. Adding due diligence on the start-up's recruiting and hiring processes and its leadership team to the investment decision is as important as any hiring decision. It's time well spent from an investor point of view. (That's hard-earned experience and a load of tax write-offs speaking.)

So there it is. I've answered some questions. More were probably raised. Once more we turn to technology. I've created the Web site www.million-dollarhire.com to help answer the questions raised but left unanswered. Visit the site, and post your questions. I'll answer them. In addition, I've provided examples of the tools reviewed on the site and offer links to some of the vendors and service providers profiled. There are others, and the ones listed haven't paid for the referral. They simply represent ones I know who deliver what they promise.

Most important, I have a request. Readers who are interested in sharing their own payoff examples can use www.million-dollarhire.com to post their stories, explain what worked, describe what didn't, and spread the philosophy that making better million-dollar hires will build businesses, one employee at a time.

Now, go find some talent. You know how to do it.

NOTES

Chapter One

1. Why small businesses fail: SBA says 50% fail during first year. http://usgovinfo.about.com/od/smallbusiness/a/whybusfail.htm.

2. Wieczorek, M. (2006). *Why most businesses fail (a theoretical model)*. www.marktaw.com/Work_and_Business/Why-Businesses-Fail.html.

3. Hogan, J., Hogan, R., & Kaiser, R. (2010). Management derailment: Personality assessment and mitigation. In S. Zedeck (Ed.), *American Psychological Association handbook of industrial and organizational psychology*. Washington, DC: American Psychological Association.

4. Bureau of Labor Statistics Databases. http://data.bls.gov/cgi-bin/surveymost.

5. Hogan, Hogan, & Kaiser. (2010).

6. Hansell, S. (1995, February 28). The collapse of Barings; for rogue traders, yet another victim. *New York Times*.

7. Gladwell, M. (2008). *Outliers: The story of success*. New York: Little, Brown.

8. Hogan, R., & Hogan, J. (1995). *Hogan Personality Inventory manual* (2nd ed.). Tulsa, OK: Hogan Assessment Systems. Hogan, R., & Hogan, J. S. (1997). *Hogan development survey manual*. Tulsa, OK: Hogan Assessment Systems. Bourdeau, N. R., & Lock, J. D. (2005, April 16). *Evaluating applicant faking via "bright-" and "dark-side" measures of personality*. Paper presented at the 19th annual conference of the Society for Industrial and Organizational Psychology, Los Angeles.

9. Thurstone, L. L. (1924). *The nature of intelligence*. London: Kegan, Paul. Guilford, J. P. (1967). *The nature of human intelligence*. New York: McGraw-Hill. Hogan, R. (2007). *Personality and the fate of organizations*. Mahwah, NJ: Erlbaum.

10. Spies, R. A., Plake, B. S., Geisinger, B. F., & Carlson, J. F. (Eds.). *The seventeenth mental measurements yearbook*. Lincoln: University of Nebraska Press. Murphy, L. L., Plake, B. S., & Spies, R. A. (Eds.). (2006). *Tests in print VII*. Lincoln: University of Nebraska Press.

11. Eder, R. W., & Ferris, G. (1989). *The employment interview: Theory, research and practice*. Thousand Oaks, CA: Sage.

12. Howard, A., & Bray, D. W. (1988). *Managerial lives in transition: Advancing age and changing times*. New York: Guilford Press.

Chapter Two

1. Oakland, J. S. (2003). *TQM: Text with cases* (3rd. ed.). Burlington, MA: Butterworth-Heinemann. Pyzdek, T., & Keller, P. (2010). *The Six Sigma handbook* (3rd. ed.). New York: McGraw-Hill.

2. Guion, R. M. (1998). *Assessment, measurement, and prediction for personnel decisions*. Mahwah, NJ: Erlbaum.

3. Gladwell, M. (2009). *What the dog saw: And other adventures*. New York: Little, Brown.

4. Barrett, G. V., Polomsky, M. D., & McDaniel, M. A. (1999). Selection tests for firefighters: A comprehensive review and meta-analysis. *Journal of Business and Psychology, 13*, 507–513.

5. Hunter, J. E., & Schmidt, F. L. (1982). Fitting people to jobs: Implications of personnel selection for national productivity. In E. A. Fleishman & M. D. Dunnette (Eds.), *Human performance and productivity. Volume 1: Human capability assessment* (pp. 233–284). Mahwah, NJ: Erlbaum. Schmidt, F. L., Hunter, J. E., McKenzie, R. C., & Muldrow, T. W. (1979). The impact of valid selection procedures on work-force productivity. *Journal of Applied Psychology, 64*, 609–626.

6. *Griggs v. Duke Power Co.* (1971). 401 U.S. 424. *Albemarle Paper Co. v. Moody* (1975). 422 U.S. 405.

7. *Ricci v. DeStefano* (2009). 530 F. 3d 87.

8. Equal Employment Opportunity Commission, Civil Service Commission, Department of Labor, & Department of Justice. (1978). *Uniform guidelines on employee selection procedures.* Washington, DC: Department of Labor. Equal Employment Opportunity Commission, Civil Service Commission, Department of Labor, & Department of Justice. (1980). *Uniform guidelines on employee selection procedures interpretation and clarification (questions and answers).* Washington, DC: Department of Labor.

Chapter Three

1. Hogan, J., Hogan, R., & Kaiser, R. B. (2010). Management derailment: Personality assessment and mitigation. In S. Zeldeck (Ed.), *American Psychological Association handbook of industrial and organizational psychology.* Washington, DC: American Psychological Association.

2. Blackjack. www.math.cornell.edu/~mec/2006–2007/Probability/Blackjack.htm.

3. Cohen, P., Cohen, J., West, S., & Aiken, L. S. (2002). *Applied regression/correlation analysis for the behavior sciences* (3rd ed.). Mahwah, NJ: Erlbaum.

Chapter Four

1. U.S. Bureau of Labor Statistics, Employment Projections Program Databases. (2009, December). *Occupations: Numerical and percentage change, by major occupational group.* www.bls.gov/emp/emptab1.html.

2. Cascio, W., & Boudreau, J. (2008). *Investing in people: Financial impact of human resource initiatives.* Upper Saddle River, NJ: Pearson Education.

3. Hulin, C. L. (1979). *Integration of economics and attitude/behavior models to predict and explain turnover.* Paper presented at the annual meeting of the Academy of Management, Atlanta, GA.

4. Hulin. (1979).

5. Cascio & Boudreau. (2008).

6. Corporate Executive Board. (2004). *Engaging the workforce: Focusing on critical leverage points to drive employee engagement.* Washington, DC: Author.

7. U.S. Bureau of Labor Statistics. (2009, December). *Most requested statistics: Injuries, illnesses and fatalities.* www.bis.gov/cgi-bin/surveymost.

8. Thanks to professional staff at Aon Consulting Worldwide and Hogan Assessment Systems for contributing some of the payoff examples in this chapter.

Chapter Five

1. Taylor, H. C., & Russell, J. T. (1939). The relationship of validity coefficients to the practical effectiveness of tests in selection. *Journal of Applied Psychology, 23,* 565–578. Naylor, J. C., & Shine, L. C. (1965). A table for determining the increase in mean criterion score by using a selection device. *Journal of Industrial Psychology, 3,* 33–42. Cronbach, L. J., & Gleser, G. C. (1965). *Psychology tests and HR decisions* (2nd ed.). Urbana: University of Illinois Press.

2. Schmidt, F. L., & Hunter, J. E. (1983). Individual differences in productivity: An empirical test of estimates derived from studies of selection procedure utility. *Journal of Applied Psychology, 68,* 407–415.

3. Cascio, W., & Boudreau, J. (2008). *Investing in people: Financial impact of human resource initiatives.* Upper Saddle River, NJ: Pearson.

4. Hunter, J. E., Schmidt, F. L., & Judiesch, M. K. (1990). Individual differences in output variability as a function of job complexity. *Journal of Applied Psychology, 75,* 28–42.

5. Welch, J. E. (2005). *Winning.* New York: HarperCollins.

6. Taylor & Russell. (1939).

7. Hunter, J. E., & Hunter, R. F. (1984). Validity and utility of alternative predictors of job performance. *Journal of Applied Psychology, 96,* 72–98. Schmidt, F. L., Hunter, J. E., Outerbridge, A. N., & Trattner, M. H. (1986). The economic impact of job selection methods on the size, productivity, and payroll costs of the federal work-force: An empirical demonstration. *Personnel Psychology, 39,* 1–29. Schmidt, F. L., & Hunter, J. E. (1998). The validity and utility of selection methods in personnel psychology: Practical and theoretical implications of 85 years of research findings. *Psychological Bulletin, 124,* 262–274.

8. Cascio & Boudreau. (2008).

9. Hunter, J. E., & Hunter, R. F. (1984). Validity and utility of alternative predictors of job performance. *Journal of Applied Psychology*, 96, 72–98.

10. Hunter & Hunter. (1984).

11. Hunter & Hunter. (1984).

12. Hunter, J. E., Schmidt, F. L., & Judiesch, M. K. (1990). Individual differences in output variability as a function of its complexity. *Journal of Applied Psychology*, 75, 28–42.

Chapter Six

1. Schweyer, A. (2004). *Talent management systems: Best practices technology solutions for recruitment, retention, and workforce planning.* Chanda, A., Krishna, B. S., & Shen, J. (2007). *Strategic human resource technologies: Keys to managing people.* Thousand Oaks, CA: Sage. Van Tiem, D., Moseley, J. L., & Dessinger, J. C. (2008). *Fundamentals of performance technology: A guide to improving people, process, and performance* (2nd ed.). Silver Spring, MD: International Society for Performance Improvement.

2. Schwabel, D. (2009, May 11). *The demise of job boards and the ride of people searching.* www.personalbranddog.com. Hansen, K. (2009). *The long, slow death march of job boards—and what will replace them: A quintessential careers annual report 2009.* www.quintcareers.com/job-board_death_march.html.

3. Landauer, T. K., Foltz, P. W., & Laham, D. (1998). Introduction to latent semantic analysis. *Discourse Processes*, 25, 259–284.

4. Hough, L. M. (1984). Development and evaluation of the "accomplishment record" method of selecting and promoting professionals. *Journal of Applied Psychology*, 69, 135–146.

5. Jones, K. (2005). *Pre-employment testing and assessment: The state of the art.* Boston: Aberdeen Group.

Chapter Seven

1. Below, P. J., Morrisey, G. L., & Acomb, A. L. (1987). *The executive guide to strategic planning.* San Francisco: Jossey-Bass. Napier, R., Sidle, C., & Sanaghan, P. (1997). *High impact tools and activities for*

strategic planning: Creative techniques for facilitating your organization's planning process. New York: McGraw-Hill.

2. Lawler III, E. (1990). *Strategic pay: Aligning organizational strategies and pay systems.* San Francisco: Jossey-Bass.

3. Bechet, T. P. (2008). *Strategic staffing: A comprehensive system for effective workforce planning.* New York: American Management Association. Burkholder, N. C., Edwards Sr., P. J., & Sartain, L. (2004). *On staffing: Advice and perspectives for HR leaders.* Hoboken, NJ: Wiley. Emmerichs, R. M., Marcum, C. Y., & Robbert, A. A. (2004). *An operational process for workforce planning.* Santa Monica, CA: RAND.

Chapter Eight

1. Lucia, A. D., & Lepsinger, R. (1999). *The art and science of competency models: Pinpointing critical success factors in organizations.* San Francisco: Jossey-Bass/Pfeiffer. Sanghi, S. (2007). *The handbook of competency modeling: Understanding, designing and implementing competency models in organizations* (2nd ed.). Thousand Oaks, CA: Sage.

2. The competency model architecture found at www.million-dollarhire.com parallels the basic job families that frame the government's EEO-1 Report framework used in reporting workforce composition. Hence, the overall architecture can be used to create competency models for families of jobs already grouped together for equal employment opportunity reporting purposes.

3. See the First Research Industry Profile—Personnel Staffing Agencies, for SIC Code 7363, NAICS Code 5613, Oct. 2, 2010, at www.firstresearch.com/industry-research/Personnel-Staffing-Agencies.html.

4. Burkholder, N. C., Edwards Sr., P. J., & Sartain, L. (2004). *On staffing: Advice and perspectives from HR leaders.* Hoboken, NJ: Wiley.

5. See the excellent update on the topic provided in *Summary report: Social network recruiting: Managing compliance issues.* (2010). Taleo Business Edition at www.taleo.com/whitepaper/social-network-recruiting-managing-compliance-issues.

6. Schepp, B., & Schepp, D. (2009). *How to find a job on LinkedIn, Facebook, Twitter, MySpace, and other social networks.* New York: McGraw-Hill. Shih, C. (2010). *The Facebook era: Tapping online social networks to market, sell, and innovate* (2nd ed.). Upper Saddle River, NJ: Pearson Education.

7. Schepp & Schepp. (2009).

8. See *Summary report: Social network recruiting: Managing compliance issues.* (2010). www.workforce.com/section/06/feature/26/68//67.

9. For more information on the Internet Applicant Recordkeeping Rule, see the OFCCP frequently asked questions (FAQs) at the Department of Labor Web site: www.dol.gov/ofccp/regs/compliance/faqs/iappfaqs.htm.

10. www.dol.gov/ofccp/regs/compliance/faqs/iappfaqs.htm.

Chapter Nine

1. Ackerman, P. L., & Heggestad, E. D. (1997). Intelligence, personality, and interests: Evidence of overlapping traits. *Psychological Bulletin, 121,* 219–245. Chamorro-Premizic, T., & Furnham, A. (2006). Intellectual competence and the intelligent personality: A third way in differential psychology. *Review of General Psychology, 10,* 251–267.

2. Hunter, J. E., & Hunter, R. F. (1984). Validity and utility of alternative predictors of job performance. *Journal of Applied Psychology, 96,* 72–98. Schmidt, F. L., & Hunter, J. E. (1998). The validity and utility of selection methods in personnel psychology: Practical and theoretical implications of 85 years of research findings. *Psychological Bulletin, 124,* 262–274. Schmidt, F. L., & Hunter, J. E. (2004). General mental ability in the world of work: Occupational attainment and job performance. *Journal of Personality and Social Psychology, 86,* 162–173.

3. Hunter & Hunter. (1984).

4. Schmidt & Hunter. (2004).

5. Blakeley, B. R., Quinones, M. A., Crawford, M. S., & Jago, I. A. (1994). The validity of isometric strength tests. *Personnel Psychology,*

47, 247–274. Anderson, C., & Briggs, J. (2008). A study of the effectiveness of ergonomically based functional screening tests and their relationship to reducing worker compensation injuries. *Work*, 31, 27–37.

6. Thanks to Veronica Schmidt-Harvey at Aon Consulting for contributing the payoff examples produced by her work with light industrial worker screening. Those interested in additional information about workplace assessment tools can contact her at veronica .harvey@aon.com.

7. Thanks to Joyce Hogan at Hogan Assessment Systems for the payoff examples on injury rate reduction reported in Chapter Four and for information about the structure and validation of the Hogan Safety Assessment.

8. Thanks to Terry Mitchel at e-Selex.com for contributing the payoff example regarding the use of biodata assessment in selecting retail sales associates. Those interested in additional information on biodata assessment can contact him at www.e-selex.com.

9. Thanks to Veronica Schmidt-Harvey at Aon Consulting for contributing the payoff examples produced by her work with telesales, customer care, and technical support employee assessment. Those interested in additional information about workplace assessment tools can contact her at veronica.harvey@aon.com.

10. Dotlich, D. L., & Cairo, P. C. (2003). *Why CEOs fail: The eleven behaviors that can derail your climb to the top—and how to manage them.* San Francisco: Jossey-Bass. Hogan, J., Hogan, R., & Kaiser, R. (2010). Management derailment: Personality assessment and mitigation. In S. Zedeck (Ed.), *American Psychological Association handbook of industrial and organizational psychology.* Washington, DC: American Psychological Association.

11. Schmidt & Hunter. (1998).

12. Schmidt, F. L., Hunter, J. E., Outerbridge, A. N., & Trattner, M. H. (1986). The economic impact of job selection methods on the size, productivity, and payroll costs of the federal work-force: An empirical demonstration. *Personnel Psychology, 39,* 1–29.

Chapter Ten

1. American Educational Research Association, American Psychological Association, & National Council on Measurement in Education. (1999). *Standards for educational and psychological testing.* Washington, DC: American Education Research Association. Equal Employment Opportunity Commission, Civil Service Commission, Department of Labor, & Department of Justice. (1978). Uniform guidelines on employee selection procedures. Washington, DC: Department of Labor and Equal Employment Opportunity Commission, Civil Service Commission, Department of Labor, and Department of Justice. (1980). *Uniform guidelines interpretation and clarification (questions and answers).* Washington, DC: Department of Labor. Society of Industrial and Organizational Psychology. (2003). *Principles for the validation and use of personnel selection procedures* (3rd ed.). Bowling Green, OH: Society of Industrial and Organizational Psychology.

2. Guion, R. M. (1998). *Assessment, measurement, and prediction for personnel decisions.* Mahwah, NJ: Erlbaum.

3. Cascio, W. F., Alexander, R. A., & Barrett, G. V. (1988). Setting cutoff scores: Legal, psychometric, and professional issues and guidelines. *Personnel Psychology, 41,* 1–24.

4. Horney, K. (1950). *Neurosis and human growth.* New York: Norton. Conger, J. A. (1990). The dark side of leadership. *Organizational Dynamics, 19,* 44–55. Hogan, R., & Hogan, J. (2001). Assessing leadership: A view from the dark side. *International Journal of Selection and Assessment, 9,* 40–51.

5. Corporate Leadership Council. (2004). *Engaging the workforce: Focusing on critical leverage points to drive employee engagement.* Washington, DC: Corporate Executive Board. Corporate Leadership Council. (2006). *Attracting and retaining critical talent segments: Building a competitive employment value proposition for in-store employees—a special supplement.* Washington, DC: Corporate Executive Board.

6. Dotlich, D. L., & Cairo, P. C. (2002). *Unnatural leadership: Ten new leadership instincts.* San Francisco: Jossey-Bass. Dotlich, D. L., &

Cairo, P. C. (2003). *Why CEOs fail: The eleven behaviors that can derail your climb to the top—and how to manage them*. San Francisco: Jossey-Bass.

7. Van Vugt, M., Hogan, R., & Kaiser, R. B. (2008). Leadership, followership, and evolution: Some lessons from the past. *American Psychologist, 63*, 182–196.

8. Hogan, R., & Hogan, J. (2009). *Hogan development survey manual*. Tulsa, OK: Hogan Assessment Systems.

Chapter Eleven

1. Sharf, J. C., & Jones, D. P. (2000). Employment risk management. In J. F. Kehoe (Ed.), *Managing selection in changing organizations: Human resource strategies* (pp. 271–318). San Francisco: Jossey-Bass.

2. For an explanation and comparison of disparate treatment versus disparate impact, see Nelson, A. H. (2009). *Adverse impact and disparate treatment: Two types of discrimination*. www.shrm.org/Education/hreducation/Pages/AdverseImpactandDisparate TreatmentTwoTypesofDiscrimination.aspx.

3. For the full text of the act, see www.eeoc.gov/laws/statutes/titlevii .cfm.

4. For comprehensive information on the Americans with Disabilities Act, see the government resource Web site www.ada.gov.

5. For comprehensive information on the Age Discrimination in Employment Act, see the government resource Web site www.eeoc .gov/policy/adea.html.

6. For information on executive order 11246 and compliance requirements, see the government resource Web site www.dol.gov/compliance/laws/comp-eeo.htm.

7. Gutman, A., & Dunleavy, R. (2008). *On the legal front: EEO enforcement activity in 2007: A sign of things to come?* Society for Industrial and Organizational Psychology. www.siop.org/tip/July08/14gutman.aspx.

8. Higher and higher: Record financial remedies for a record number of American workers in FY2008. www.dol.gov/esa/ofccp/regs/compliance/FY2008_Accomp.html.

9. Sharf & Jones. (2000).

10. Society of Industrial and Organizational Psychology. (2003). *Principles for the validation and use of personnel selection procedures* (3rd ed.). Bowling Green, OH: Society of Industrial and Organizational Psychology. U.S. Equal Employment Opportunity Commission, Civil Service Commission, Department of Labor, and Department of Justice. (1978). *Uniform guidelines on employee selection procedures.* Washington, DC: U.S. Department of Labor. U.S. Equal Employment Opportunity Commission, Civil Service Commission, Department of Labor, and Department of Justice. (1980). *Uniform guidelines interpretation and clarification (questions and answers).* Washington, DC: U.S. Department of Labor. American Educational Research Association, American Psychological Association, and National Council on Measurement in Education. (1999). *Standards for educational and psychological testing.* Washington, DC: American Education Research Association.

11. U.S. Equal Employment Opportunity Commission, Civil Service Commission, Department of Labor and Department of Justice. (1978).

12. See analytical tool kits for examining the adverse impact of a given recruiting or hiring practice provided at www.management-advantage.com/products/AdverseImpactCD.htm.

13. *Connecticut v. Teal,* 457 U.S. 440 (1982).

Chapter Twelve

1. Corporate Leadership Council. (2004). *Driving employee performance and retention through engagement: A quantitative analysis of the effectiveness of employee engagement strategies.* Washington, DC: Corporate Executive Board. Corporate Leadership Council. (2004). *Engaging the workforce: Focusing on critical leverage points to drive employee engagement.* Washington, DC: Corporate Executive Board.

2. The 10 commandments of employee onboarding. www. careerbuilder.com/jobposter/small-business.

3. For more information on this topic, see www.talentkeepers.com.

4. Cordin, E., Odgers, P., Redgate, R., Rowan, L., & Barnes, A. (2008). *Whitepaper: $37 billion: Counting the cost of employee misunderstanding*. London: IDC.

5. Taleo Research. (2006). *Onboarding: Speeding the way to productivity*. www.taleo.com.

ACKNOWLEDGMENTS

Most authors close their books by acknowledging people. I'd like to acknowledge organizations. And I'd like to thank those I've had the privilege to work with—many, one project at a time—in creating the ideas, tools, and technology I describe in this book.

These are organizations where a focus on payoff, risk reduction, and continuous improvement created new strategies and tactics for driving hiring practices. The list is long and diverse, and it reflects all parts of the economy. Some were part of developing new approaches, groundbreaking at the time, that are standard practice today.

Thanks, for example, to technology companies like Motorola and Texas Instruments, where we designed quality-of-hire programs in manufacturing and created ways to bring Six Sigma and continuous improvement techniques to hiring. We even transported the systems across international borders.

Thanks to manufacturing companies such as GM, Ford, Chrysler, Saturn, and their many tier 1 suppliers for helping to develop approaches to assessing not only basic skills and abilities, but concepts such as teamwork and creative problem solving, and for helping to create the concept of recruitment process outsourcing to reduce costs and deliver new hires when needed and where needed. And thanks to companies such as America West, Delta, UAL, and Home Depot for helping to create new ways for evaluating candidates for customer-facing roles.

Thanks to companies like Taco Bell, Pizza Hut, KFC, Pepsi, and Frito-Lay, where meeting the needs at thousands of hiring locations called for finding ways to merge technology and hiring in a straightforward, cost-effective way, even creating ways to track the resulting payoff as thousands of new hires joined the organization.

Thanks to the many companies, including Anheuser-Busch and Philip Morris, for providing the stage to create hiring programs to guide plant start-ups, expansions, or acquisitions, and to those that provided the opportunity to try out the packages in places as varied as Lithuania, Turkey, Kazakhstan, and Russia.

Thanks to the industry consortia—for example, the scores of electric utility companies and life insurance companies—whose industry-wide platforms helped build hiring systems that save industry members the cost and time of creating their own individual programs.

Thanks to major public sector employers, from New York, to Chicago, to Los Angeles, that provided venues for designing hiring programs where civil service rules, legal oversight, and the need to handle tens of thousands of candidates called for creating ways to deal with challenges seldom encountered in the private sector.

Thanks to the employment law firms and the federal agencies— the Equal Employment Opportunity Commission, Department of Labor, and Department of Justice—for opportunities to serve in expert witness roles focused on linking recruiting and hiring practices with the equal employment opportunity laws and regulations that affect nearly every employer. Working on both the defendant and plaintiff sides of the issues offered me unique insights that I have tried to capture in this book.

From the pharmaceutical manufacturers, to the financial and professional services firms; from the food processing companies, to the drillers, miners, and refiners; from the health care providers to the gambling industry: I thank all those who, while there was always a bottom-line objective in the assignment, were willing to try something new and see what happened. It's good to know you're still out there and still interested in finding what works best.

ABOUT THE AUTHOR

David P. Jones has worked as an organizational psychologist and human resource consultant for over thirty years. He received a doctorate from Bowling Green State University in Ohio. One of the few in his profession to found and develop a major business enterprise, he draws on that experience in offering up the real-life examples that populate *Million-Dollar Hire*.

Jones was formerly the global head of human resource consulting with Aon Consulting Worldwide, one of the world's largest human resource advisory and outsourcing firms. Before that, he founded HRStrategies, a human resource consulting and outsourcing firm with offices throughout the United States and Europe, recognized as one of the fastest-growing consulting companies in the United States prior to its acquisition by Aon Corporation. Today he is president of Growth Ventures Inc., a human capital advisory firm working with start-up and established companies, as well as units of government.

Jones's accomplishments have been highlighted in the *Wall Street Journal*, *New York Times*, *Investor's Business Daily*, *Crain's Business*, and other publications. He has followed his passion for entrepreneurship for over thirty years, pioneering technology solutions to employee recruitment, candidate assessment, and employment process outsourcing in the 1990s, and introducing technology solutions to both U.S. and international clients. He established offices in the Baltics and Moscow in the early 1990s, where he helped recruit and hire new talent for Western companies moving into Central and Eastern Europe and Russia.

Jones has designed recruiting and hiring programs for most of the Fortune 100. He serves as a frequent expert witness in matters associated with employment law and works with both the government and private law firms in matters of employment compliance. He is an active investor in start-up initiatives, where his background leads to board of directors roles in which he helps build new management teams and design start-up hiring programs.

This book's Web site, www.million-dollarhire.com, provides more information about Jones and introduces readers to some of the tools and technology he has created to drive million-dollar hires.

INDEX

Page reference followed by *fig* indicates an illustrated figure; followed by *t* indicates a table.

48, 104, 122–126, 160, 188–191;
rates during prerecession and
recession, 2. *See also* Candidates;
New hires; Return-on-investment
(RPO)
Hiring decisions: compensatory
approach to, 198–200, 207–208;
considering personality traits as part
of, 211–216; hybrid approach to,
200; improving the odds of making
the, 34–35; legal compliance
through consistency of, 216–217;
materiality model of, 32–34;
more-is-better concept and, 6, 209;
more-is-worse model considered for,
6–7, 209–210, 211–212t; multiple-
hurdles approach to, 196–198, 207,
226; payoff for good, 47–84; putting
the principles at work for, 206–209;
reducing legal risk during stage of,
236–238; research on failure of,
210–211; retention for validating
the, 255–257; setting the bar on
qualifications for, 201*fig*–206;
Uniform Guidelines on Employee
Selection Procedures on, 26–27,
189, 228; valid and correctly used
candidate data as key to, 194–196.
See also Legal compliance;
Million-dollar hires; Recruiting;
Validity model
Hiring funnel: candidate prescreening
stage, 88*fig*, 91–94; candidate
sourcing stage, 88*fig*–91; continuous
improvement stage, 28, 88*fig*,
102–104; full-scale assessment
stage, 88*fig*, 94–97; legal
compliance stage, 26–28, 88*fig*,
100*fig*–102; onboarding and
retention stage, 88*fig*, 97–99; role of
technology during stages of, 88*fig*.
See also specific stage
Hiring mistakes: even when using
validity model, 41*fig*; financial
consequences of, 2–3, 33–34,
246–247; raising the bar resulting

in different kinds of, 202*fig*–203.
See also Turnover
Hiring payoff dollar-value formula:
analysis of results, 77–79; assessing
whole candidate process and,
185–188; assumptions used for,
76–77; description of, 74, 77;
proven evidence of accuracy of,
79–80; terminology used in, 74–76
Hiring payoff measures: blending
validity concept with, 72–79;
formula for computing improved
validity and, 74–80; improving sales
results, 47–51; increasing
production, 47, 55–56, 57t;
lowering accident and injury rates,
56, 58–60; objective metrics used
for, 46–47; reducing turnover, 47,
51–55; reviewing hiring practices
for, 60–61; simple approach to
estimating, 80–81. *See also* Job
performance payoff measures;
Payoffs
Hiring practices: adding even more
value to valid, 81–84; continuous
improvement principles applied to,
28; hidden costs associated with,
2–3, 33, 246–247; how technology
has changed process of, 86–88*fig*;
materiality concept for, 32–34;
Uniform Guidelines on Employee
Selection Procedures on, 26–27,
189, 228. *See also* Legal compliance;
Thinking models
Hiring programs: average new hire
tenure, 75; calculating hiring
payoff dollar-value formula of new,
72–80, 185–188; candidate
screening selectivity of, 75–76;
fundamental questions for framing,
81–82; increase in validity of, 75;
net dollar value gain for year's hires,
74; recouping investment with first
million-dollar hire, 266–267; year's
increased cost of administrating, 76;
year's number of new hires, 75